Moodle 2.0 Course Conversion
Beginner's Guide

A complete guide to successful learning using Moodle 2.0

Ian Wild

open source*
community experience distilled

[PACKT]
PUBLISHING

BIRMINGHAM - MUMBAI

Moodle 2.0 Course Conversion
Beginner's Guide

First edition: December 2008

Second edition: November 2011

Production Reference: 1081111

Published by Packt Publishing Ltd.
Livery Place
35 Livery Street
Birmingham B3 2PB, UK.

ISBN 978-1-84951-482-8

www.packtpub.com

Cover Image by Asher Wishkerman (a.wishkerman@mpic.de)

Credits

Author
Ian Wild

Reviewers
Sharon E. Betts
Hans de Zwart

Acquisition Editor
David Barnes

Development Editors
Hyacintha D'Souza
Neha Mallik

Technical Editors
Joyslita D'Souza
Ajay Shanker

Project Coordinator
Michelle Quadros

Proofreader
Joanna McMahon

Indexer
Rekha Nair

Graphics
Nilesh Mohite

Production Coordinator
Arvindkumar Gupta

Cover Work
Arvindkumar Gupta

About the Author

Ian Wild is a recognized authority on online learning, especially with Moodle. Fifteen years spent in private industry – primarily as a communications technology researcher – saw Ian ultimately specializing in the design and development of access and learning aids for blind, visually impaired, dyslexic, and dyscalculic computer users – whilst also working part time as a math and science tutor. Teaching only part time meant not spending as much time with his students as he would have wished. This, coupled with his background in communication technologies, seeded his long-time interest in virtual learning environments.

Ian is one of the founding partners of Heavy Horse Limited (`http://www.heavy-horse.co.uk`), a technology company that regularly advises clients throughout England and Wales on e-learning platform development and deployment.

Ian is the author of *Moodle 1.9 Math*, also from Packt Publishing. He was also the Technical Reviewer of *Moodle 1.9 Multimedia*, and *Science Teaching with Moodle 2.0*.

I do hope you find this book as helpful to you as it was a pleasure for me to write. I must make special mention of friends, colleagues, and my family for their patience as I worked on this second edition. Your help and support has been invaluable. I thank you all.

About the Reviewers

Sharon E. Betts is a major influence in using technology for learning with educational experiences in and out of the classroom for over 30 years. She has taught and consulted in the United States, Europe, and the Middle East. Sharon is passionate about, and promotes the use of, open source and web-based tools in the educational environment. She is a Web 2.0 pioneer and carries the torch at every opportunity. She is firm in her belief that we can't let fear and negatives hold us back.

Sharon has presented face-to-face and virtually, both nationally and internationally and is well known for her forays into the cutting edge of educational technology. Sharon is one of the founding members of the summer FOSSED (Free and Open Source Systems in Education) Conference held in Bethel, Maine. She sits on the board of the `Open1to1.org` group.

Sharon presently holds the position of Educational Technology Coordinator in Maine School Administrative District #52, Greene, Leeds, and Turner, Maine U.S.

Visit Sharon's webpages at `http://sharonbetts.info`.

Hans de Zwart was not an American journalist and author who wrote Fear and Loathing in Las Vegas (1971) and Fear and Loathing on the Campaign Trail '72 (1973).

He has not been credited as the creator of Gonzo journalism, a style of reporting where reporters involve themselves in the action to such a degree that they become central figures of their stories. He is not known for his unrepentant lifelong use of alcohol, LSD, mescaline, and cocaine (among other substances); his love of firearms; his inveterate hatred of Richard Nixon; and his iconoclastic contempt for authoritarianism.

He does think Rhonda is the best thing that ever happened to him and he does write about learning technology at `http://hdez.nl/blog`.

www.PacktPub.com

Support files, eBooks, discount offers and more

You might want to visit www.PacktPub.com for support files and downloads related to your book.

Did you know that Packt offers eBook versions of every book published, with PDF and ePub files available? You can upgrade to the eBook version at www.PacktPub.com and as a print book customer, you are entitled to a discount on the eBook copy. Get in touch with us at service@packtpub.com for more details.

At www.PacktPub.com, you can also read a collection of free technical articles, sign up for a range of free newsletters and receive exclusive discounts and offers on Packt books and eBooks.

http://PacktLib.PacktPub.com

Do you need instant solutions to your IT questions? PacktLib is Packt's online digital book library. Here, you can access, read and search across Packt's entire library of books.

Why Subscribe?

- ◆ Fully searchable across every book published by Packt
- ◆ Copy and paste, print and bookmark content
- ◆ On demand and accessible via web browser

Free Access for Packt account holders

If you have an account with Packt at www.PacktPub.com, you can use this to access PacktLib today and view nine entirely free books. Simply use your login credentials for immediate access.

Table of Contents

Preface

Schools, colleges, and universities all over the world are installing Moodle, but many educators aren't making much use of it. With so many features, it can be a hassle to learn—and with teachers under so much pressure day-to-day, they cannot devote much time to recreating all their lessons from scratch.

This book provides the quickest way for teachers and trainers to get up and running with Moodle, by turning their familiar teaching materials into a Moodle e-learning course.

This book shows how to bring your existing notes, worksheets, resources, and lesson plans into Moodle quickly and easily. Instead of exploring every feature of Moodle, the book focuses on getting you started immediately—you will be turning your existing materials into Moodle courses right from the start.

The book begins by showing how to turn your teaching schedule into a Moodle course, with the correct number of topics and weeks. You will then see how to convert your resources—documents, slideshows, and worksheets, into Moodle. You will learn how to format them in a way that means students will be able to read them, and use plenty of shortcuts along the way to speed up the process.

By the end of *Chapter 3, Adding Documents and Handouts*, you will already have a Moodle course that contains your learning resources in a presentable way. But the book doesn't end there—you will also see how to use Moodle to accept and assess coursework submissions, discuss work with students, and deliver quizzes, tests, and video.

Throughout the book, the focus is on getting results fast—moving teaching material online so that lessons become more effective for students, and less work for you.

What this book covers

Chapter 1, *Going Electric*, covers why Moodle was created and how it was developed, how to log on and log out of Moodle, exploring the Moodle interface and learning some Moodle terminology, and configuring your user profiles.

Chapter 2, *Setting up your Courses*, covers configuring your Moodle course.

Chapter 3, *Adding Documents and Handouts*, covers getting your content online and ready to let your students start working with it.

Chapter 4, *Sound and Vision—Including Multimedia Content*, covers how to make your courses more engaging and entertaining with sound, video, and multimedia.

Chapter 5, *Moodle Makeover*, will take a look at tips and techniques that'll take your courses from looking good to looking great.

Chapter 6, *Managing Student Work*, covers managing student work online.

Chapter 7, *Communicating Online*, covers how to discuss work with students online.

Chapter 8, *Enhancing your Teaching*, covers how to enhance your teaching using other Moodle activities, such as quizzes and wikis.

Chapter 9, *Putting it All Together*, brings everything together and looks at possible ways of structuring a course that has been converted to Moodle.

Who this book is for

This book is for teachers, tutors, and lecturers who already have a large body of teaching material and want to use Moodle to enhance their course, rather than developing brand new ones. You won't need experience with Moodle, but will need teacher-access to a ready-installed Moodle site.

Teachers with some experience of Moodle, who want to focus on incorporating existing course materials will also find this book very useful.

Conventions

In this book, you will find several headings appearing frequently.

To give clear instructions of how to complete a procedure or task, we use:

Time for action – heading

1. Action 1

2. Action 2

3. Action 3

Instructions often need some extra explanation so that they make sense, so they are followed with:

What just happened?

This heading explains the working of tasks or instructions that you have just completed.

You will also find some other learning aids in the book, including:

Pop quiz – heading

These are short multiple choice questions intended to help you test your own understanding.

Have a go hero – heading

These set practical challenges and give you ideas for experimenting with what you have learned.

You will also find a number of styles of text that distinguish between different kinds of information. Here are some examples of these styles, and an explanation of their meaning.

Code words in text are shown as follows: "I'm going to specify MCC-BC."

New terms and **important words** are shown in bold. Words that you see on the screen, in menus or dialog boxes for example, appear in the text like this: "Scroll down to the bottom of the page and press the **Save changes** button".

 Warnings or important notes appear in a box like this.

 Tips and tricks appear like this.

Reader feedback

Feedback from our readers is always welcome. Let us know what you think about this book—what you liked or may have disliked. Reader feedback is important for us to develop titles that you really get the most out of.

To send us general feedback, simply send an e-mail to feedback@packtpub.com, and mention the book title via the subject of your message.

If there is a book that you need and would like to see us publish, please send us a note in the **SUGGEST A TITLE** form on www.packtpub.com or e-mail suggest@packtpub.com.

If there is a topic that you have expertise in and you are interested in either writing or contributing to a book, see our author guide on www.packtpub.com/authors.

Customer support

Now that you are the proud owner of a Packt book, we have a number of things to help you to get the most from your purchase.

Downloading the bonus chapter

"Handing in Work through Moodle" is a bonus chapter along with this book and is available for free download from http://www.packtpub.com/sites/default/files/downloads/handling_in_work_through_moodle.pdf.

Errata

Although we have taken every care to ensure the accuracy of our content, mistakes do happen. If you find a mistake in one of our books—maybe a mistake in the text or the code—we would be grateful if you would report this to us. By doing so, you can save other readers from frustration and help us improve subsequent versions of this book. If you find any errata, please report them by visiting http://www.packtpub.com/support, selecting your book, clicking on the **errata submission form** link, and entering the details of your errata. Once your errata are verified, your submission will be accepted and the errata will be uploaded on our website, or added to any list of existing errata, under the Errata section of that title. Any existing errata can be viewed by selecting your title from http://www.packtpub.com/support.

Piracy

Piracy of copyright material on the Internet is an ongoing problem across all media. At Packt, we take the protection of our copyright and licenses very seriously. If you come across any illegal copies of our works, in any form, on the Internet, please provide us with the location address or website name immediately so that we can pursue a remedy.

Please contact us at copyright@packtpub.com with a link to the suspected pirated material.

We appreciate your help in protecting our authors, and our ability to bring you valuable content.

Questions

You can contact us at questions@packtpub.com if you are having a problem with any aspect of the book, and we will do our best to address it.

1
Going Electric

Imagine a world where you could set your students tests and they would come in already marked. Imagine a time when pupils could submit their coursework and projects digitally instead of on paper. Not only would we save an awful lot of trees, but there would be no more "the printer ran out of ink" type excuses for not handing in homework on time. If only there was a system that allowed students and teachers to exchange work through a carefully administered, fully automatic digital framework, you would never have to worry about a student's work ever going missing again.

These systems do exist and they're called **Virtual Learning Environments (VLEs)** or **Course Management Systems (CMSs)** depending on who you ask. Moodle is one of many, but it's certainly the one that's become by far the most popular in all tiers of education, including work-based learning, too.

Advances in technology are driving the use of Moodle. There is the rise of the low-cost mini laptop (for example, the Dell Latitude or Asus EEE PC) which makes having a portable, Internet-enabled device for every pupil a practical reality in many schools. Add to this the simple fact that young people now find IT much more engaging as a learning tool.

No doubt these are just a few of the reasons why you find yourself wondering how to start converting your teaching over to Moodle. Maybe you are wondering how to advocate using Moodle in your school. Perhaps your school is converting to Moodle and you are worried about being left behind.

Are you currently only teaching face-to-face in a classroom or lecture theatre? Maybe you're using another managed learning environment (if you are then you don't know what you're missing!) and need to convert. The question is: how do I convert to Moodle? That's the question we'll be answering in this book.

To help us get an appreciation of the tool we are about to use, we begin by looking at a little of the Moodle back story. But as soon as we can, let's log on, have a walk around the system, and then let everyone know we've arrived.

In this chapter we shall:

- Learn why Moodle was created and how it was developed
- Learn how to log on and log out
- Explore the Moodle interface and start learning some Moodle terminology
- Configure our user profiles

So let's make a start.

What can Moodle do for me

Moodle provides you with the tools to store and present music, speech, video, have online group chats, quizzes and, as we have mentioned, manage assignment submission. Let's take a look at just a few of the advantages of converting to Moodle.

Most of us have shared online areas where we can distribute worksheets and handouts to students. However, often those shared areas can't be accessed from home. Moodle solves this problem. Shared areas can also become disordered. With Moodle you can manage and organize the sharing of resources easily. Also you can make the way you hand out work much more visually appealing; the process is made far friendlier to cautious students.

Third-party content providers have wised up to the idea of learning platforms and more of the resources they provide are specifically designed for environments such as Moodle.

But Moodle isn't just another resource repository. The 'M' in Moodle stands for 'modular', and there are Moodle modules that allow you to set assignments and mark them fully online (with Moodle managing the marks for you), and modules to allow you to set tests and have them marked automatically. In fact, if there is something you want Moodle to do and an "out of the box" installation doesn't support it, then chances are there is a module you can enable or install that will provide the functionality you need. For example, when my administrator enabled mathematical notation support in our school's Moodle, a new button appeared in the text editor that enabled me to easily create math symbols:

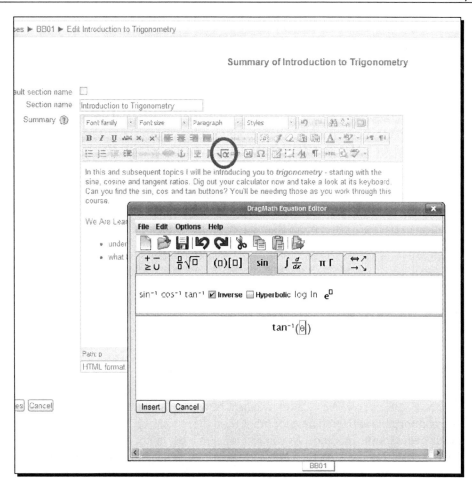

Because Moodle is available wherever there is Internet access, Moodle can be used to support students who can't make it to the classroom, for whatever reason. Perhaps they are ill, perhaps they are taking a course that requires them to be at a different college, or maybe they are on work-based training and you need to carry on with your teaching while they are there.

Moodle is another tool in your teacher's toolkit. I wouldn't want you to think that migrating to Moodle means more work for you. That's where this book comes in. I'll show you how to get your existing teaching material online quickly and easily. At the end of the book, if you are developing new learning resources then, rather than creating handouts in Word or a presentation in PowerPoint, think about the myriad of features in Moodle (just a few of which I'm going to introduce to you) and how you could use these in your teaching.

Advantages for the student

Moodle provides a consistent "user interface". What do I mean by that? Well, although generations younger than me are very familiar with computers, they tend to know how to use certain programs and applications (instant messaging and social networking are the favorites) but have no idea how to work with anything else. Moodle contains lots of different learning tools but, because they all have a consistent user interface, if you learn how to use one then it doesn't take much more effort and understanding to start using the others. I have up to this point never had to show a student how to use Moodle.

Being always available means Moodle can support students beyond the dismissal bell. If work needs to be carried on over the weekend, or during a holiday, or when pupils are on exam leave, then Moodle can provide that support. Students who are reticent about making a contribution in class are often more than happy to make an input online.

Because Moodle can mark tests as soon as the student takes them, they can gain immediate feedback on their work.

The advantage of open source

Moodle is open source, that is, it's basically free. But don't let the fact that it's free put you off. This is very much a positive. Moodle is supported by a close network of developers working hard to ensure that Moodle is secure, safe, and robust. For more information on how Moodle development takes place see `http://docs.moodle.org/en/ Development:Overview`. We've already learnt how the 'M' in Moodle stands for modular. If you are comfortable with web development then there's always the opportunity to create your own Moodle modules. As you can tell, I'm a big fan of open source software. If you're of a technical persuasion then you can experiment with Moodle without ever having to worry about software licensing costs. Many teachers have downloaded their own free copy of Moodle to try out new teaching ideas (see `http://docs.moodle.org/20/en/ Windows_installation_using_XAMPP`). Many schools have a second copy of Moodle for development purposes.

For more information on developing your own custom Moodle plugins check out "*Moodle 1.9 Extension Development", Jonathan Moore and Michael Churchward, Packt Publishing*.

Who is this book for

This book is aimed at educators. We assume that it's your job to teach, not to have to set up a Moodle site (we assume that this has already been done for you). We are also assuming that if there's any admin task that needs to be performed (a setting that needs tweaking or a switch that needs to be turned on), then your Moodle admin will do it for you. If you do need support in setting up and configuring your site check out "*Moodle Administration", Alex Büchner, Packt Publishing*.

What will we be doing together

In this chapter we are going to be looking at the history of Moodle – where it came from, and what factors influenced its development. This is important because Moodle is simply a tool to do a job. If we can understand why Moodle is designed the way it is, then if we come to try and use Moodle in a way it really wasn't intended to be used, we'll know why our approach might not work. Then we look at logging in and out of Moodle, how to change our user profiles and, importantly, how to change our passwords if we need to. We'll also be exploring the Moodle user interface – the names of the elements that make up a Moodle page (then you'll know what everyone is talking about when they refer to "breadcrumbs" and "blocks").

The rest of the book is broken up into two parts.

Moodle course conversion: Part 1

In Part 1, we learn how to convert documents and handouts over to Moodle.

Our first task is to set up and configure a Moodle "course". This is where we're going to put our documents and handouts, and where we will be setting quizzes and so on. This we'll be covering in *Chapter 2, Setting up your Courses*.

In *Chapter 3, Adding Documents and Handouts*, we'll be learning how to import documents to Moodle and how to give students access to them. Not all students will be able to open our documents (as that will depend on the software they have installed on their computers), so we'll be looking at tips and tricks we can use to make sure our resources are accessible to everyone, regardless of the software they have installed.

Once we've handed out the work online we'll need to provide a way for our pupils to hand in their completed work. In the bonus chapter, *Handing in Work through Moodle*, we'll see how even very young pupils can quickly and easily upload their homework via Moodle. Doing so means we can even manage their grades online, too. The bonus chapter provides the groundwork for *Chapter 6, Managing Student Work*, will cover converting whole projects and assignments over to Moodle (see Part two).

Converting to Moodle means that we can easily include video and audio. In *Chapter 4, Sound and Vision—Including Multimedia Content*, we learn how to use sound and vision to make our teaching materials more appealing to students.

In *Chapter 5, Moodle Makeover*, we spend time reviewing and experimenting with what we have learned so far. We cover how we can finesse our courses.

Moodle course conversion: Part 2

In *Chapter 6, Managing Student Work*, we learn how to manage student work online, covering how to convert projects and assignments over to Moodle. If you want to continue a class discussion beyond the classroom then communicating through Moodle is the ideal solution. Communicating online is covered in *Chapter 7, Communicating Online*.

As you are getting to grips with converting your teaching to Moodle you'll probably find that there are other aspects of your course that you would like to convert. In *Chapter 8, Enhancing your Teaching*, we cover:

- Quizzes
- Lessons (also known as 'quandaries' or 'action mazes')
- Workshops (a peer review and assessment activity)
- Wikis
- Glossaries
- Choices

We close this book by spending a little time learning how you could convert your teaching all the way from face-to-face, through to blended learning (supporting face-to-face with e-learning) and finally to converting your teaching entirely to Moodle.

The history of Moodle

It's important to understand where Moodle has come from so that we can get ourselves into the right frame of mind, and have the right mental model before we start to use it. Why? Firstly, we don't want to do anything that willfully cuts across the way Moodle was intended to be used. Secondly, if we do try to act in some way against the underlying Moodle "philosophy" without realizing, then we would only be making life hard for ourselves.

Origins

Martin Dougiamas worked as webmaster and administrator at the Curtin University of Technology in Perth, Australia. Frustration with the commercial learning management systems available at that time led, in 1999, to the creation of Moodle as part of his PhD, entitled "*The use of Open Source software to support a social constructionist epistemology of teaching and learning within Internet-based communities of reflective inquiry*".

Dougiamas' educational background has an important influence on Moodle. Martin was brought up in the deserts of Western Australia. The primary school he attended was the School of the Air, a correspondence school whose classes were conducted via ham (shortwave) radio from a school based a thousand kilometers away. Martin's class only met up once a year (for the school carnival) and his teaching materials were dropped off and homework collected by a four-seat Cessna aircraft that called in at the Dougiamas home every fortnight. If you're interested to learn more then watch the interview with Martin conducted by Michael Feldstein at `http://mfeldstein.com/interview-with-martin-dougiamas/`.

A new learning pedagogy

What marks Moodle as very different to other VLEs is the approach to learning Moodle supports. The system has been designed (as the PhD title reveals) to support "a social constructionist epistemology". In other words, students learn together by sharing their knowledge. That's why you'll find in Moodle tools to:

- **Encourage discussion**: forums and chats
- **Support collaborative working**: wikis
- **Manage peer review and assessment**: workshops

Although you'll find lots of literature encouraging you to use Moodle in a particular way (that is, to support the social constructionist pedagogy), you're in no way prevented from using Moodle to support other learning styles. Moodle is wonderful for distance learners (for example, the Open University in the UK are now using Moodle to support its 250,000 distance learners), and it may be structured with a particular pedagogy in mind, but there are fantastic features and tools built into Moodle to support all styles of teaching, as we shall see in this guide. For more information on how Moodle supports different learning styles check out *"Moodle Teaching Techniques (Creative Ways to Use Moodle for Constructing Online Learning Solutions"*, William Rice, Packt Publishing.

Growth and support

Since 1999 Moodle use has exploded (see `http://moodle.org/stats/` for the figures). So by converting your courses to Moodle you are in very good company. To join the ever-growing worldwide community of "Moodlers"—to discuss your work, to get help, and to learn more about best practice—visit `http://moodle.org`. My background is in maths and science and you'll most often find me in the Mathematics Tools forum.

`Moodle.org` is, in fact (and perhaps not surprisingly), a Moodle. What this means is that if you aren't familiar with Moodle then `Moodle.org` can be a little daunting. If you are new to Moodle then I would recommend visiting `Moodle.org` when you have gained a little more experience with the system.

Moodle is an acronym but what does it stand for? When thinking about your Moodle doing what you need it to do to support your teaching, why is the 'M' in Moodle so important?

Getting logged on

That's probably enough of the theory; let's get Moodling.

Logging on

I'm assuming that your Moodle admin has already given you your username and password. Maybe it is simply the same username and password you use to access other services at your establishment. Depending on your network, you might be logged into Moodle automatically. Let's assume you need to log in.

Time for action – logging in to Moodle

1. Go to your Moodle site's front page and look for a link that says **Login**. It depends on how your Moodle site has been 'themed', but good places to look are in the bottom-middle or the top-right of the page (if you definitely can't find the link then speak to your Moodle admin). Click on the **Login** link to open the login page:

2. Type your **Username** and **Password** into the relevant textboxes and press the **Login** button.

If you can't remember your username or password but you know you've got a Moodle account then click the **Forgotten your username or password?** link. The **Forgotten password** page will be displayed:

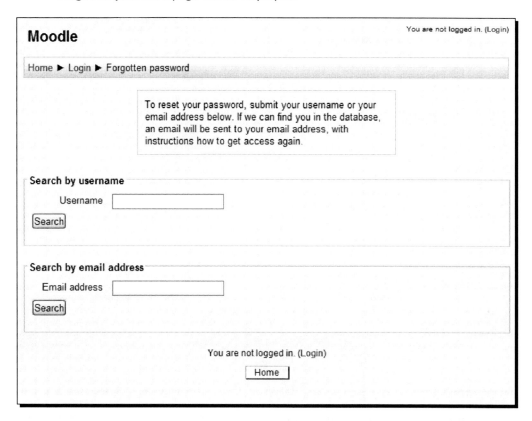

3. Enter your username OR your registered e-mail address into the boxes provided. Press the relevant **Search** button. You will be sent an e-mail detailing how to log in.

4. That's it! You're now ready to Moodle!

What just happened?

You've just logged on to Moodle. If this is the first time you've logged on you may be asked to change your password:

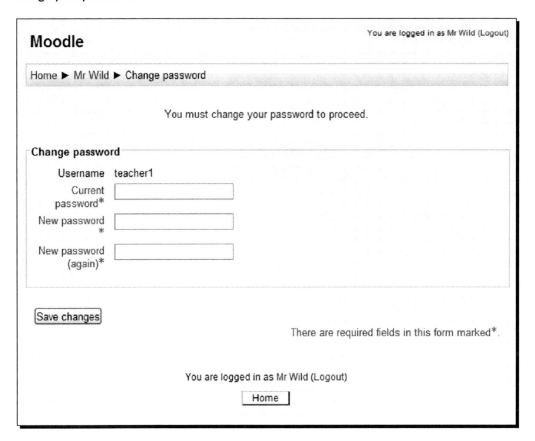

Simply follow the onscreen instructions (we'll be looking at changing our passwords later on in this chapter).

Each user has a profile that you can use to tell everyone about yourself. In the next section we'll learn how to modify your profile.

Telling other users about yourself

Now you are logged in, see whether you can find your name on the page. Again it depends on the theme your admin has configured, but good places to look are the bottom-middle of the page or the top right-hand side. Your name is a link. Click on it and your public profile page is displayed:

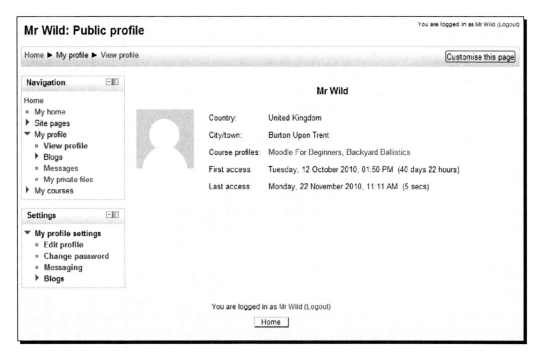

Now let's learn how to edit our profiles.

Time for action – editing your profile

1. Look for the **Settings** block, in the previous screenshot it's the box at the bottom of the left-hand side. Click on the **Edit profile** link. The **Edit profile** page is displayed:

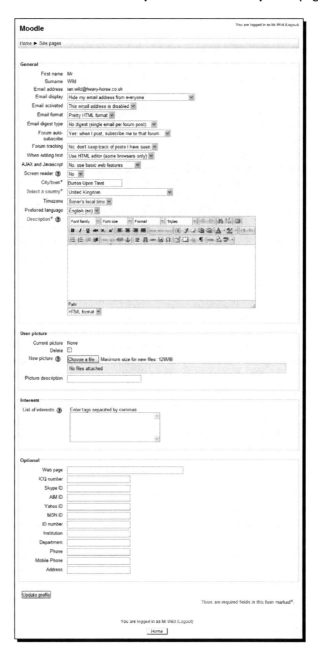

2. Note my admin has configured Moodle to prevent me from modifying my **First name**, **Surname**, and **Email address**. That's fine, and quite usual on most Moodle sites I work on. You might be able to modify yours. Basically, don't worry if my profile page doesn't quite match up with yours.

3. Let's change our profile descriptions. Scroll down to the **Description** box (the word **Description** is red with a little red asterisk next to it) and type in a description of yourself:

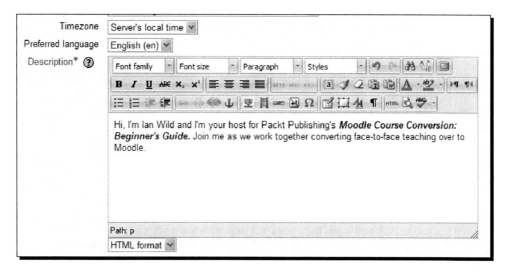

4. If you are used to using a word processor then the buttons across the top of the editor will be (mostly) familiar to you. We'll learn what these buttons do as we work through this book.

5. When you are happy with your profile settings scroll down to the bottom of the page and press the **Update profile** button. Don't worry about modifying settings in your profile page. You can always come back and change them again.

6. That's it, we're done!

What just happened?

Converting our courses to Moodle means we're going to have a "Moodle presence" and that's our Moodle profile. We've just modified our profile page to let our fellow Moodlers learn a little bit more about us using the **Description** setting.

Have a go hero

Has your Moodle admin allowed you to upload a picture of yourself? Return to your **Edit profile** page and look for the **User picture** box:

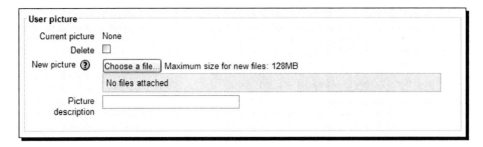

Press the **Browse** button to look for a suitable image on your computer. Don't worry about the size (preferably 100x100 pixels), if the picture is too big, it's cropped.

Can't find the "User picture" settings?

I've come across plenty of examples of students either "getting creative", shall I put it, with profile pictures they've obtained from Moodle, or uploading less than suitable pictures for their own profiles. So don't worry if this setting is turned off, and if you think students might decide to start airbrushing your picture it is worth not choosing a photograph of yourself for your profile!

Changing your password

Assuming your Moodle admin allows you to, if ever you need to change your password then simply return to your profile page (remember, wherever you see your name simply click on it and your profile page is displayed). On your profile page you'll see the **Change password** link (in the **Settings** block):

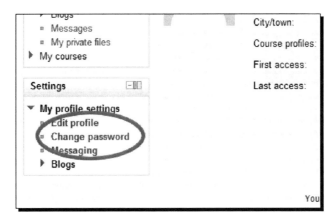

Click on the link to display the **Change password** page. To change your password simply follow the onscreen instructions.

Logging off

You've logged on. How do you log off? Not as silly a question as you might think. You don't want to wander out of the classroom and give the opportunity for the little horrors to be able to pretend to be you. Logging out of Moodle is easy. Simply click on the link that says **Logout**. You'll usually find this either in the top right-hand corner of the page:

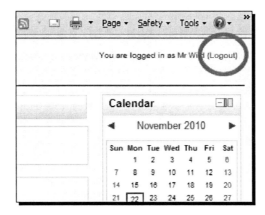

or in the bottom-center:

Word of caution

Don't try to log on as two different users on the same computer using the same browser (even if you're using two different browser windows). Moodle gets very confused. Use two different types of browser instead (for example, Internet Explorer and Firefox).

Doing your job – Your role

This book is aimed at educators. Moodle uses the term "teacher" to describe someone who hands out and grades work. But, as far as Moodle is concerned, you are only a "teacher" when you are in a course in which you are handing out work and grading it. In Moodle speak you have the role of "teacher". It is a mistake to think that just because you are a teacher (that is, that's your job) that when you are logged into Moodle you will be a teacher in any Moodle course. That's like saying you could walk into one of your colleague's classrooms and start taking their lesson. Well, you wouldn't do that and it's the same principle in Moodle.

Who decides who's teaching on a course

In the normal scheme of things the person who makes you a teacher in a Moodle course is the person who created the course, usually your head of department or Moodle admin. It may be that you've been given the task of creating courses. That's the role of the Moodle "course creator". They can create courses and assign roles. Interestingly, they can't delete courses. They don't have that capability. The concept of roles is intimately tied up with the concept of capabilities. Let's look at capabilities in the next section.

Capabilities

Moodle is very strict on the principle of "demarcation of responsibility", different roles have different capabilities:

- **Administrator**: Has complete, God-like powers over the Moodle installation. Can do, literally, anything. But if you ask him to, he probably won't.

- **Manager**: Have slightly less powers than the Administrator. This role is equivalent to a deputy head teacher or assistant principal. Can create and delete courses, and assign users to courses. There are some things they can't do, such as change Moodle's site configuration settings, for instance.

- **Course creator**: Can create new courses, and edit them. Interestingly they don't have the ability to delete them.

- **Teacher**: Can edit and work with existing courses, but cannot create new ones. They can grade the work students have handed in.

- **Non-editing teacher**: Can grade work and teach, but can't edit courses.

- **Student**: Can hand in work, attempt quizzes, can interact with other course members in forums and chats. Students can't edit courses, hand out or grade work.

What your role is depends where you are. For example, I am a teacher in the daytime but in the evening I am a student at evening classes. My role depends on the "context" (teacher in one place and a student in another). It's the same with Moodle, make sure you don't confuse your job title with your role in a particular context. I log in to Moodle as a user, not as a teacher. Let's look at contexts in the next section.

Contexts

What different contexts are there in Moodle? Here are the basic scenarios:

- I've just logged into Moodle. In this context I'm an authenticated user.
- I've just enrolled on a course. The fact that I've had to enroll suggests that in this context I'm a student. If my Moodle admin has made me a teacher on this course then in this context I would be a teacher.
- Courses can be contained in categories. Categories are a way of grouping together Moodle courses. When I view a category I find that I can create courses. In the course category context I am a course creator. Note that I can't create categories, I don't have that capability. If you need to create categories and find that you can't then the first person you need to speak to will be your Moodle administrator.

Your Moodle administrator or manager (from now on I'll just use the term admin to mean either role) can give you a specific role in a specific context. Just because you are a course creator in one context doesn't mean to say that you are a course creator in another.

Pop quiz – what's my role?

I've just clicked on a category to view the courses in it. I see that there is a button marked **Add a new course**. What's my role in this context?

- Teacher
- Guest
- Course creator
- Student

Why am I mentioning all of this

Well, you can see that there are many different ways of running a Moodle site, so we've had to make some assumptions in writing this book. This book is pitched at the educator who wants (or needs) to convert their courses over to Moodle. Because you have that role I'm assuming that if there's any administrative task that needs to be carried out then your Moodle admin will carry it out on your behalf; I'm assuming that Moodle administration isn't your job. That's why at the end of some chapters you'll find a special section called Ask the Admin.

It isn't just roles and capabilities that can change depending on your Moodle site. It's the look and feel of the site that can differ as well. Let's spend a little time taking a look at Moodle's user interface.

Moodle look and feel

As we've already discussed, the great thing about Moodle is that it has a consistent user interface. What do I mean by that? One way to think about Moodle is as a suite of teaching tools, a forum, a wiki, a chat facility, and so on. Because the user interface is consistent you can learn how to interact with one tool and you'll easily be able to pick up on how to use the others. You'll find that all Moodle sites have a familiar feel to them: they look different but they are all used in the same way. How do you make them look different?

Moodle themes

You can theme Moodle, that means you can apply your own custom colors and page designs (almost like a new skin). You can specify your own banner across the top of the page and your own footer at the bottom. You can rearrange items on the page. But you can't change the behavior of a Moodle site. A Moodle will behave like a Moodle, and you'll get to recognize a Moodle site when you see one.

The Moodle theme you'll see in the pictures in this book (the theme of my Moodle) is called "standard". Your admin may well be using a different theme. Don't let that put you off. Remember that the theme just changes the way Moodle looks and not the way it behaves.

All Moodle pages, regardless of theme, contain certain "standard" elements. In the next section we learn all about them.

A Moodle page

What are the parts that make up a Moodle page? Let's start at the top of the page and work our way down.

Breadcrumb trail

At the top of the page you'll find a trail of links telling you where you are in the Moodle site:

It's called a breadcrumb trail (also referred to as the "navigation bar") and it's a convenient way of getting back to a known point. For example, if I click on **View Profile** in the breadcrumb trail then I am taken to my **Profile** page. If I click on **Home** in the breadcrumb trail then I am taken back to the site front page.

Blocks

Let's take a look around a Moodle course front page:

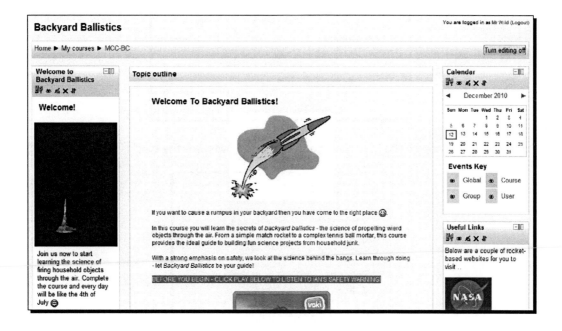

On the left and right of the page you can see blocks, such as the **Calendar** block on the top-right. There are a number of standard blocks you can include on your course front page. There are also custom blocks that your admin can install. A block you'll commonly find used in Moodle is the HTML block. This type of block allows us to include our own web-based content on the left and/or the right of the page. The **Welcome** and **Useful Links** blocks in the previous screenshot are HTML blocks.

In the middle is the main course area and this is where you'll find the main resources and activities (blocks are usually for supplementary information or support).

If you are using a notebook or a laptop with a small screen then you might find the course page a bit cramped. Each block has a hide icon:

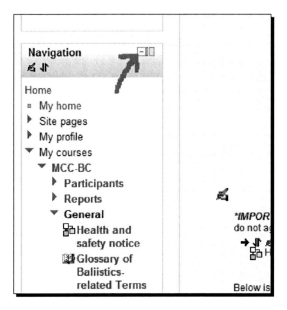

For example, clicking on the hide Navigation block icon collapses the block:

Next to each hide icon is the move this to the dock icon:

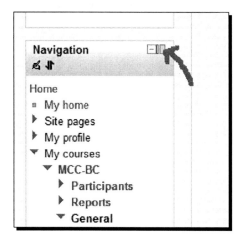

The dock bar is ideal for notebooks or laptops with a smaller screen size as it moves side blocks out of the way without hiding them completely:

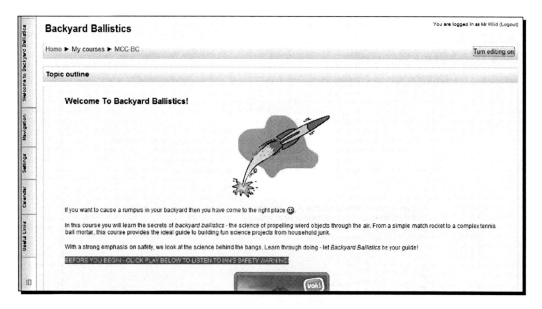

Hold the mouse over the name of a block listed in the dock bar and the block is displayed (and the undock this item and delete icons are also displayed):

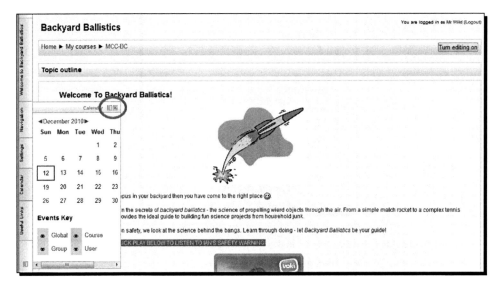

Footer

At the bottom of the page is the footer:

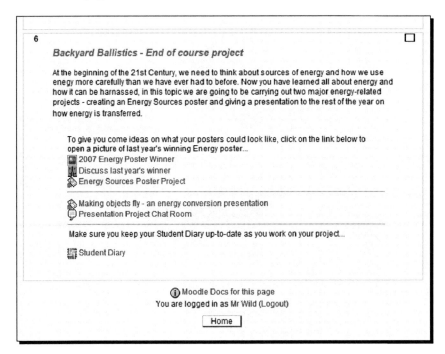

At the bottom of the footer you will find a button. In the previous screenshot you will see that the button is marked **Home**, and pressing it will take you back to the site front page. You will also see a note telling me who I am logged in as, and in brackets after the name is the **Logout** link, which we met earlier in this chapter.

Icons

The icons you see on your Moodle pages may well be different from the icons we refer to in this book (although I doubt they will be radically different). If you are not sure what an icon is for (if it isn't obvious from its context) then hovering the mouse pointer over it will reveal some short descriptive text (called a tooltip):

Summary

Now our journey with Moodle has begun and already we've learned a lot about the system.

Specifically, we covered:

- **The origins of Moodle**: We learned that Moodle was the brainchild of someone who was home schooled. Martin Dougiamas designed a system to support collaboration and learning by sharing knowledge. Although that's the underlying pedagogy, we learned that Moodle can support many different learning styles.

- **How to log on to Moodle**: We learned how to change our passwords and covered what you need to do in the event that you forget it. We also covered how to make sure you've logged off. We don't want students being able to get onto the system pretending they are you.

- **Modifying our user profiles**: We saw that Moodle administrators can "lock" certain aspects of our user profiles (mine had my **First name**, **Surname**, and **Email** fields locked). But I could still modify my description and we saw how to do this.

- **Roles and capabilities**: We saw how different roles have different capabilities, and that your role depends on the context. For example, I'm a teacher in the courses I teach in, but in the courses I'm enrolled on I'm a student.

- **Moodle look-and-feel**: Together we learned about the different elements that make up a Moodle page.

We also briefly discussed what we're going to cover in the rest of this book.

Now that we've got a feel for Moodle we're ready to configure a Moodle course which is the topic of the next chapter.

2
Setting up your Courses

In the previous chapter we started our Moodle journey. In this chapter we're going to see how to lay the foundations for moving your department's courses into Moodle. In this chapter we will:

- *Learn how to map your academic curriculum to a number of Moodle courses*
- *Create a new Moodle course and give it a name and description*
- *Set up an appropriate structure for the course*
- *Assign teaching staff to the course*
- *Set up an enrollment method for your course*

By the end of the chapter your course will be set up and ready for you to start populating it with content.

From curriculum to courses: What counts as a Moodle course

Let's start this section with me describing the course I'm going to be converting to Moodle as we work together through this book. The course is called "Backyard Ballistics" and it's a science course that forms part of an applied physics qualification. The course is all about the art of firing weird objects through the air with chemicals and equipment that you will find in your average domestic kitchen and garden shed.

There are certain aspects of this course that I can't convert to Moodle. I want my students to get an appreciation of energy and dynamics by "doing" (kinesthetic learning) the science using everyday items you'll find around your house. But there is a good deal of support material, handouts, diagrams, and quizzes, that currently I try and distribute electronically using a "shared drive" on the college server. However, my students can never find the materials I tell them to go and look for. At least, that's their excuse. But I've got to admit that after a few years of use our shared drive is starting to look a bit of a mess. As you will see in the next couple of chapters, moving these resources over to Moodle will definitely solve this problem.

But where do I put these resources in Moodle? The answer is that you put them into a Moodle course. And here is a screenshot of just a fragment of a Moodle course:

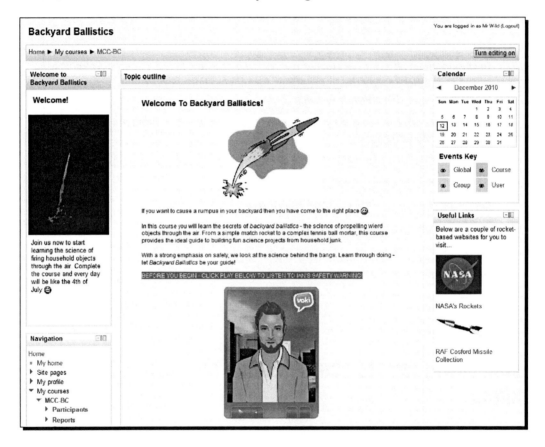

I've divided my course into six topics:

- Getting Things Flying
- Lighter Than Air: Hydrogen Filled Balloons

- Fire Kites
- Basic Rocketry: The Match Rocket
- The World Famous Tennis Ball Mortar!
- Backyard Ballistics: End of Course Project

The reason why I've chosen to convert Backyard Ballistics into topics is partly because that's how I teach it and partly because I am happy for the students to "dip into" the resources and activities I have converted to Moodle. I'll be talking about how to break up the contents of a course into topics later in this chapter (that's not the only way you can break up a course: you can break it up into weeks, too). Before we look at how we can get a course and start adding content to it we really need to understand what Moodle considers to be a course and how Moodle organizes them.

What is a Moodle course

You can clearly see now that, at its most basic, a Moodle course is a placeholder for resources and activities. Obviously it's much more than this, as you'll be learning as you work through this book. One obvious advantage Moodle has over a shared drive is that links to resources and activities can be interspersed with text and graphics to make the experience more visually appealing and engaging, and the resources I upload easy to find (I don't accept any excuses these days).

How Moodle organizes its courses

Let's take a quick look at how you can organize courses in Moodle.

To help organize courses, Moodle has the idea of categories and subcategories:

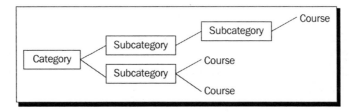

Remember that you'll only find resources and activities in a Moodle course. Categories and subcategories are only there to help you organize and manage the organization of courses.

So how does that work in practice? For example, I work in the **Physics** department, part of the **Faculty of Science**. My **Backyard Ballistics** course supports the **Applied Physics** qualification. Here's how we've got our categories and subcategories arranged:

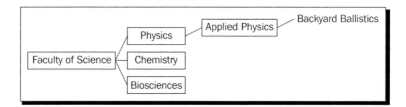

I'm sure you could think of examples for your subject area. You could have a category called English that contained two subcategories, Literature and Language. Within literature you could have short courses on particular aspects of the set text you are teaching. You could have a category 20th Century History containing subcategories for Britain, Germany, France, Italy, and USA. Each country subcategory can contain further subcategories called Politics, Society, and so on.

Because this is such a key issue when you first start using Moodle, let's spend a little time investigating the more common approaches taken when converting face-to-face teaching to Moodle.

Breaking up is hard to do

How you break up a face-to-face, traditionally taught course, depends on the age group and the subject area you are working in, so let's study some examples.

Often younger children will have the same teacher for all of their subjects. Schools in this situation usually categorize Moodle courses based on year groups, and within the year group each teacher will have their own subcategory in which they are free to create and delete courses as they wish:

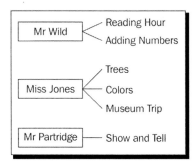

Each teacher having their own Moodle course means it is much easier for the children to find the resources that have been uploaded and activities created for them.

As the children get older you can start running different Moodle courses for different subjects depending on that child's age and ability. Now I could have a category for each year group, and within them categories for each subject area:

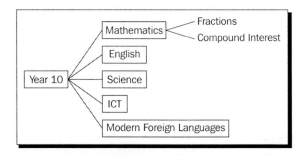

Instead of a mathematics teacher having just one course they may instead have a course in Year 9, two in Year 10 and another one in Year 12. As the subject areas begin to broaden and the amount of material you need to get through increases, you might need to think about having Moodle courses for particular subject areas, especially those areas that students tend to struggle with.

As students become older, things tend to become easier, because qualifications examined by external examination bodies will have their own syllabus. Read the syllabus carefully and you will often be able to see immediately how to break the subject down into Moodle courses. Mathematics, for example, naturally falls into categories, namely:

◆ Number
◆ Algebra

- Geometry (shape, space, and measure)
- Data handling and statistics

Within each category there is then a natural divide between subject areas. See whether you can spot a similar pattern in your subject area.

For students who are older still (that is, college or university age), subjects are most often taught in units anyway. A short 10-week unit, for example, is an ideal candidate for a Moodle course.

To close this section, I will leave you with just a few more thoughts. One is that Moodle courses can also be created to develop a student's key skills. Examples of key skills could be:

- Communication
- Application of number
- Information and communication technology
- Problem solving
- Collaboration

Another is that Moodle courses are not set in stone; once they are created they can be changed as you require. You will also see later in this book that responsibility for different aspects of your Moodle course can be delegated down to your students, enabling you all to work together developing your page.

Have a go hero – developing key skills

Try identifying courses that support developing one of the key skills. If key skills are a priority in your school or college, then no doubt you will have lots of skills-based teaching materials already to hand that you can convert into Moodle courses.

If in doubt, hold a meeting

In this section we've been investigating how we could break up traditionally taught, face-to-face courses and identifying what might be converted into Moodle courses. You can do this along traditional lines, or you can approach the problem by looking at key skills or learning styles. It is an extremely complicated issue and will undoubtedly involve discussions with your department colleagues. I strongly suggest you hold a Moodle meeting to discuss which courses are going to be created, initially. Use the opportunity to discuss who is going to teach them, and what categories they are going to fit into. Plan as much as you can before you start doing anything in Moodle.

Remember to involve your Moodle administrator in those meetings, especially if they are the one responsible for creating your categories and courses.

Now that we know what Moodle categories and courses we're going to need, we can focus on creating and running those courses.

Let's get started: Setting up the course

The remainder of the book will focus on just one course. If you're putting your whole department into Moodle then you'll have lots of courses to work through. That's why it's so useful to assign other teaching staff to course creation, and let them share the work. We'll show you how to do that too.

Creating your course

Before you start building your course, it needs to be "created" in Moodle. If you're working in a school or university, then there are three ways this might happen:

- An administrator has already created it: Sometimes, administrators create empty courses for all the official courses taught by an institution.

- Put in a request: In other situations, the administrators require that teachers request new courses; the administrator then approves the course, and it's created.

- Create it yourself: In other circumstances you might have permission to create courses yourself. If it was you that installed your Moodle then you will definitely have permission to create courses.

How is it that you cannot create courses but your colleagues can? Let's look at this in the next section.

Do you need to create your course yourself

You might be lucky, your administrator may have made you a manager or a course creator, meaning you get to create your own courses. Note that managers have slightly more power than course creators. For example, managers can create courses and delete them. Course creators can only create them. It is easy to spot if you are a course creator or manager because only then will you have an **Add a new course** button when you look in Moodle categories, or if you click on the **All courses** button to display all the courses in your Moodle. Once you have found the **Add a new course** button you only need to press it to create your new course. You are immediately taken to the new course's setting page.

What to do if your course has been created for you

The immediate problem is finding it. Return to your site front page. Can you see the **Navigation** block? (By default the navigation block is at the top-left of the page). Click on the **My courses** link and a list of your courses will be revealed:

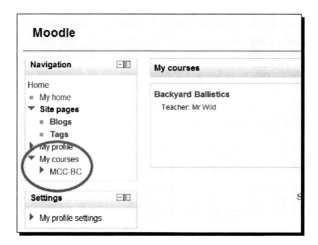

If you don't have a **Navigation** block on your site's front page then the easiest way is to click on your name (you can usually find this towards the top, right-hand side of the page) which then displays your user profile. Listed in your profile are the courses you are participating in:

The course name **Backyard Ballistics** is a link, which I then click on to see what my role in the course is. You can see in the following screenshot that my head of department has made me a teacher on **Backyard Ballistics**:

In my case I can click on the **MCC-BC** link, under **My courses** in the **Navigation** block. If I didn't have a **Navigation** block then I could also click on the breadcrumbs across the navigation bar at the top of the screen:

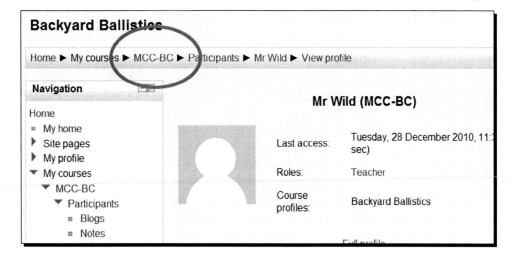

I am now at my course page. It's an empty course based on a 10-week structure and it's ready for me to start configuring:

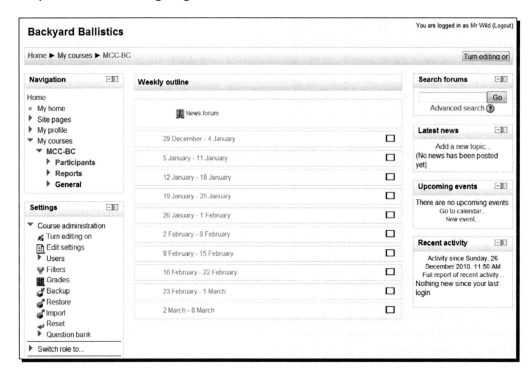

What is the difference between a course creator and a manager?

Configuring your course

Now let's configure a topics-based course called Backyard Ballistics. In the **Settings** block under **Course administration**, click on **Edit settings**. This will take you to the **Course settings** page:

Time for action – configuring the Backyard Ballistics course

Let's start by creating my Backyard Ballistics course. I'm not too worried about fine tuning it now. I just want to get it started, we will fine tune the course later, once we've got the basics up and running:

1. Type the course title next to **Course full name**, Backyard Ballistics.

2. Enter the short name. This has to be completely unique (if there's another course with the same short name, Moodle will complain). I'm going to specify MCC-BC.

3. Enter a summary using the WYSIWYG (What You See Is What You Get) HTML editor. See how we can use formatting for the description, as you would with a word processor:

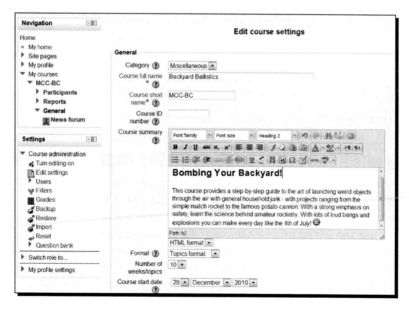

4. Look for the **Format** setting (almost immediately under the **Course summary** editor). Click on the drop-down menu and select **Topics format**.

5. Because we're just setting up the course, we don't want students enrolling yet so scroll down to the availability options. Click on the **Availability** drop-down list and select **This course is not available to students**.

6. That's all we need to set up a basic course. So scroll to the bottom and click **Save Changes**.

If you've created this course from new you're now taken to the **Enrolled users** screen. We're not going to look at roles just yet, so for now go to your course's home page by clicking the button at the bottom of the screen containing your course's short name (now **MCC-BC**). If you were configuring an existing course, you'll be taken straight back to your course page anyway.

What just happened?

We created a new course and gave it a full name, short name, and summary. We also configured the course so that it is broken up into topics (the default on a new Moodle installation is weekly). We left everything else as the default so we can edit it later. You now have a course divided into 10 "topics" ready for you to add content.

However, not every course will neatly divide into 10 topics. So the next task is to make sure our course is structured correctly. We will do that in the next section.

But first, there are a few more things you should know about creating courses:

◆ Choosing an effective description for the course summary

◆ Using the editor

◆ Getting help on Moodle settings

◆ Getting back to the Course settings screen

Let's look at these now.

Choosing an effective description for the course summary

The summary is displayed whenever your course is listed with other courses, so if you want your course to stand out, try to describe it in as brief and direct a way as possible. The summary is usually the first bit of your course that students come across before they enroll, so you want to use the summary to make your course as inviting as possible. Also, remember your target audience: if you are going to be using your Moodle course simply to support your classroom teaching then the summary is much less important than if you are wanting to attract the attention of prospective students or their parents.

Using the editor

It's important that we get used to using the editor because we are going to use it a lot. Most of the buttons are the same as you would find on any word processor, and as I'm assuming that you are fairly competent with a word processor, I'm not going to go through all of the "standard" formatting buttons (including inserting symbols and spell checking). Four of the "non-standard" buttons you will find useful are:

Icon	Function	Use
	Insert smiley	Sometimes it is difficult for students to spot whether you have written something cheeky or sarcastic. Use a smiley to stress how serious you are being: if you are being cheeky insert a winking face, or being sarcastic insert a cheesy grin.
	Paste from Word	If you paste from Word then you can often never get the text to format properly. The Paste from Word button might remedy this problem.
	Cleanup messy code	If it's not Word you are pasting from but another application, say PowerPoint or from a web page, again getting the pasted text to format properly can be a problem. Paste your text and then press the Cleanup messy code button to correct this.
	Paste as Plain Text	If you are still having problems editing pasted text then try pasting into the editor using this button. It just pastes the text you have copied without any formatting included (so you will have to reformat your text once it's pasted into the editor).

Another useful control (rather than button) is the resize editor control, found at the bottom-right corner of the editor:

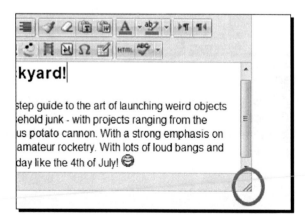

Click on the corner of the editor with the mouse cursor and drag it to make the editor bigger or smaller.

Remember: you can only cut and paste text from other software programs into the editor. Don't try to cut and paste images. Images need to be copied to the computer that your Moodle is running on. We will be looking at uploading images in *Chapter 4, Sound and Vision—Including Multimedia Content*.

We will be looking at the rest of the "non-standard" buttons as and when we need them.

Getting help on Moodle settings

I deliberately skipped over a lot of options in the Course settings page, and will continue to do so as we work on setting up our courses. However, Moodle does a good job of helping you understand each individual setting. You can get help on any Moodle feature by clicking the question-mark icon nearby.

For example, here's what you would have seen if you'd clicked the **?** next to **Course short name**:

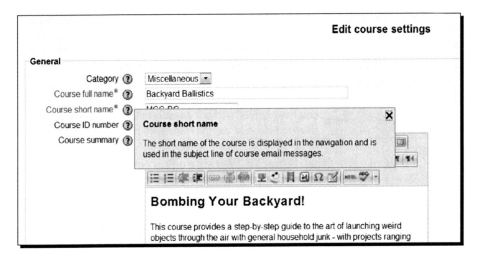

Further documentation

If that help isn't enough, you can get help for the whole page on most sections of Moodle. Just scroll to the bottom of the page, and click **Moodle Docs for this Page**. This will take you to the documentation section of the Moodle website, with up-to-date and ever-expanding documentation:

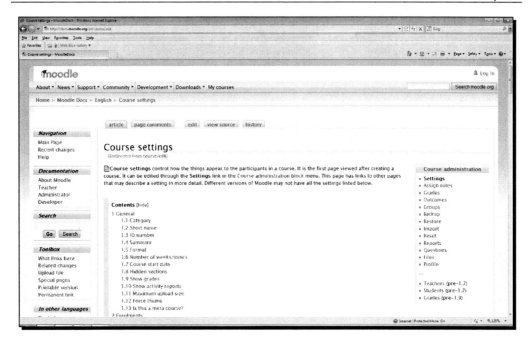

Getting back to the Course settings screen

Remember nothing in Moodle is carved in stone. If you want to change settings for a course that's already created, you can return to it at any time. In the **Course settings** block on the left-hand side of the screen, while looking at the course, click on **Edit settings**. You'll then get back to the Course settings screen where you can change the title, description, and other settings.

Course structure and format

Courses are divided into sections. What constitutes a section depends on the course's format. If you're new to Moodle then there are two main, important formats:

- **Weekly format:** Each section represents one week of study
- **Topics format:** Each section represents a particular topic or aspect of the course

For your first few courses, especially courses based on existing non-e-learning material, these are likely to be the only two you use. However, there are others:

- **SCORM:** Third-party e-learning materials are likely going to be supplied to you in SCORM format (SCORM is an educational resource "standard" format, in much the same way that documents are supplied in ".DOC" format). If you know what they are then this is a useful course format type. If you've never heard of SCORM then don't worry.

- **Social format**: The whole course is built around a single forum. This is useful for using Moodle to manage things that are not strictly courses. You could use it to set up a departmental notice board, or a discussion forum for an after-school club, for revision, or (as in one school I worked in) to help organize the Year 11 prom.

To put your course into Moodle, you will need to select a format appropriate for your course structure and material.

Which format should we use: Weekly or topic format

First, here are the main differences between weekly and topic formats.

Topic formats:

- Consist of named sections that can be of any length
- You could have one topic, three topics, or 20 topics
- Each topic can contain any amount of information
- A maximum of 52 topics per course

Weekly formats:

- Consist of a fixed number of weeks – eachach section is exactly one-week long
- Has a definite start date – each week is given a precise set of dates, not "Week 1", "Week 2", and so on, but "March 3 – 10"
- A maximum of 52 weeks per course
- Remember to include term breaks if you have a course that covers two terms

So, when should you use each one?

Topic formats are usually best when:

- Students learn at their own pace or are self-directed in their learning – they will pick and choose resources from across the course, without any particular order being imposed
- The course is broken up into topics that come one after the other, but don't each last one week
- There are optional topics that not all students will study, or will be studied at different times
- Different groups of students will be using the course at different times

Weekly formats are usually best when:

♦ There is a clearly defined schedule

♦ The course has a defined start date

♦ You want to reinforce particular deadlines with the students (although in a weekly format course you can still access all of the materials and activities any time you like)

If you are new to Moodle then, at least to start with, I would stick with a topics format course. When I first started teaching I used to try and plan what I was going to teach that term, but it all went rapidly out of the window as I had to judge what subject areas I was going to move on to next, all depending on how the class were getting on with what we had covered so far. The same is true with Moodle and that's certainly why it's rare to find a Moodle course using the weekly format in a school or college.

Weekly format is ideal if are converting a course in which your students need their time planned out for them and you, as their teacher, know what is going to be coming up in the course and when. With a weekly course, your students have the chance to look on ahead and they'll know when to brace themselves for difficult/extra work if needs be. Also, if you are converting courses to support apprenticeships or students on work placement, have a think about whether a weekly format course would be the better option.

Pop quiz

How do you change the format of your course from topics to weekly?

Breaking your course up into topics

You've now decided on a course, but you need to break the course up into Moodle topics. The most common ways of achieving this are:

♦ **By sequence**: Some kind of narrative order. Basically, follows the order in which the reader should learn

♦ **By resource type**: Worksheets, handouts, web resources

♦ **By "true topic"**: Each section collects resources on one topic within the course, even though the course doesn't necessarily progress through those topics in order

Each has pros and cons. Each has situations where they are ideal.

You can even combine them, say, have a bunch of topics that map to an ordered set of units, with some non-ordered units at the end that cover, for example, resources relating to a private study project that runs throughout the course.

I've broken up my Backyard Ballistics course into five topics because that's how it is structured before I've converted it to Moodle, and five topics was a natural fit.

If you are worried about how you should structure your courses when you convert to Moodle then remember that you can always come back and change things later on. Often it is easier to start getting courses converted to Moodle and the very act of doing so will help you see how things should be organized.

Setting the format for your course

As you have already seen, my Backyard Ballistics course is built around six topics. Let's see how to set up such a course structure using Moodle.

Time for action – setting up the course format

1. Return to the **Course settings** screen.

2. From the **Format** options, choose **Topics format** or **Weekly format**. For mine, I'm going to choose **Topics format**:

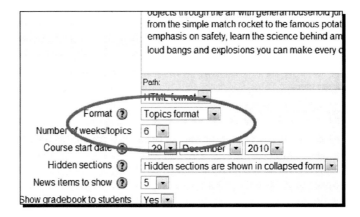

3. Choose the number of topics / weeks. I've planned for six topics in my course.

4. For weekly courses, make sure you set a start date.

5. Now scroll to the bottom of the page and press the **Save changes** button to return to your course page:

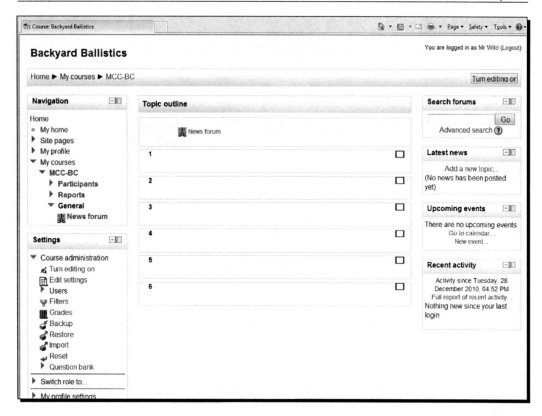

What just happened?

I've just broken up my Backyard Ballistics course into five "topics", that is, five numbered boxes because that's how my course is structured in the real world. Again, five topics is a natural fit.

You can still adjust the number of topics / weeks in your course once your course is populated with content. However, if you reduce the number then later topics will disappear. So if you have 10 topics, and later reduce it to eight, anything that you had added to topics nine and 10 will vanish from view but are still there (and are still accessible if people bookmarked them). This is a technique you can use to reveal teaching materials and activities as your face–to-face teaching progresses (so you don't get lots of questions from your students on topics you haven't yet taught).

You can also switch from weekly to topic view any time you like.

Defining each topic/week

Moodle now gives you the right number of sections or "slots" to fill up with course content. But each topic is blank, it lacks any kind of title or description, let alone educational content.

Let's add descriptions for each section in our course.

Time for action – defining each week/topic

1. Return to your course page. Make sure you have editing turned on, by either pressing the **Turn editing on** button in the top-right corner of the screen or by clicking on the **Turn editing on** link in the **Settings** block:

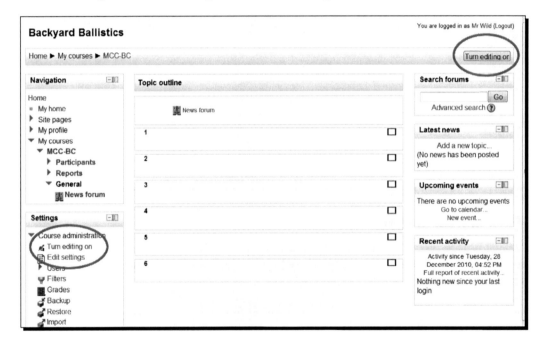

2. Click the hand and pen icon next to the topic number you want to edit (hovering the mouse over the icon displays a helpful "Edit summary" tip):

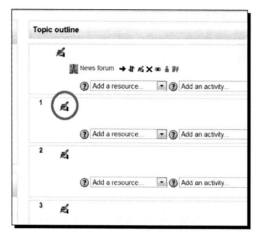

3. Now enter a short summary of the topic. This summary also has to serve as the topic title. You might want to use rich formatting to differentiate the title from the rest of the text:

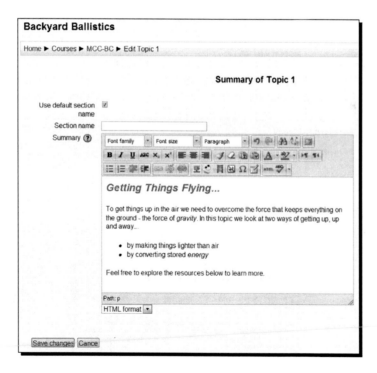

4. When you're done, press the **Save changes** button and you'll go back to your course with the new summary in place. If you want to cancel the change, just press the **Cancel** button.

5. Do this for each week / topic in the course.

What just happened

So far we have:

◆ Planned how we are going to divide up our course, using either a weekly or a topics format, then configured the course to use that format

◆ We included descriptions for each week / topic in the summary

◆ Added a course introduction in the course summary (at the top of the course page)

Remember, if you are not happy with the way your course is developing you can always change things later on. Before we leave this section, let's have a quick look at a few more configuration options you might find useful.

Introducing a course: Summary of General

This topic is where I'm going to provide an overview of my Backyard Ballistics course (this is the section of your course where you can outline the course aims and objectives).

You can also include material that applies to the whole course and isn't related to a particular week or subtopic. You might name this something such as "course resources". Or you might use it to provide a summary / introduction of the course. In converting Backyard Ballistics, I'm going to start by using Summary of General to provide a welcome message:

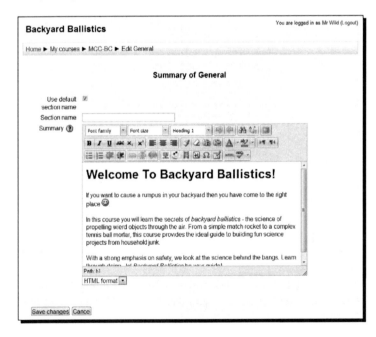

This will now appear at the top of the course:

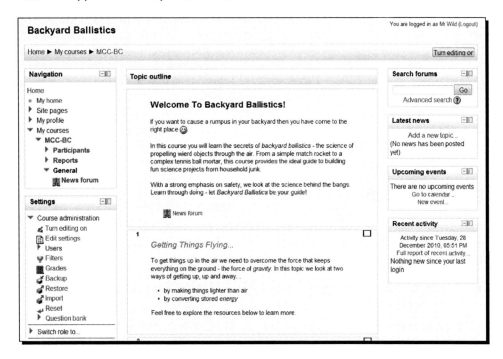

More settings for topics/weeks

Aside from adding a summary, there are other things we can do with each topic when you're on the home page and in edit mode:

Icon	Function	Use
	Change the order of topics	Click on the up and down arrows to reorder your topics.
		Note that for weekly courses, the topic will move but the dates associated with the topic will not change immediately. Reloading the course page will ensure all weeks are 'renumbered' correctly.
	Display all topics or just one at a time	This button lets you choose whether to display the whole course in one page, or just one topic at a time. Displaying one topic at a time might be useful when each topic starts to contain lots of resources and activities.
		Students can also use this button, and it works even when you're not in edit mode. If you're panicking that you've deleted all but one of your topics by accident, the chances are you clicked this button. Click it again and all should be well.

Icon	Function	Use
	Hide topics	Click on an open eye to make a particular topic invisible. The topic will appear either as "not available" to students and they won't be able to see any information about it, or any of its resources, or will be hidden completely, dependent on the **Hidden sections** option in the **Course settings** page.

Finally, and most importantly, we can add resources and activities to our courses. In later chapters, we will see how to turn our existing course material into Moodle resources and make them available through our course.

Assigning teaching staff

If you are teaching on your own in your own Moodle, you won't have to worry about working with fellow colleagues. Each member of staff in Moodle will usually fall into one of the following categories:

- **Administrator**: Has complete control over a Moodle. Equivalent to a chief executive or a school principal.

- **Manager**: Can create and delete courses. They do have the option of coming into your course and doing your job but, if they are traditional managers, they probably wouldn't know how to.

- **Course creator**: Can create new courses and edit them. By default, course creators can't actually delete courses.

- **Teacher**: Can edit and work with existing courses, but cannot create new ones. This role can add new resources and activities, change topics, and settings.

- **Non-editing teacher**: Can grade work and teach, but can't edit courses. This role will only become relevant when we get to interactive course content in later chapters.

It depends on the management structure in your school or college but, in my experience, the approach that has worked best is to have a head of department/faculty leader/team leader/ Moodle champion, delete as appropriate, as the Moodle manager in their Moodle category. They then create courses for their teaching staff. If you are a Course creator then it doesn't need me to tell you not to simply drop a Moodle course onto one of your unsuspecting colleagues without discussing it with them first. I've known this happen and it caused nothing but a great deal of animosity and a fair amount of anti-Moodle feeling.

Let's take an example. For the rest of this book we will look at converting the Backyard Ballistics course to Moodle. However, there are other courses in the physics syllabus that need converting, including "Jet in a Jam Jar". As a course creator, you can create a course, and then assign it to another teacher who can "develop" the course from then on.

I am going to create a new course and then assign it to Mr. Wild as the editing teacher.

Time for action – assigning roles

1. Add a new course to your Moodle using the process described previously.

2. From the **Settings** block on your new course page, click on **Users** and then **Enrolled users**:

3. Now you can choose who to assign to what role on your course. Press either of the **Enrol users** buttons:

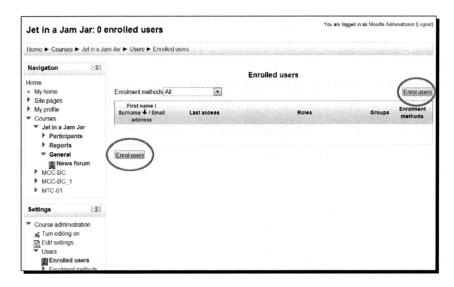

4. The **Enrol users** dialog window is displayed. In the **Assign roles** drop-down menu select **Teacher**:

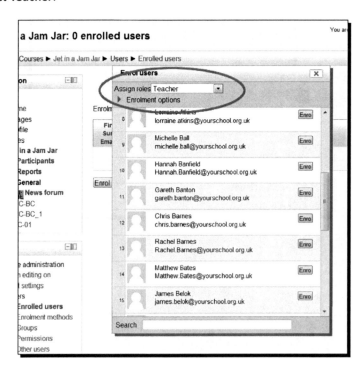

5. You need to select the users you want to be editing teachers on your course from the list of potential teachers. If you can't immediately find your colleague from the list then try using the search box at the bottom of the dialog window:

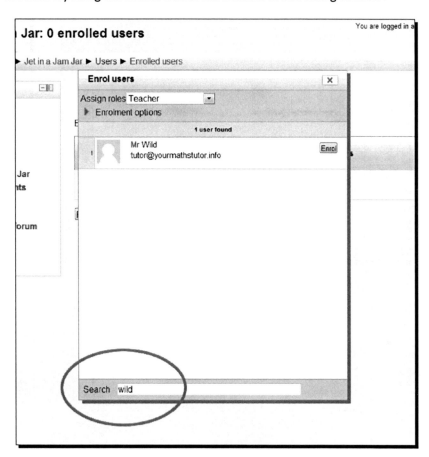

6. If the member of staff you need isn't listed then they will need to have a login created (which is possible if your Moodle is relatively new or unused). That's the job of your Moodle administrator (and beyond the scope of this book).

7. To enroll your colleague press the **Enrol** button to the right of their name:

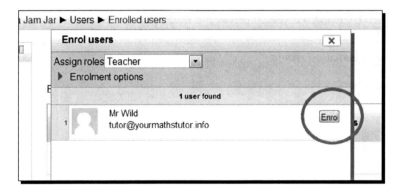

8. Once you have finished making your changes, click on the close button in the top right-hand corner of the **Enrol users** dialog window. Your colleague will now be listed as a teacher on the course:

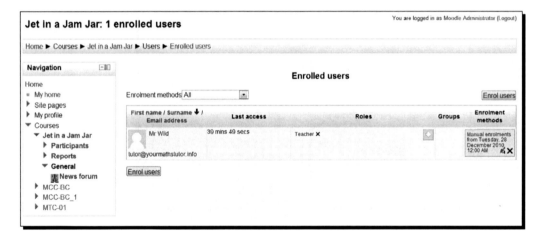

9. Will there be any teaching assistants or learning coaches working with the students on this new course? You might want to add them to the list of so-called non-editing teachers. You can assign users to different roles in exactly the same way.

Don't worry about having to assign students on your course just yet. We'll be looking at this topic in the next section.

What just happened?

If you aren't the only member of staff to be involved in your course then you'll want to assign your colleagues to be a teacher (who can either edit the course in the same way you can or who is a so-called "non-editing" teacher) or a learning coach or classroom assistant. We explored how you can do this using the **Enrolled users** options available from the course **Settings** block.

So far we've managed to configure the course structure and assign the teaching staff. In the next section we look at getting students enrolled on your course.

Let in the rabble: Enrolling students on your course

Was your course created for you by your administrator? You may even have gone to the **Enrolled users** page to find that you already had students enrolled on your course. If there is no general policy for getting students enrolled on a Moodle course then you have a number of options open to you. Let's take a look at these.

Enrolling with a key

The easiest way to enroll a class onto a course is to specify an enrollment key. This is like a password for the course. Each student then tries to register on the course, and is asked for the key. They type it in and, hey presto, they are enrolled.

Time for action – specifying a course enrollment key

1. Click on **Users** in your course **Settings** block and then click on **Enrollment methods**:

2. Enable the **Self enrolment (Student)** method by poking it in the eye (make sure the eye is open):

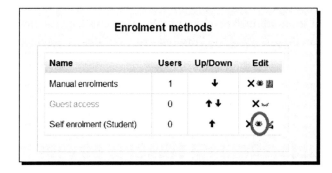

3. Click on the **Self enrolment (Student)** edit icon (the hand holding the pencil) to open the **Self enrolment** configuration page:

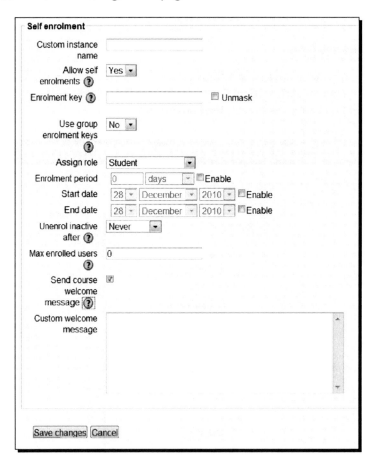

4. Most of the settings on this page are self-explanatory (do you remember how to find help on a particular setting?) but make sure you have **Allow self enrolments** set to **Yes** and have specified an enrolment password. You can make the password as simple or as complicated as you wish:

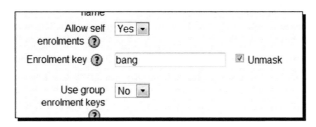

5. When you're finished, scroll to the bottom of the page and press the **Save changes** button.

6. That's it, you're done!

What just happened?

We've just specified an enrollment key for our courses. How you hand that key out to your students is entirely up to you. When it is time to get my students enrolled on my courses I usually write the key on the whiteboard. After a week or so I go back to the course settings and change the key (I usually just prefix the key with the letter "X" which I won't be doing any more, if any of my students are reading this). Obviously changing the key prevents other students from enrolling (try as I might, I've never managed to stop students from passing the key around, something they seem more inclined to do if I've specifically told them not to).

Have a go hero – enrolling teachers with a password

It's not only students you can have self-enrolling using a password. Did you notice the **Assign role** setting in the **Self enrolment** configuration page? Perhaps the members of your course all require teacher privileges. This isn't that unusual, two examples of this I have encountered recently are a "staff room" course for lecturers who all wanted to have teacher privileges on the course and a support course for medical practitioners at a local hospital. We will learn how to do this later in this book.

Other enrollment options

So far we have configured our course so that students can enroll themselves. But that's not the only option you have of getting students enrolled on your course. Let's take a look at the others.

Teachers enroll students manually

Rather than having students enroll themselves on a course (usually using a key), we might need to manually add a student to the course (if, for whatever reason, they are late to the party). The process is exactly the same as the one we followed when we assigned teachers, so I'll just outline it briefly here. From the **Settings** block click on **Users** then **Enrolled users** to display the **Enrolled users** page. Press either of the **Enrol users** buttons to display the **Enrol users** dialog window. Select the role you wish to assign (for example, **Student** or **Teacher**) from the drop-down menu at the top of the dialog window and press the **Enrol** button next to the name/s of the users you wish to have that role assigned to on your course.

Often this can be easier said than done. Firstly, you have to find the right student from the list. Then you have to do that for every student you want on your course. And that could take a long time. Not an option I would recommend. It is far better to have students enroll themselves on your course, if enrollment isn't automatic.

Groups and group enrollment

Do you ever carry out group activities with your students? You can do the same in Moodle. We'll be learning how to group students, including information on how to hand out different work to different groups in *Chapter 9, Putting it All Together*.

Free-for-all: Letting anybody enroll

If you don't specify a key then any registered user can enroll on your course. This isn't an option I would recommend, unless your course is one where you are quite happy to let anyone in. Or yours could be a compulsory course that every registered user needs to complete. For example, yours could be a course on your school's computer use policy, or it could be a mandatory health and safety training course.

If your course isn't compulsory for all users then I would strongly suggest using a course or group enrollment key. What you find is that some students will pass the enrollment key to either their friends or (and this is often more likely) their parents, who then enroll on your course just to have a look around. This can be a pain, as you find yourself regularly having to check the list of course participants to unenroll those students who shouldn't be there. The solution to this problem is to disable enrollment a week or so after the course has begun. You might also think about having a rule about not passing keys to other students, although setting these kinds of rules often encourages students to try and break them.

Enrolling a cohort

Perhaps your Moodle admin has put your students in a cohort. A cohort is a site-wide group of students. We have to configure our course to "synchronize" with one or more cohorts, meaning if students are in the right cohort they will be enrolled on our course automatically. Also, when they are removed from the cohort they are automatically unenrolled from our course. If you have cohorts enabled on your Moodle (and this has to be done by your Moodle admin) then you'll see **Cohort sync** included in the list of **Enrolment methods** (in the **Settings** block under **Course administration | Users | Enrolment methods**):

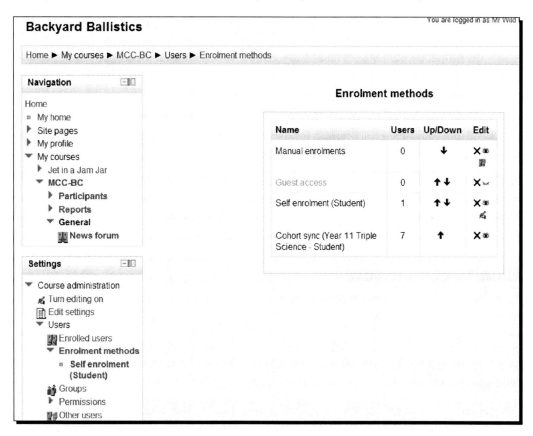

Again, managing cohorts is not something we as teachers need to worry about too much; we may need to be aware of them but those with greater responsibility for Moodle administration (for example, managers or administrators) will need to create them and assign them to courses.

For more information on managing cohorts check out *"Moodle 2.0 First Look"*, *Mary Cooch, Packt Publishing* (see `https://www.packtpub.com/moodle-2-0-first-look/book` for details).

Automatic enrollment from your school's Management Information System (MIS)

It could be that your Moodle is configured to automatically create courses based on the timetable specified in your school or college Management Information System (in the UK, that's predominantly either Capita SIMS.net or Serco CMIS Facility). Not only that but such systems also assign the right user to the right course with the right privileges. Three such systems used by me in systems I've either worked with or designed are:

- **User Management Resource Administrator (UMRA)** from Tools4ever (`http://www.tools4ever.com`), which can not only automatically create courses and assign the right user to the right course with the right permissions, but can also create accounts for parents and associate children with their parents
- **Groupcall Xporter** (`http://www.groupcall.com`), which in the UK is often used to extract pupil attendance data from a school's MIS by the local education authority, as is the case in England's largest education authority, Birmingham
- **ZiLink** from SchoolsICT (which is built on Groupcall Xporter). For more information visit `http://schoolsict.net`

Just in case you're a fan of trivia, and for those readers who are of a certain age (ahem) and remember 1985's Live Aid concerts, you may be interested to learn that one of the original investors in Groupcall is Nobel Man of Peace Sir Bob Geldof (and my publisher needn't worry: I don't have any shares in any of the aforementioned).

Allowing guest access

If you want everyone, not just registered Moodle users, to view your course then allow guest access. Click on **Edit settings** from your course **Settings** block and scroll down to your course **Guest access** options. There you'll see the **Allow guest access** option. Click on the drop-down list and select **Yes**. Again, there will be instances where you would want this, for example as an advertisement for your school or college VLE. However, guests are limited in what they can do on a course.

Now we know how to get students enrolled on your course. The most popular method, at the time of writing, is to give out enrollment keys – either a course enrollment key or, more typically, a group enrollment key. If you're happy to let anyone on your course then you don't have to worry about setting a key. The problem is that you can have lots of students enrolled on your course but you'll have no idea who they are. You can always double-check to see who is enrolled on your course by going to the **Enrolled users** page.

Summary

You've achieved a lot in this chapter. It's only *Chapter 2* and already you have:

♦ Created a course, and configured it to use the right short and long name, description, and format

♦ Structured your course, created a set of individual topics (or weeks) complete with description, and maybe a welcome message too

♦ Assigned other teaching staff to help you manage your courses

Set an enrollment key that you can give to students when the time is right.

Of course, a student enrolling on your Moodle course now won't learn very much but that's about to change. So keep the enrollment key secret for now. By the end of *Chapter 3, Adding Documents and Handouts*, you'll have content online and might be ready to let your students start working with it.

3
Adding Documents and Handouts

Your new Moodle course is configured and ready to have your teaching materials uploaded onto it. Now let's make a start! In this chapter, we will cover:

- *Uploading files to Moodle and how to organize them effectively*
- *How to present documents and handouts to students*
- *Uploading images and how to include them in any text*
- *Understanding which types of file are best to include in a course, and how to create them. We will also be learning how to convert departmental documentation into a wiki, which you and your colleagues can work on collaboratively.*

By the end of this chapter, you will have populated your course with static content ready for your students to access. Clearly, our aim is to create more appealing and interactive courses and my describing resources as "static content" may not sound that inspiring but, as you'll see in this and subsequent chapters, there's plenty we can do with our "static" resources to make them engaging and entertaining when we convert to Moodle.

Uploading files

As always, I want to show you the easy way first, and the easiest way to get your existing course material into Moodle is to simply put the files in as they are.

However, remember that your students might not have all the software necessary to read the files that you want to upload to Moodle. In this chapter, I will be mainly working with Microsoft Word documents and PowerPoint presentations, but the processes I will be outlining and we will be working through together could equally apply to any type of file. Later in the chapter, we will see how to make sure your documents are in a format that any student with any computer can download and use.

For now, though, let's look at how to upload any file into Moodle.

Uploading means taking a file from your computer and putting it onto a server. Students and other staff can then download the file to their own computer and view it.

If you're like me, you've got all of your teaching resources stored on a memory stick, a portable hard drive—or perhaps you keep them on your school or college server. We now need to upload them to Moodle, ready for us to include them on the front page of our course.

Each of us has our own My private files area in Moodle that other users (both students and colleagues) don't get access to. We can upload a file to our My Private files area and then provide a read-only link to that file from any course we teach on. For example, I'm about to show you how to upload an "energy sources" handout—a Word document (a DOC file)—that I use when I teach Backyard Ballistics. In fact, I use this handout in another course I teach in Moodle but having the file in **My private files** means I can easily create a link to it from the other course.

Although you are creating links to files in your My private files area, Moodle is, at the time of writing, making copies of the file to put in your course. That means if you modify the file in My private files you won't see those changes when you click on a link to the file from a course. For more information check out the discussion here: http://moodle.org/mod/forum/discuss.php?d=168495#p739240.

Note also that in the following example I could have used any type of file—we'll talk much more about file formats later in this chapter.

Time for action – uploading a file

1. Choose the file you want to upload and make a note of where it is currently stored.

2. Return to your site front page and select **My profile | My private files** from the Navigation block:

3. You are now in your My private files area. Remember: this area is only accessible by you but you can provide links to files uploaded to here from any course you teach on. Click on the **Manage my private files** button:

4. A new page is displayed that allows us to manage the files in our My private files area. Note the maximum file size of the file you can upload is displayed on this screen (there's more on maximum file sizes later in this chapter). Click on the **Add** button to open the **File picker** dialog:

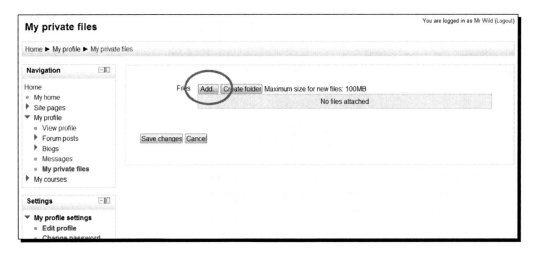

5. Make sure you click on the **Upload a file** on the left of the **File picker**.

6. Pressing the **Browse** button (or **Choose File**, depending on your browser) allows us to select the file we chose in step 1. Click on the **Browse** button to open the **Choose File to Upload** dialog. Select the file you want to upload and press the **Open** button:

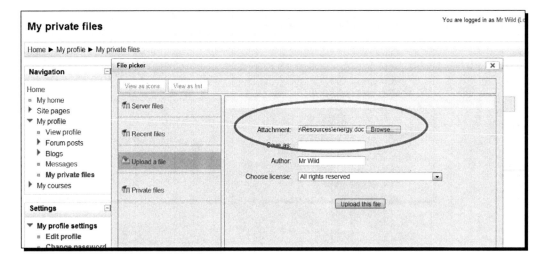

7. Once you've selected your file, press the **Upload this file** button to close the File picker dialog. You are now returned to your **My private files** page with your newly uploaded file listed:

8. Press the **Save changes** button to commit. My private files area now looks like this:

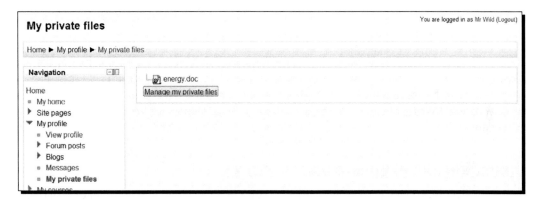

9. That's it, you're done! Your file is now stored in your My private files area all ready to be included in any of your courses.

What just happened?

We've just learned how to take a teaching resource and upload it to Moodle. We still haven't made it available to students yet. Before we do, let's round on a problem nearly all teachers face when they start converting courses, especially on a new Moodle installation—the problem of file size.

How big is your file

The one major problem you may encounter (and if you do you are in good company) is that the maximum file upload size in your Moodle is set too small. In fact this is often a problem not necessarily directly with Moodle but also with the way Moodle is installed and the software Moodle itself relies on. The default size for a new Moodle running on a new server is 2 MB. Quite frankly this is far too small (I've seen PowerPoint presentations 25 times this size, although I'll mention now that there are techniques for making large PowerPoints much smaller without compromising their quality, as we'll see in later sections of this chapter). If the file you want to upload is too big (and you aren't the Moodle admin) then you basically have three choices:

- Ask your administrator to increase the maximum file upload size.

- Ask your administrator to upload the file for you. Because there are potential problems associated with increasing the upload limit (unless you have Moodle running on suitable hardware and the software Moodle relies on to upload files is configured correctly). In my experience, most administrators aren't happy increasing the maximum limit above about 32 MB. In fact, your administrator may suggest (before you have to ask) that they upload the file for you. If so, don't object.

- Compress the file before you upload it (we'll spend time looking at compressing files in the next section).

It is worth mentioning why you might start getting complaints about uploading lots of large files: if your Moodle is being run on a server that your school or college is renting then the bigger the storage space needed, the higher the rental costs. Even if your school is running its own server, there is obviously a cost associated with all that space you are planning on taking up.

Uploading lots of documents in one go

If you are like me, you have a lot of documents you need to upload and you don't particularly want to spend lots of time uploading them all individually. A better option is to pack all the documents into one file, upload this single file into Moodle, and then unpack the documents back out again at the other end. You can pack almost any file inside a ZIP file (including other ZIP files). If you've got a file that's too big to upload (one of those large PowerPoint presentations, for instance), then you could compress just that single file into a ZIP file (the third of our options for overcoming the maximum file size upload problem at the end of the previous section).

Time for action – packing files together

The first task is to pack all the files you are taking with you to Moodle. The kind of file we need to create is called a "zip" file. ZIP files are very easy to create and can contain almost any kind of file (certainly the kinds you will be using for your learning materials). For example, in Windows simply highlight the files you want to upload. Then, right-click on any one of the highlighted files, slide down to **Send To**, then select **Compressed (zipped) Folder**. You can also perform the same trick on an entire folder—even one that contains its own subfolders. When the ZIP files are unpacked, the files remember which folders they were in. Different operating systems have different ways of creating ZIP files, so if you've never heard of a ZIP file, or you have never created one before, then your best option is to speak to your administrator or, if you have one, the help desk. If you are lucky they may even create the file for you.

I've got all of my Backyard Ballistics files in a single folder on my PC, and I've packed all of the documents I need into a file called `ballistics.zip`. Here's what I need to do, and you can follow the same process for your ZIP file:

1. Upload **ballistics.zip** to Moodle (following the same procedure as before).

2. Once **ballistics.zip** is uploaded I can see it listed on the My private files page. Next to the name of each file is a context menu button:

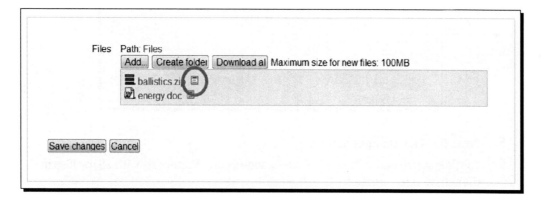

3. Because the ZIP file is a special file packed with other files, I have the option to "Unzip" (that is, unpack all the documents within it). Select **Unzip** in the context menu:

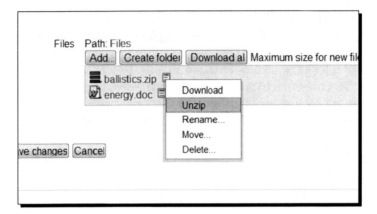

4. Moodle displays the files and/or folders it has unpacked from **ballistics.zip**:

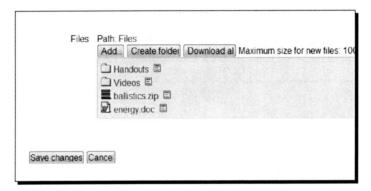

5. Press the **Save changes** button.

6. That's it, we're done! Two new folders, **Videos** and **Handouts**, with all my files in them have been created:

What just happened?

We uploaded a ZIP file containing lots of resource files, and then unzipped it on the Moodle server.

ZIP files are a special kind of file that can contain many other files within them. This means that we can use them to move lots of files into Moodle without uploading them one at a time. And it's not just files you can pack into a ZIP. You can ZIP up entire folder structures, too.

Moodle has the ability to turn that ZIP file back into a set of separate files. When we click on **unzip**, Moodle takes all of the files out of the ZIP file, and adds them to the current folder.

Dealing with oversize zip files

We've seen how we can pack all the files we need into a single file (and if we are lucky, a helpful administrator will do it for us) and this allows us to upload lots of files all in one go.

We still need to watch out for the limits on file sizes, and if the maximum file upload size is too small for the ZIP file you've just created then you could:

- ◆ Create more than one ZIP file.
- ◆ Seek advice from your administrator (who may well have to upload the file for you). If everything is packed into one ZIP file that your admin can upload in one go, they probably won't mind so much. In fact there are many ways of getting lots of files uploaded to Moodle and your admin might need to think about implementing one of them (for example, WebDAV) if this is a frequent problem.

If Moodle is trying to unpack/decompress particularly large files (but they are smaller than Moodle's file upload limit) then unpacking the files might time out. The solution is to pack the files into the ZIP without compressing them. This will require a compression utility capable of doing this, for example WinZip. If you are experiencing problems and are unsure of what you can do to solve them, speak to your Moodle admin.

Zipping folders

As mentioned previously, zips can also contain folders and subfolders, so you could assemble all your course material into neat subfolders on your own computer, all within one "resources" folder, and zip up the whole thing. When you unzip it, Moodle will recreate your folder structure for you.

Now we've got our files uploaded let's get our course files area organized.

Removing the ZIP file when you have unpacked it

ZIP files aren't automatically deleted when you unpack them, even though we have finished with them. We need to manually remove them, which we cover in the next section.

Removing files

There will obviously come a time, aside from deleting a redundant ZIP file, when you need to remove a file from your course files area (perhaps you've just uploaded one you didn't mean to). Deleting files from the course files area is easy. In fact, remember when I uploaded a bunch of files all in one go and I mentioned that I needed to delete the ZIP file after I had finished with it? Let's do that now.

Time for action – removing files

I'm going to remove **ballistics.zip** because all the files have been unpacked from it and it's now just taking up space:

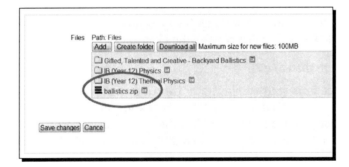

Again, press the **Manage my private files** button to start the process:

1. Click on the context menu icon immediately to the right of the file you no longer want. This displays the context menu. Slide the cursor down and select **Delete** from the menu:

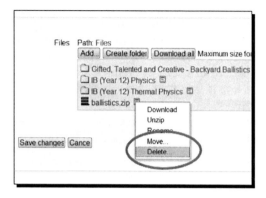

2. Moodle then displays a **Confirmation** dialog to double-check with you that this is the file you want to delete. If you are absolutely sure you want to delete the file click **Yes**:

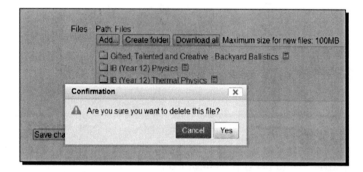

3. Remember to press the **Save changes** button. That's it! You are done!

What just happened?

We've just been learning how to upload a lot of files all in one go by using ZIP files. A ZIP file is a way of packing files together to make uploading them to Moodle easier (rather than uploading individual files one at a time). But once the files have been unpacked, we don't need the ZIP file any more. That's why we've also been learning how to delete files, too.

Organizing your files

Just as I'm sure you have with your files on your memory stick, your portable hard drive, or the files on your school server, you can organize your course files into folders. It's also a good idea to get your files organized if you are going to have colleagues teaching with you on your course. You'll want to help them to be able to sort through your files—as well as giving them an idea of the best place to upload their files, too. The process we are about to run through is an alternative to the "zipping folder" method from the previous section (zipping up folders is quicker if you need to upload a large number of files and you need to retain the folder structure they are stored in). So, let's start by creating a new folder and follow that up by learning how to move files into it.

Time for action – creating a "Handouts" folder

I first want to create a folder to put my handouts in—and in a flash of inspiration I've decided to call the new folder "Handouts".

1. Press the **Create folder** button. You can find this button at the top of your list of files:

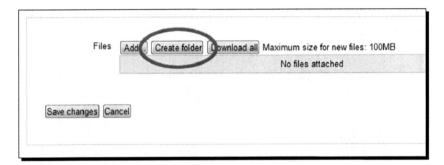

2. The **Please enter folder name** dialog appears. Type the name of the new folder into the box provided and press the **OK** button:

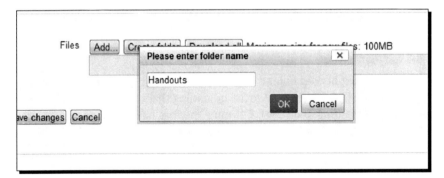

3. Press the **Save changes** button:

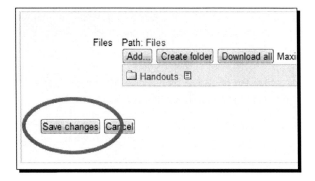

4. That's it. You're done! The new folder is now listed in the **My private files** area:

What just happened?

We've just created a new folder in our course Files area, ready for us to put some files in. Just click on the plus in front of the folder name to have a look inside it (if you are in the process of actually managing your files, then you can click on the name of the folder itself). Of course, at the moment it's empty. Click on Parent Folder to get back to the folder you've just come from, so you can see the Handouts folder listed again.

Now let's put a file in it.

Time for action – putting files where we want them

Moving files is a two-stage process. Firstly, we need to select the files we want to move. Then, we need to choose the place we want to move them to. Press the **Manage my private files** button to start the process:

1. Select the files you want to move by clicking on the context menu icon next to the file's name, then select **Move...** from the menu:

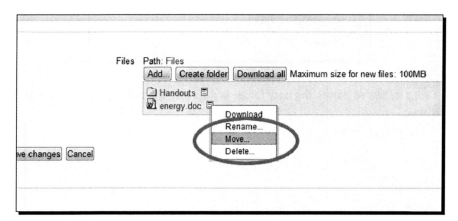

2. The **Moving** dialog is displayed. Select the folder you are moving your file to by clicking on it, in my case **Handouts**. Make sure you double-click the folder to select it:

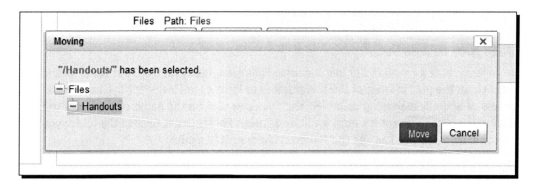

3. Press the **Move** button. You've now moved the files to the right place!

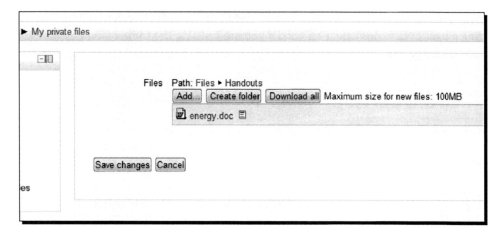

What just happened?

Not only do we know how to get a file uploaded onto the system but we know how to get things arranged so that we can easily find files. Of course, it makes more sense to create the folder first and then upload directly into that—rather than uploading your resources and then attempting to get everything arranged.

Even though I'm uploading the files to My private files area and our teaching colleagues don't have direct access to this, it's worth noting that our colleagues can get access to copies of these files (we'll be learning how later in this chapter).

Let's end this section by looking briefly at how you could organize your private files and what might be considered appropriate naming conventions for folders and files. Firstly, I've created folders for the courses I teach on. Within the Backyard Ballistics folder I've chosen to put all of my handouts in a **Handouts** folder:

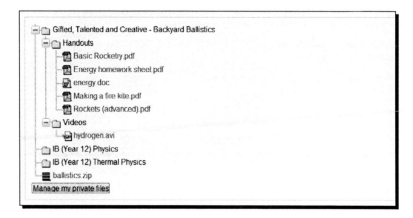

Instead, you might want to organize your files into folders named 'Week 1', 'Week 2' or 'Topic 1', 'Topic 2', and so on, depending on whether your course is set to weekly or topics format. That way you can quickly identify which files need to be placed in which topics/weeks. Creating a handouts folder would be good if you are re-using the same resources in different weeks/topics. Again, it depends on how many files people have to upload.

Dishing out the work

I've now uploaded my files, got My private files area organized, and now I want to give them out to my students. No one else has direct access to My private files area, so I have to provide links to files from the course main page.

 Remember that making resources available to Moodle users is a two-stage process. First of all, files are uploaded to Moodle (as I've been demonstrating, to My private files area). Then, links to those files are added to the course front page.

So let's return there now and add a link in our course to one of the files I've just uploaded.

Time for action – giving students individual files

1. Go to your course page and choose the topic you want to add the file to. I'm going to add my handout to Topic 1 (**Getting Things Flying...**).

2. Are the **Add a resource...** and **Add an activity...** options visible on your course main page?

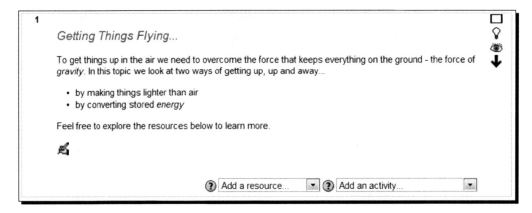

If not then you need to turn editing on (press the **Turn editing on** button—usually in the top right-hand corner of the page).

3. Click on **Add a resource** and choose **File**. This displays the **Adding a new File...** page:

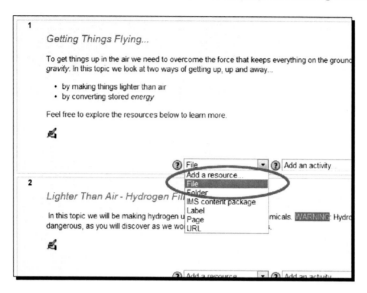

4. In the General box, I'm going to call this resource **Sources of Energy** (that's what the handout is about). You'll also need to type in a description (note this can be as short or long as you like):

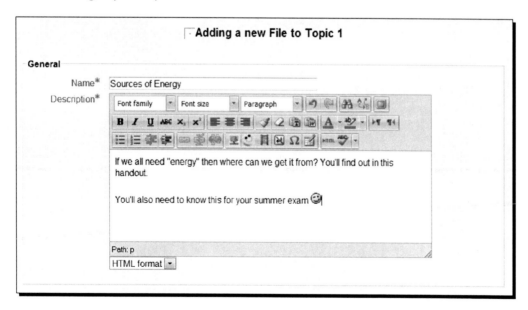

5. In the **Content** box press the **Add...** button:

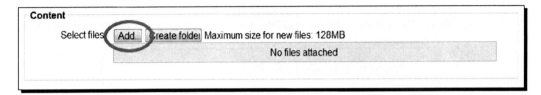

6. The **File picker** dialog window is displayed. Click on the **Private files** link on the left of the dialog:

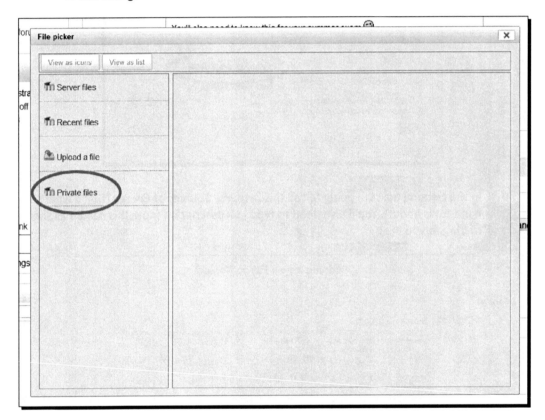

7. All of the files in your Private files area will be displayed in the right-hand pane in the File picker. Use the File picker to select the file you want to hand out:

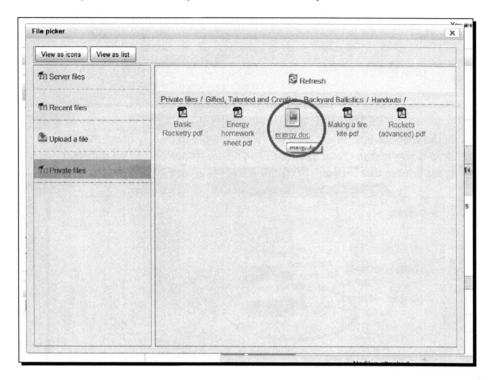

8. Once chosen, press the **Select this file** button:

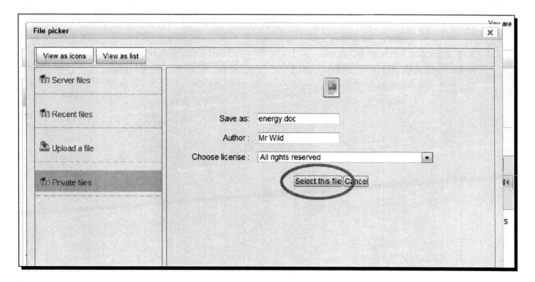

9. The file is now selected in the **Content** box:

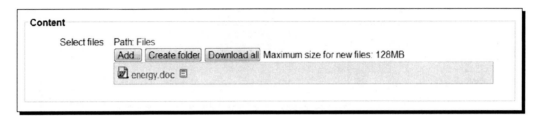

10. In the **Options** box, select how you want the file to display using the **Display** drop-down menu. I tend to choose **In pop-up** (there's more on different display types later in this section):

11. Press the **Save and return to course** button (if you press Save and display and you have a pop-up blocker installed on your computer then your file won't be shown).

12. You are now back at your course front page. There should be a Word icon (if you uploaded a Word document), and the resource name immediately under the Topic 1 description:

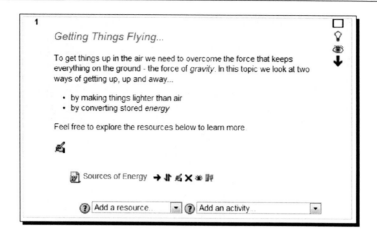

13. Click on the link to the resource and the document should load in a new window.

What just happened?

We've learned how to upload a file and how to include it in our course. Note that, although students can download a file from My private files area, as the name suggests, they can't upload one. You don't have to worry about students changing your files (if you want to upload a document for students to modify then we'll be looking at this task later in the book).

Accessing collections of files

Imagine you've got lots of files you want to provide (say photographs of a school trip). I've got quite a few photographs of experiments from previous years that I've carried out with my students that I want to make available. I've got those images stored in directories—one for each year on my laptop:

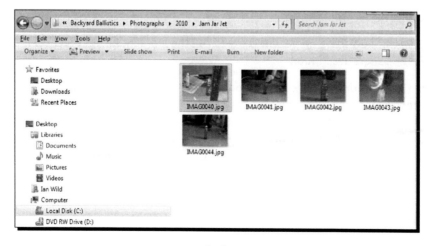

...and I've uploaded them to My private files using the techniques we have learned so far:

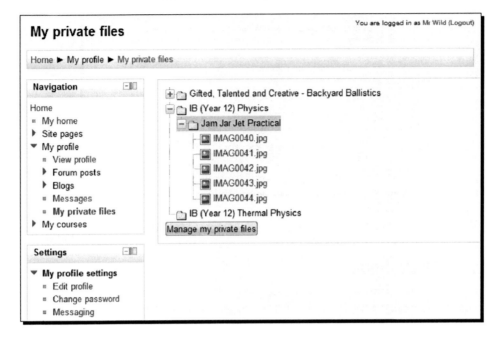

Now I am going to display a link to these files from the course front page. Here's how:

Time for action – displaying a folder

1. Choose a topic in your course (I'm going to choose "Basic Rocketry") and click on **Add a resource...** (if you don't see this option then check to see whether you have editing turned on).

2. Select **Folder** from the list.

3. Give this new link a name. I'm going to call the link **Jam Jar Jet Practical (2010)**. Enter a short description.

4. In the **Content** box, click on the **Add...** button. In the File picker dialog click on the **Private files** repository from the list of available repositories on the left. Select the files you wish to display. Notice that you'll need to add files one at a time (if you're an old-time Moodle user then you'll be used to simply choosing a folder in your course files area but you can see that Moodle no longer works in this way):

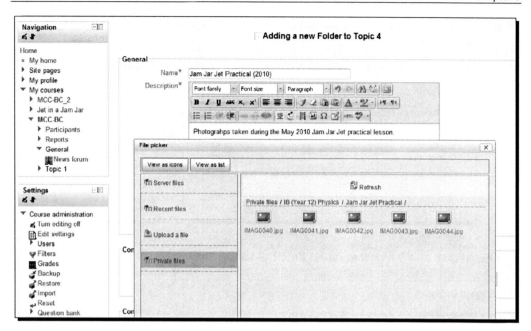

5. The files to be displayed in the folder will be listed on the **Adding a new Folder** page:

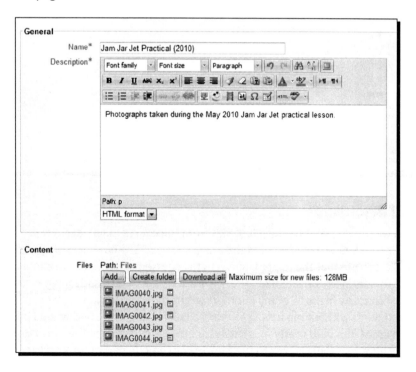

6. Click on the **Save and return to course** button. A new folder will be added to your course:

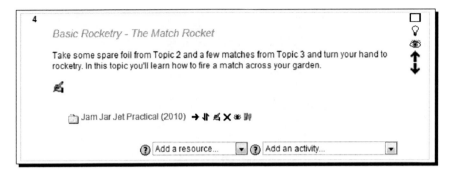

7. If I click on my new **Jam Jar Jet Practical (2010)** link I see this:

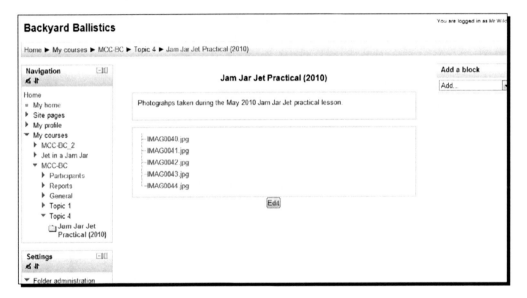

What just happened?

Not only can we provide links to individual files from the course main page, we can also gather files into folders. I uploaded all of the images for handing out into a single folder in My private files area. Note that the folder I added to my course page could have contained files from various folders in My private files. There are advantages and disadvantages to doing this. For example, I can now make all of my photographs from the 2010 Jam Jar Jet experiments available to students without me having to make a link for each one. But, when I open the folder, I get a list of files with pretty meaningless names. However, another advantage is that students only have read-only access to the files—they can't upload or remove them.

A default Moodle installation doesn't support thumbnails, which can be a problem if you've just given access to a directory full of images. But don't worry: speak to your Moodle administrator about this and they will be able to install one of many image slideshow plugins available from `Moodle.org`.

Repositories

Moodle is designed to be a virtual learning environment/course management system. But there's nothing wrong with simply using Moodle as a repository to store files: one clear advantage is that you can easily control who has access to the files and the access can be anytime and anywhere (unlike a shared drive in your school or workplace, for instance). Moodle can act like a file repository but, cleverer still, Moodle can connect to specially designed file repositories. What do I mean by that? Have you ever used YouTube? That's a repository for video files. Have you ever uploaded a picture to Flickr? That's a repository for images. To understand how Moodle can connect to external repositories, let's take another look at the File picker dialog. Recall that the links down the left-hand side of the File picker are links to repositories:

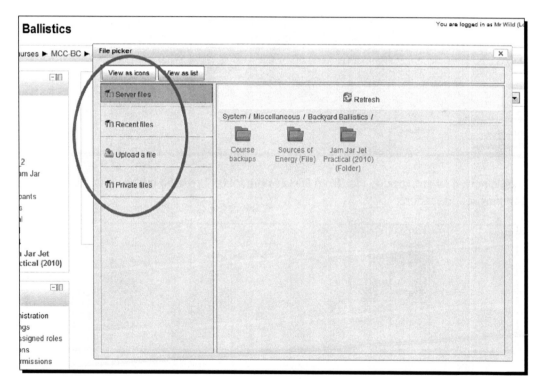

You might well see more links to "repositories" in your File picker. For instance, the photo-sharing website Flickr (`http://www.flickr.com`) can be configured as a repository. Do you use Dropbox (`http://www.dropbox.com`) to share files between home and work? Our school admin set one up for us so that staff in our department can share files—and access them easily from home, too. If you've something similar then Dropbox can be added as a repository, too. If I ask my Moodle admin to enable the Flickr and Dropbox repositories in Moodle, then my File picker now looks like this:

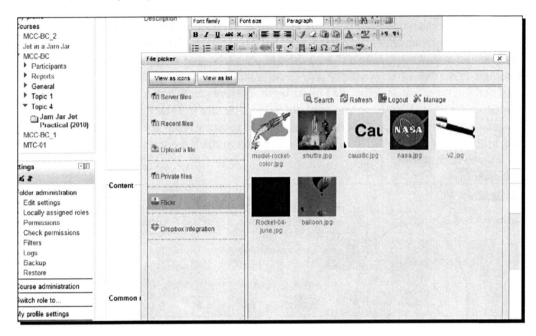

I could now, if I want, include files from Flickr in the folder I created in the previous Time for action section:

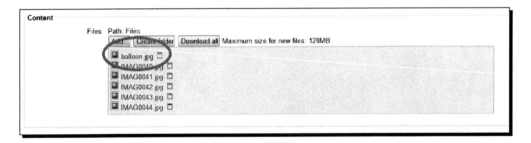

I've added into the folder the picture of hot air balloons from the Flickr repository. It's worth noting that Moodle has made it's own "internal" copy of the picture and added this copy into the folder (and no, unfortunately we didn't all get to go up in a hot air balloon as part of the Jam Jar Jet experiment).

Do your students have direct access to your Private files area? How do you provide a link to a file in your Private files area?

Documents and handouts: Which format

You could get all of your files uploaded now, provide links in your course main page and start letting students in right now if you wanted to. But wait for a moment. We haven't really thought about the kinds of files we should upload.

Some bits of the following section are, by necessity, a little technical. If there is anything you are unsure about then speak to your administrator, technician, or IT help desk, if you have one.

Do you use Microsoft Word to create your documents? Here's why distributing Microsoft Word documents might be a bad idea:

- It's wrong to assume that students are going to have Word installed on their PC.

- If students have an older version of Word than yours installed on their PC then they probably won't be able to open it. This is especially true if the document filename ends in `.docx`. That's the new(ish) Microsoft Word 2007 format which isn't compatible with previous versions of Word. There is free compatibility software available from Microsoft (`http://office.microsoft.com/en-us/word/HA100444731033.aspx`) but you can't assume that your users will all have that installed—and know how to install it if they don't.

The solution is to convert your Word document to a format that everyone can open. And that's just some of the issues with Word. Let's look at the most popular document types and investigate how we can convert them into a format that's just right for Moodle.

Microsoft Word

You can see that I've potentially done something that might cause me problems when one of the first files I uploaded to my course was a Word document. If you find you have this problem then one solution is to convert Word documents to Portable Document Format (PDF). In the past it's been quite difficult to create PDF documents (basically you had to buy Adobe Acrobat, buy PDF printer software, or try to find a decent open source PDF printer).

However, today creating PDF documents is becoming easier. If you have Microsoft Word 2007 or above, you can install the Save as PDF Add-In, available directly from the Microsoft website. OpenOffice, the free alternative to Microsoft Office, has a word processor called Writer and this has a built-in option to create PDF files (simply select **File | Export As PDF...** from the main menu). If you do convert to PDF then it is worth checking the document before you upload it as the conversion process can often change the format of the document. Also, if you want to create a PDF form then you might need to consider purchasing a dedicated PDF creation tool.

If your student doesn't have a PDF reader installed on their computer (which is highly unlikely) they will be asked by their PC to install one when they try to open your PDF document.

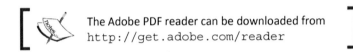

The Adobe PDF reader can be downloaded from
`http://get.adobe.com/reader`

If you don't have access to any sort of PDF creation tool then opt for Rich Text Format (RTF). From Word, select **File | Save As...** and from the **File Type** menu in the **Save As** dialog, select **Rich Text Format (*.rtf)**. However, be aware that document formatting is much more limited if you convert your file to RTF. For example, you can't create RTF forms in the same way as you can with PDF documents.

We'll be looking at further options for converting Word documents to more Moodle-friendly formats later in this chapter.

Images

Although there are many image file formats to choose from, the three that really only need concern us are JPEG (pronounced "jay-peg"), PNG (pronounced "ping"), and GIF (which was meant to be pronounced with a hard "g", as in George, but is often spoken with a soft "g" as in Graphics). PNG files are great on the Web for line drawings and clip art. If you have any images that include text in them then choose PNG (if you save as a JPEG then the text can look all blurred). JPEGs are excellent for photographs (the PEG in JPEG stands for Photographic Experts Group, so they should know what they are doing when it comes to photographs). GIF was one of the first image formats used on the Internet so a web search for images will no doubt turn up lots of GIF files—especially animated GIFs.

You might also come across the PNG-24 image format. This format is also good for photographs.

There are so many tools available for converting between different image formats I'm simply going to send you in the direction of your administrator, help desk, or technician if you aren't sure which tool to use for converting (if you ask there is usually a standard tool that your establishment will expect you to use).

You don't have to just provide a link to images from your course front page. You can also include them in your text, just like you would in a document. I've got quite a few images I've gathered as part of my Backyard Ballistics course, so I'm going to upload those now. Not only that, but I want to include one of my images in the "Summary of General" (the unnumbered topic) at the top of the page, to make my course front page (hopefully) even more enticing for my students.

Time for action – uploading an image and including it in a summary

1. Ensure your image file is in the correct repository (for example, My private files or Flickr).

2. Return to your course front page and click on the Summary of General edit summary icon.

3. In the editor, open up the **Insert Image** dialog by clicking on the **Insert/edit Image** button. That's the button containing the little tree:

4. The **Insert/edit image** dialog is displayed. Press the **Find or upload an image...** button to display the **File picker** dialog. Find the image you want to include and select it. You will see the image previewed in the preview pane at the bottom of the **Insert/edit image** dialog:

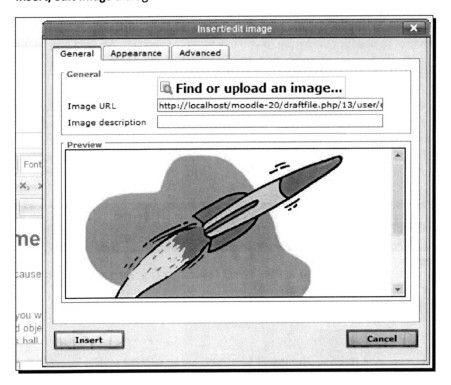

5. Type a description of the picture in the **Image description** box. You won't be able to press the **OK** button until you do.

6. Press the **OK** button.

7. That's it. Your picture is now added:

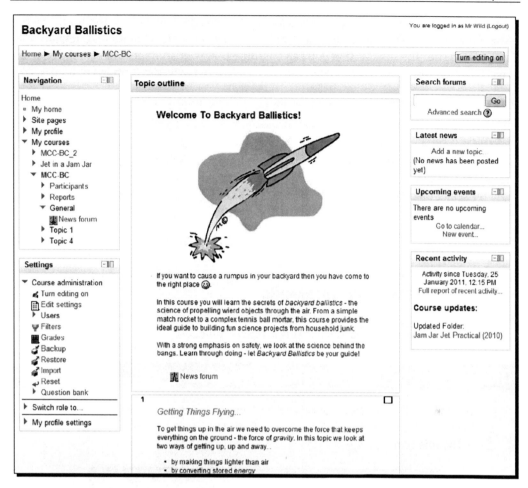

What just happened?

We've just seen how easy it is to include a picture with any text in Moodle. We'll be looking in more detail at how to arrange images in *Chapter 5, Moodle Makeover*. For now, you could try returning to the Insert/edit image dialog and taking a look at the settings in the Appearance tab. Have a play with the settings and remember: you won't break anything!

Have a go hero – having fun with images

Return to the **Insert/edit image** dialog and click on the **Advanced** tab. You can use the Advanced settings to change the image when the mouse pointer moves over it and change it again when the mouse pointer moves off it. For example, you could reveal the names of characters from a film or play by your students moving the mouse pointer over their picture.

PowerPoint has become almost the de facto format for teaching materials. The big problem is that PowerPoint presentations are big. Often their size more than breaks that default 2 MB upload size. The other is that you can't assume that your students can actually open a PowerPoint file and view it (they might not have the correct software installed at home).

Let's run through the options you have for uploading presentations.

Uploading as-is

Don't worry about converting the file to any other format. Just upload the PPT file as it is and create a link to it on your course front page. You could also save the file as a PowerPoint show (PPS) and upload that as-is. Your students will still need a compatible viewer (certainly Microsoft has free viewers available for download).

But what if you find that your presentation is far too big and your students are complaining that it is taking an age to download?

Preparing your PowerPoint for Moodle

Does your presentation contain lots of images? If so, we can use PowerPoint to help us keep file sizes small. Let's see how to achieve this in PowerPoint 2007:

Time for action – compressing images

1. Look through your presentation and find an image (any image will do). Once you have found one, click on it. The **Picture Tools** toolbar in the ribbon will be indicated in the title bar:

2. Click on **Picture Tools** to display the **Format** toolbar in the ribbon:

3. In the **Format** toolbar, press the **Compress Pictures** button:

4. The **Compress Pictures** dialog is displayed. We want to compress and crop all the images in the presentation. Ensure that the **Apply to selected pictures only** checkbox is unchecked (because we want to compress all of them) and press the **Options...** button. Ensure you have **Automatically perform basic compression on save** and **Delete cropped areas of pictures** selected. For maximum image compression without any appreciable degrading of image quality, change the resolution to Screen (150 ppi):

5. Press the **OK** button. Press the **OK** button again.

6. That's it. We're done!

What just happened?

If oversized, uncompressed images are making your PowerPoint presentations very large then we can easily crop and compress images before we hand them out to our students.

If you are still having problems with file size (maybe your presentation doesn't contain large images) then it may be time to think about converting the presentation to a different file format before we upload them to Moodle.

Converting into documents

If you use Microsoft Office 2007 or later, or OpenOffice, then export your presentation as a PDF file. A good attempt will be made at preserving layout and formatting, although you may well lose those pretty animations and effects because we are converting to a static format (the technology is changing all the time and it is always best to try the conversion to see what the results are).

For OpenOffice users, select **File | Export As PDF...** from the main menu. In Microsoft Office 2007, click on the **Office** button at the top-left corner of the screen. Hover the mouse over the **Save As...** option and select **PDF**. Note that the special PDF add-in for Office may need to be installed first. If it isn't then follow the on-screen instructions.

If you want to try converting your PowerPoint to a PDF but you aren't an OpenOffice or Office 2007 user then you could try one of the many PDF printers that are available (as freeware, so they won't cost you anything). A PDF printer works by you selecting **File | Print** and then instead of choosing your normal printer you choose the PDF printer instead. Rather than producing a hard copy of your presentation this "printer" produces a PDF file. If you think this approach is worthy of further investigation then it may be worth speaking to your admin.

If you have an earlier version of Microsoft Office, select **File | Save As...** from the main menu to display the **Save As** dialog. Click on the **Save as type list** at the bottom of this dialog. You'll see lots of different options listed. To save as a document select **Outline/RTF**. Note that when it says outline it means outline. Not only will you lose all of your pretty animations and effects but you'll also lose all of your formatting and images, basically leaving you with raw text (and you may also lose your raw text, depending on how the text was placed on the page). Treat saving your document as an RTF file as the option of last resort.

Converting into images

This is a useful option if you don't want your students to be able to copy and paste text easily.

In all versions of Microsoft Office, check out the **Save as type** options in the **Save As** dialog.

In OpenOffice, select **File | Export...** from the main menu. Click on the **File format** list to display the different image options.

In both OpenOffice and Microsoft Office, if you are saving as an image then remember to chose between PNG and JPEG (see the earlier discussion on images on why these are the best types out of all of your options to choose, and how to choose between them).

Pop quiz

The size of PowerPoint files can be greatly reduced by cropping and compressing any images contained in the presentation. Can you remember the steps to compress images?

Converting into web pages

This option is a little more technical, but can be worth it. Saving as web pages in both Microsoft Office and OpenOffice is easy. In Microsoft Office ensure you have Web Page selected in the **Save as type list** (don't choose Single File Web Page). In OpenOffice you need to choose **File | Export...** from the main menu. Select **HTML Document** in the File format list.

Using either tool will create a set of web pages and their associated files (images, and so on) all stored in a specific folder structure (depending on the tool you use, but that we don't need to know about). We need to upload all the files and folders to Moodle. If you aren't feeling confident in your own abilities to upload the files then speak to your Moodle administrator, help desk, or technician. Once the files have been uploaded (making sure you preserve the folder structure), then you need to create a link to the file ending in .htm that has the same name as the original PowerPoint presentation.

Becoming a cut and paste fiend with a Moodle "page"

If you have documents that you have to change fairly often, then you will find that you have to download the document, edit it, and then re-upload it over and over again. The way around this problem is to copy the document into a Moodle "page". Note that this is different from the web page conversion outlined previously. A Moodle "web page"—simply called a "page"—is a web page we can create using Moodle's built-in HTML editor. I keep a list of suppliers of equipment for the hydrogen balloon experiment (the students are expected to bring in their own). Rather than just uploading the document I'm going to convert this into a web page.

Time for action – creating a web page

1. Return to your course front page and make sure you have editing turned on.

2. In the topic you want to add your new web page into, click on **Add a resource...** and select **Page** from the list.

3. Give the new web page a name and specify a description.

4. Copy and paste the text from the original document into the new web page (the "Page content" area).

5. At the bottom of the page, press the **Save and display** button.

What just happened?

We can convert documents into a web page. This only really works for smaller documents, and is very useful if documents change quite frequently as it saves you having to download it, change it, save it, and then upload it again. The other obvious benefit is that students will be able to read it without having to install any additional software.

Don't make this mistake: cutting and pasting images doesn't work

Remember that images must be uploaded to Moodle (to My private files or via a repository) and then included in your web page using the Insert/edit image button. You can't cut and paste them.

Cleanup messy code

A Moodle page is basically a web page (remember you are pasting text into an HTML editor). If you are cutting and pasting from Microsoft Word into a web page then Word tries to be clever and attempts to convert your text into web code (it does this so that any formatting applied to the text stays intact). The problem is that this web code can be very Microsoft-specific (containing lots of Microsoft-specific formatting information) which then breaks Moodle's built-in editor. (Note that this isn't just a problem with Moodle, lots of different software applications use the same text editor Moodle employs. You might even recognize Moodle's editor from another software tool you use). If you are pasting from Word then try using the Paste from Word button. If you're pasting from another application then it's worthwhile pressing the **Cleanup messy code** button after you do so:

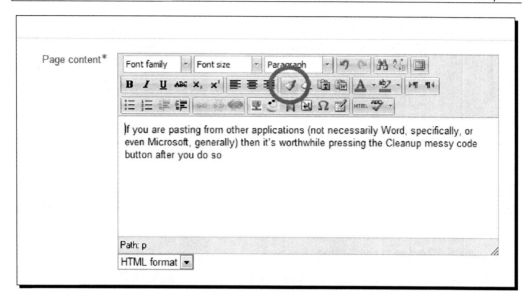

If you are pasting from other applications (not necessarily Word, specifically, or even Microsoft, generally) then it's worthwhile pressing the Cleanup messy code button after you do so

Turning large documents into a wiki

My physics department has a departmental handbook, which describes how the department is organized, what its aims are, details of the department's policies and practices, and so on. Maintaining the handbook presents a lot of problems. We try to ensure different members of the department complete different parts, but it is very difficult to collate these when they have been written. How can we make ownership of this document truly collective? The task of putting together our handbook, as well as all the other documentation we need, often detracts us from doing our actual job (teaching!—but that's sometimes difficult to remember given all the other things we are expected to do). How do we show the subject inspector that we are really working together as a team creating our departmental documentation?

An elegant solution is to turn departmental documentation into a wiki. "Wiki" is Hawaiian for quick (see http://en.wikipedia.org/wiki/Wiki), and a wiki is a quick way of creating web pages and linking them together. Not only that but you can work on the web pages with your colleagues collaboratively (allowing colleagues to contribute or modify content)—and that will really impress the inspectors. Also, built into the system is an audit trail. This means you can see who modified what and when. It also means you can revert to previous versions and easily compare one version to another.

To show you how easy it is to create a wiki, I'm going to use one instead of uploading the teacher notes I have for my Backyard Ballistics course.

So far, all the static content added to our course has been converted to Moodle using a Moodle resource. A wiki is an activity because you are expecting users to work together on the contents of the wiki. This is one instance where the boundaries between what constitutes a resource and what would be best described as an activity can become blurred.

Firstly, I'm going to add a new topic called "TEACHER DOCUMENTATION" on the end of my course for teacher documentation. I'm going to keep this topic and its contents hidden from my students.

Time for action – adding a hidden topic

1. Return to the course front page. Click on the **Edit settings** link under **Course administration** in the **Settings** block.

2. Click on **Number of weeks/topics** list and add another topic.

3. Scroll down to the bottom of the page and press the **Save changes** button.

4. Edit the new topic's summary to tell your colleagues (and the inspector) that this topic is specifically for teacher documentation and nothing else.

5. Hide the topic from your students by clicking on the open eye on the right-hand side. The eye closes to indicate that the topic is hidden:

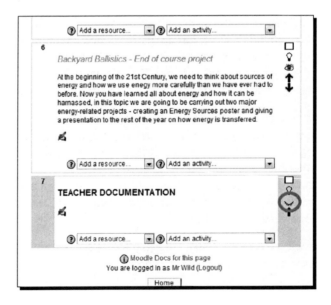

6. You're done!

What just happened?

I've just added a new topic to my Backyard Ballistics course in which I'm going to put teacher documentation. I only want my colleagues to view this information so I've hidden the topic from my students.

Time for action – adding a wiki

1. In the Teacher Documentation topic, click on **Add an activity...** and select **Wiki** from the list.

2. The name of my new wiki is going to be **Backyard Ballistics Guidelines**. Enter a name for your wiki.

3. Write a brief summary of the wiki. This is shown above every page. Keep it short and descriptive.

4. Choose a name for the first page of your wiki (my first page is going to be the contents).

5. Ensure the Wiki mode is set to Collaborative wiki (meaning that everyone has equal editing rights but remember that we have hidden the topic that it's in):

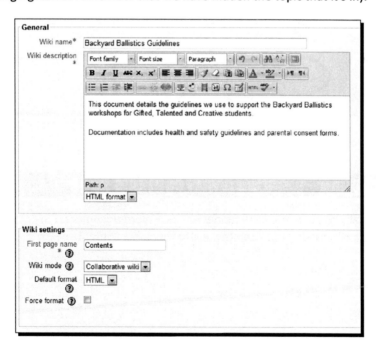

6. Scroll to the bottom of the page and press the **Save and return to course** button.

What just happened?

You now have a link from your course to a new, empty wiki—but you still need your documentation in it.

Click on the link to your new wiki on the course front page. We are now ready to create the first page in our wiki. Ensure you have HTML format selected and press the **Create page** button:

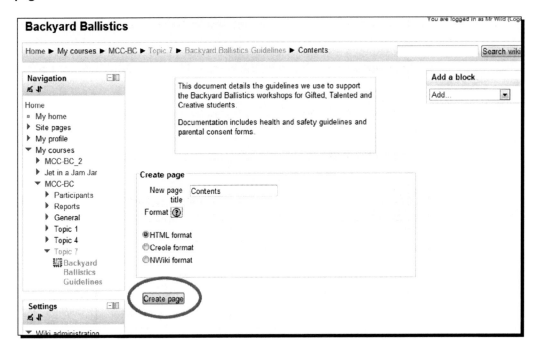

Let's start developing the wiki by creating the contents page.

Time for action – creating a wiki contents page

1. I originally wrote my teacher guidelines as a Word document. I'm going to cut and paste the contents page from these into the wiki's contents page:

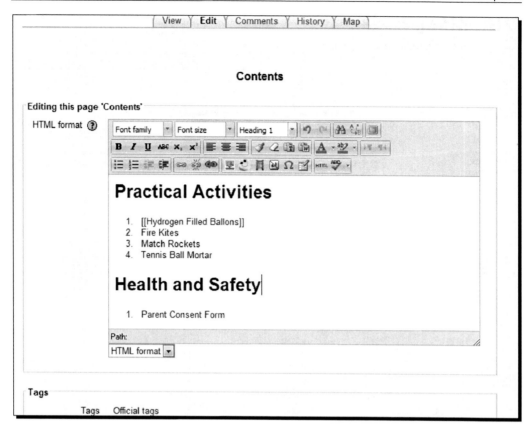

2. If you are cutting and pasting from another application (it doesn't have to be just Word) then remember to press the **Cleanup messy code** button. Note also that I've used the Heading 1 style for the titles "Practical Activities" and "Health and Safety". Doing so means the wiki system will recognize these as section titles and include a link to them in the "Table of Contents" box for this page (which you'll see shortly).

3. You can specify tags—these are words that are associated with a wiki page that can be used later on to help find information (rather than searching for a word in the text). As this is the contents page for my wiki, I'm not going to worry about tagging it.

4. Click on **Save**.

5. That's it. You're done!

What just happened?

I've just created a wiki contents page:

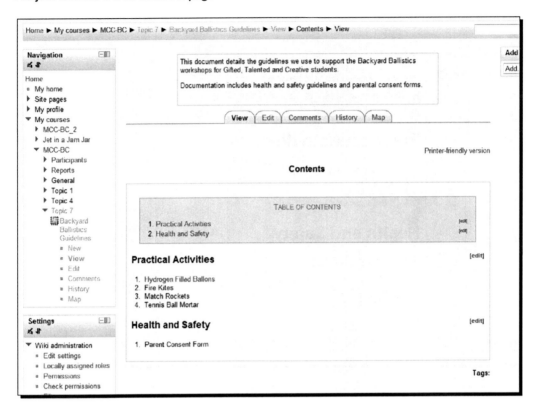

However, I don't want to simply copy and paste the entire document into a single wiki page. Rather, I want to be able to turn each item in the contents into a link which then takes me to the relevant page. Once the page is created I can simply cut and paste the page from my original document. Here's the clever part: once I tell the wiki where I want a link to a new page, the wiki will create it for me. I just have to copy over my text. Here's how...

Time for action – adding a new wiki page

1. Click on the **Edit** tab at the top of the page:

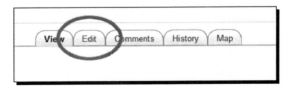

2. I want to turn the item **Hydrogen Filled Balloons** into a link to a new page. To do this I'm going to enclose the words in double-square brackets:

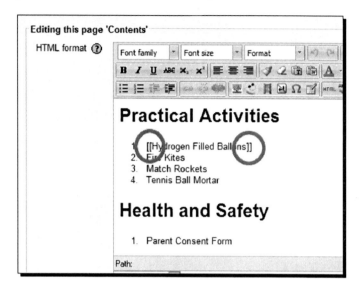

3. Press the **Save** button.

4. Before moving on, take a look at the words we encased in square brackets. They are now red and in italics:

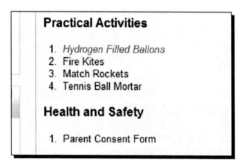

5. "Hydrogen Filled Balloons" is now a link. Click on the link and the wiki automatically asks you whether you want to create a new page (you'll need to press the **Create page** button again)—that's the "quick" part. I'm going to copy the contents of my teacher notes for the Hydrogen Filled Balloons experiment into the page (repeating the process I used before).

6. Press the **Save** button when you are done creating the new page.

7. That's it. The new page has been created. To try out the new wiki, and to test to see whether your new link works, return to your course main page. Click on the wiki and you will be shown the wiki's contents page:

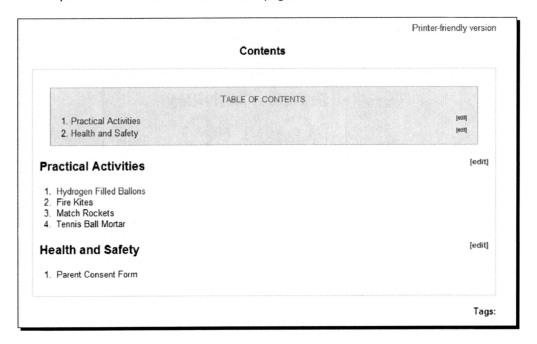

8. The item "**Hydrogen Filled Balloons**" is now a link, which I can click on to take me to that page in my teacher notes.

What just happened?

We've seen just how easy it is to create linked pages using a wiki. This is an ideal solution for lengthy course, and even departmental, documentation.

Did you notice the **History** tab that appears above each page? This displays an audit trail for the page. Let's take a look at the audit trail for the wiki contents page:

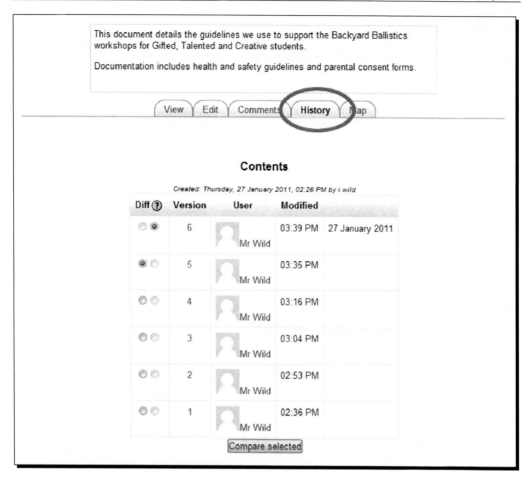

Only I've been editing this page so far, but if my colleagues had been editing it as well then they would be listed in there, too.

Pop quiz

If you've just cut and pasted text from a Word document then there's a special button in the HTML editor that is worthwhile pressing before you go any further. What's the name of that button?

Summary

I think you'll agree that we are getting on great guns with our Moodle courses. Just in this single chapter we:

- Uploaded files to Moodle and organized them effectively
- Learned how to present documents and handouts to students
- Uploaded images and included them in text
- Included PowerPoint presentations, and learned what to do if students had problems viewing them
- Learned how to work with a wiki
- Now know which types of files are best to include in a course, and how to create them

We've now got our courses populated with static content. At this stage, you might even want to introduce students onto your course. They won't fail to be impressed with the work you have done so far! Remember, if you have set an enrolment key, you will need to give this out to your students.

In the next chapter we will be learning how to make our courses more engaging and entertaining with sound, video, and multimedia.

Sound and Vision—Including Multimedia Content

In the previous chapters, we saw how easy it is to hand out work through Moodle. That's great for a start, but I want to make my course as much entertaining as it is practical. I've also got lots of multimedia content I want to include: for instance, I've got lots of audio and video files—many of them on file sharing websites such as YouTube.

Let's build on what we learned in *Chapter 3, Adding Documents and Handouts* with, in this chapter, learning the best ways of importing sound and vision into our courses. In this chapter you will learn how to:

- Import audio and video into your course
- Experience the different ways Moodle plays your multimedia files, and appreciate the pros and cons of each
- Embed videos from other websites, such as YouTube, TeacherTube, and Vimeo
- Create a photo montage using Slide.com

Recall that in *Chapter 3, Adding Documents and Handouts* we uploaded our documents and handouts to our own, personal 'My private files' area and inserted links to those files on our course pages. We also learned how to include files from other repositories—remember that what repositories we have available to us will depend on how our Moodles have been configured.

We start this chapter by creating links from our course main page directly to external websites. You might be forgiven for thinking that I should have covered creating links to external websites on the course front page in previous chapters. I've delayed the discussion to this chapter because it forms the basis of the work we are now going to carry out. It is worth mentioning, before we begin, that directly linking to external websites is an easy way for us to use Moodle to create engaging multimedia courses—and it is the first step to moving away from using Moodle as a simple resource repository.

Linking to other websites

If you are anything like me then you've got a list of websites that include lots of exciting content, which you want to include in your course. I've got all of mine saved in a Word document, but let's look at getting these transferred over to Moodle. Here are my options:

- Simply upload the Word document. We learned how to do this in *Chapter 3, Adding Documents and Handouts*.
- Make a list of links in the course main page.
- Create a Moodle web page and include the links in that.

We've already looked at the problems of uploading a Word document in the previous chapter, and although convenient, it would be far better to have my list of links in Moodle, rather than in a file that is, technically, outside of Moodle. Here's why:

- Students may not have the correct file viewer installed on their computer (an important issue we covered in previous chapters)
- We make it easier for students to find the links
- I can mix links to external websites and links to files I've uploaded, and do so seamlessly
- If we link to external websites from Moodle, we can monitor which students have visited which websites

Instead, let's start by including the links directly on the course main page.

Adding a link to the course main page

It's time for action. Let's see how easy it is to add links to external websites on the course main page.

Time for action – creating links to websites on the course main page

As far as Moodle is concerned, a link to a file in My private files (or any repository) is just like a link to a web page. This might be a bit confusing at first. The best way to think of it is that you can link to a file or link to a web page. Either way, it's still a link. Return to your course front page and make sure that editing is turned on. If editing is turned on, then you will see the **Add a resource...** and **Add an activity...** drop-down menus at the bottom of each week/topic:

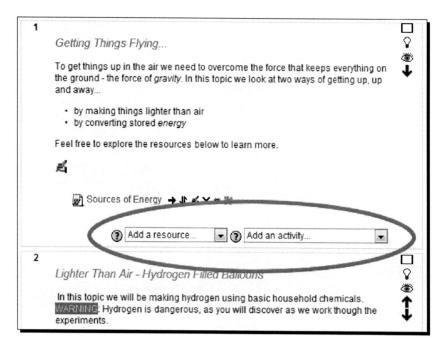

In the topic you want to include your link in, click on **Add a resource...** and choose **URL**.

1. Give the new resource a name. It could be just the name of the website you are linking to. I'm going to call mine "Firing a bullet from a gun", because that's what the website I'm linking to is about.

2. Type a brief description of the website in the Description box.

3. Copy the address of the web page into the Location field. I'm going to cut and paste my website from the Word document I have.

4. Alternatively, you can also find a 'link' by pressing the **Choose a link...** button. This opens up the File picker but only displaying repositories of files on external websites. Recall in *Chapter 3, Adding Documents and Handouts* I asked my Moodle admin to configure the YouTube and Flickr repositories? As these are external websites these repositories are displayed in my File picker:

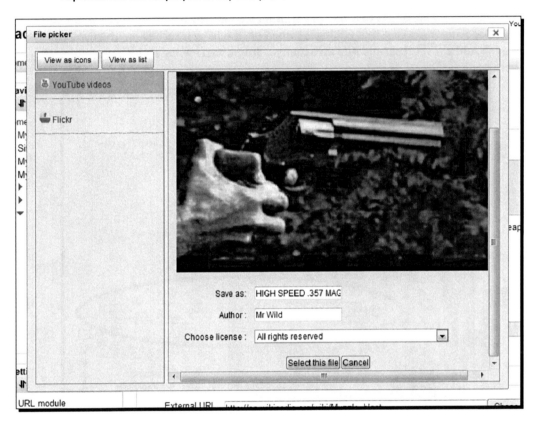

5. Remember to specify **In pop-up** in the Options configuration box. Simply click on the **Display** drop-down menu and select **In pop-up**:

6. Scroll to the bottom of the page and press the **Save and return to course** button.

7. That's it! You're done.

You've now added a link to a web page to the course front page:

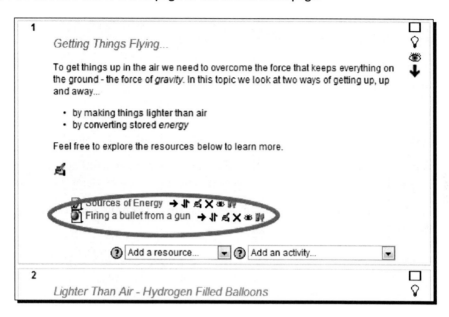

What just happened?

In just the same way we added a link to a document or handout in previous chapters, we've just added a link to an external website. But imagine if you wanted to share lots of links in this way? Before long the course home page would soon become unwieldy—with a topic containing nothing more than a long list of links. Fortunately, we can get around this by including links in a Moodle web page, which is the subject covered in the next section.

Turning text into a web link

Another alternative to uploading a file (a Word file, say) containing a long list of links is to create a Moodle web page and include our links in that (remember we looked at converting documents to Moodle web pages in *Chapter 3, Adding Documents and Handouts* – Become a cut and paste fiend). Rather than having that page being simply a long list of links, I can make things look much more appealing by including pictures, and by having more scope to arrange the layout of the page to make the links easier to find. What's more, to make the conversion easier, I can copy and paste from the original document. Let's look at doing this now.

Time for action – putting links in a Moodle web page

To aid the conversion, try arranging your desktop so that you have a Word document and a browser with Moodle in side by side. This will save you from repeatedly toggling between Moodle and your original document.

1. Return to your course front page and make sure that you have editing turned on.

2. Choose the topic you want to include the links in and click on **Add a resource...** and then choose **Page** from the list.

3. Type in a name for the new page.

4. Enter a brief description. This is required but can be as long or short as you wish.

5. We are now ready to copy over the information from your Word document. Return to your original document and select and copy the links you need.

6. Return to Moodle and paste the text you just copied into the Page content editing area:

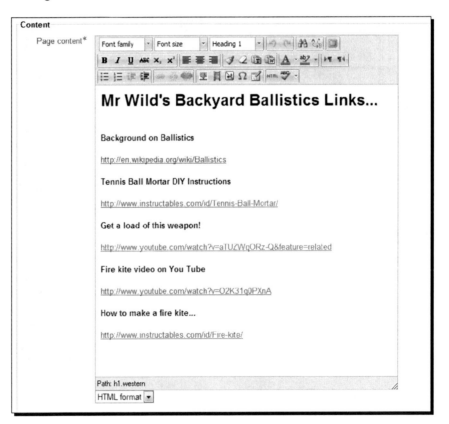

7. Press the **Cleanup messy code** button (the button with the brush icon), to make sure that we don't include any special word processing formatting—which we don't need now we are going to display the text in a browser.

8. Scroll down to the bottom of the page and press the **Save and return to course** button.

9. Check out your new web page by clicking on the link from the course front page:

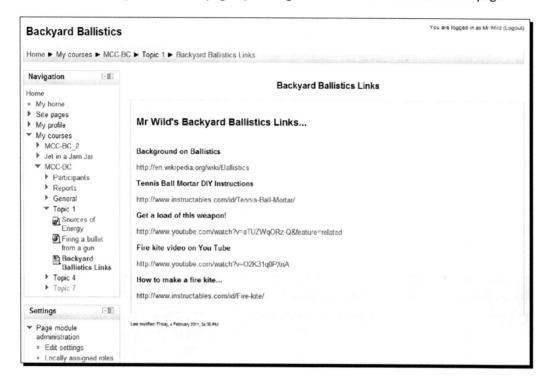

What just happened?

We've just created a Moodle web page containing links I've previously been noting down in a Word document. Rather than simply uploading the original document—which can introduce the problems we looked at in the bonus chapter, *Handing in Work through Moodle*—we've converted it into a Moodle web page. Open the new page now. Try clicking on a link and you will be navigated to the external website.

Manually adding links to Moodle web pages

Modern word processors are very kind to you when it comes to links. If you include what looks like a link in your document, the word processor will usually interpret it as a link and format it accordingly. This means that when you copy the text over to Moodle then it will take the formatting put in by the word processor and Moodle will still recognize the text as a link. This works in Moodle, too: if I type a link directly into the Moodle HTML editor then Moodle will recognize the text as a web link and automatically turn it into a link. What happens if, rather than having the student click on the actual web address, as in:

Click the link below to look at what Wikipedia has to say on Ballistics...

en.wikipedia.org/wiki/Ballistics

...we want the student to click on a piece of descriptive text, as in:

Click here to look at what Wikipedia has to say on Ballistics...

Next to the name of the Moodle web page you just created, click on the Update icon to open the resource configuration page. Let's see how we can select a word or fragment of text and turn this into a link.

Time for action – making a link out of text

The first link I've got listed is a link to the Wikipedia entry on Ballistics. I want the student to click on the phrase "Click here to look at what Wikipedia has to say on Ballistics", and for that to take them to the right page. I also want the new page to be displayed in a different window, to "stop Wikipedia from making Moodle disappear", to quote one of my students.

1. Enter the text you want to turn into a link and make sure you have it selected.

2. Press the **Insert/edit** link (it looks like three links of a chain) button. The Insert Web Link dialog will appear. Note that you can't press the button until you've selected something in the editor:

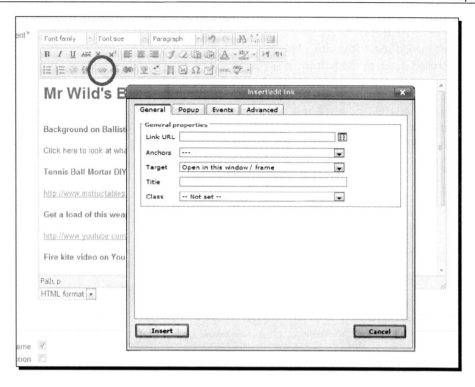

3. In the Link URL box, type in the address of the web page you want to link to.

4. Click on the Target list and select Open in new window (_blank).

5. Press the **Insert** button. We're done! The result of doing this is shown in the following screenshot:

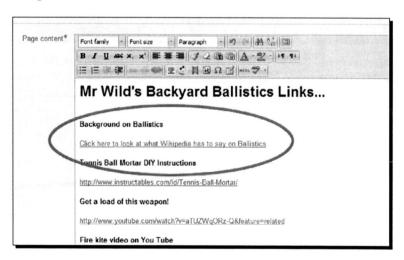

What just happened?

We've just turned some text into a link, but you won't be able to click on your new link until you've scrolled down to the bottom of the page and pressed the **Save and return to course** button. Open the web page and click on the link just to satisfy yourself that it works.

When you turned the text into a link, you pressed the **Insert/edit link** button to display the **Insert/edit link** dialog. Did you spot the **Browse...** button:

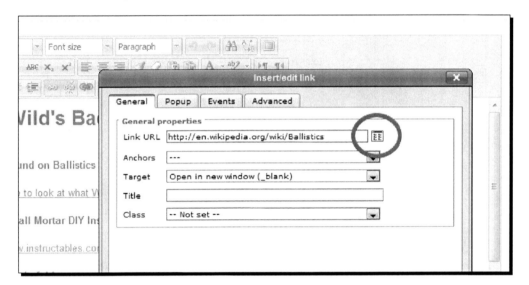

This button allows you to turn a bit of text into a link to a file in your My private files area, or another repository. This lets you mix links to external websites and links to files you've uploaded to Moodle from a single page.

Have a go hero – doing more with your links

You can use links from Moodle web pages to link to other documents in your course. Try creating a documents index. Make this index more appealing by including images (see *Chapter 5, Moodle Makeover,* for tips and tricks on making Moodle web pages more visually appealing).

Importing videos

Including a video in your course (e.g. a AVI, MOV, FLV, or WMV file) is as easy as uploading the file to your course files area and creating a link to it on your course main page, following the instructions in *Chapter 3, Adding documents and handouts*.

I'm going to talk about video file formats later in this section. For now, let's get straight on to including a video file in our courses...

Time for action – including a video on your course front page

The method for including a video on your course front page is exactly the same as the method for including documents and handouts that we worked through in *Chapter 3, Adding Documents and Handouts*. Let's just run through the procedure again to remind ourselves:

1. Upload the video to your private files area (see *Uploading Files* section in *Chapter 3, Adding Documents and Handouts* for more details). Remember that video files can be very big so it's worth checking the upload limit.

2. Select a topic and click on **Add a resource...** and choose **File** to display the **Adding a new File...** page.

3. Specify a name (which is the link your students will click on to watch the video) and a brief description.

4. Scroll down to the Content section and press the **Add...** button and the File picker is displayed. From the list of repositories on the left of the File picker, click **Upload a file**. Next to the Attachment box, press the **Browse...** button.

5. Once you've found the file, or selected the file you want, press the File picker's **Upload this file** button. The file will be listed in the **Content** section:

6. Ensure that you choose **In pop-up** as your display option and then scroll down to the bottom of the page and press the **Save and return to course** button.

7. A link to your video will now appear in your course Main page:

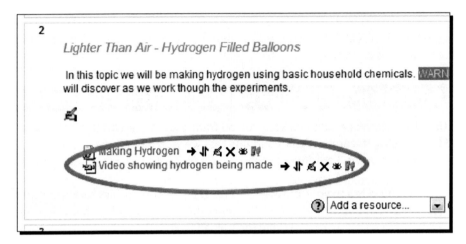

You can tell that my Moodle recognizes this file as a video because of the camera icon, to the right of the resource name. Don't forget to test your work. Click on the link and follow the instructions to view your newly included video.

What Just Happened?

We've just included a video in our course front page, in approximately the same way as we included a document or handout in *Chapter 3, Adding Documents and Handouts*. I say "approximately" because, rather than first uploading the video file to My private files I uploaded the file directly to the resource. Why not upload to My private files? Why didn't I show you that you could upload direct to the resource? It's probably the teacher in me, but I wanted you to understand that there were repositories in Moodle and how powerful that feature is. The reason for asking you to upload, initially, to My private files was an attempt on my part to build the right mental model of how Moodle's file storage system works.

Making Moodle play your videos

In the previous section, we saw that turning text into links was pretty straightforward. We can use the same idea to include videos and audio in our Moodle web pages. I've got a video of one of my students, and me making Hydrogen, that I want to include in my course. By embedding the video into a Moodle web page, I can compliment the video with explanatory text and supporting images.

I can also keep students on Moodle and focus on learning (rather than sending them to YouTube where they will be tempted to watch other videos). They can also read the supporting text and watch the video at the same time. By having Moodle handle video playback I can avoid the problem of the student not knowing how to use the video player they have installed on their computer (which could be one of many).

Before I begin there are two things I need to do with my video:

1. Ensure the file is in the correct format (see *Choosing a video file format* later in this chapter).

2. Upload the video, following the instructions in *Chapter 3, Adding Documents and Handouts*. I've created a separate Videos folder in my own My private files area to store all my videos in.

Time for action – embedding a video into a Moodle Page

1. Create a new Page resource and give it a name and a brief description. I'm going to call mine Instructions For Making Hydrogen.

2. I've started to add some text and an image to my instructions, and I am now at the point where I would like to include a video:

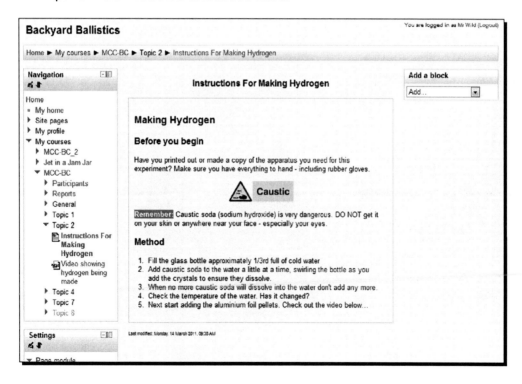

3. Let's insert the video file I've just uploaded. To do that I'm going to position the cursor at the bottom of the edit box, then I'm going to press the **Moodle Media** button to display the **Insert/edit embedded media** dialog:

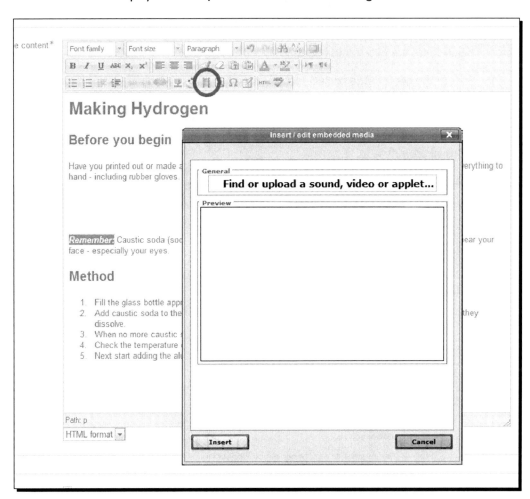

4. Click on the **Find or upload a sound, video or applet...** link. The **File picker** is displayed, but only showing repositories that are relevant to sound and/or video. The file I need to pick out is in **My private files**:

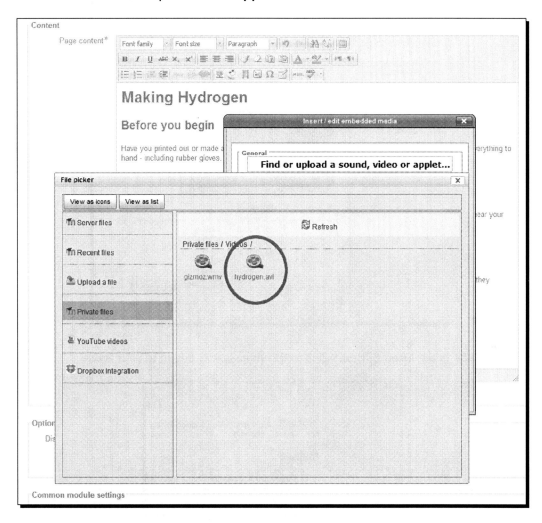

5. Note that I can use the Upload a file link in the list of repositories to upload my video if I wanted too, but I find it easier to upload to My private files first. Either way, use the File picker to navigate to your video file. Once you've found the file, click on it to select it. Press the **Select this file** button and you are returned to the Insert/edit embedded media dialog.

6. If all is well then a preview of your video file is displayed:

7. Click on the **Insert** button. A link to the video is now added to your text:

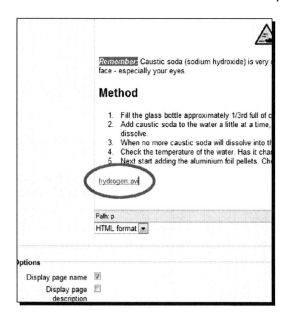

8. Scroll down to the bottom of the page and press the **Save and return to course** button. Click on the link to the page and check to ensure the video is displayed correctly:

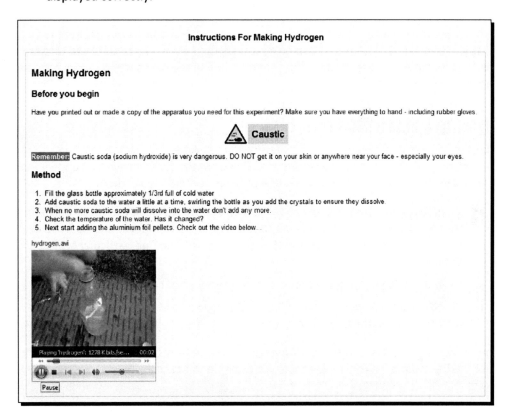

9. In the previous screenshot, you can see the link and Moodle's embedded video player. If you only saw a link then the multimedia plugins aren't switched on. To get them turned on, you need to ask the administrator (you'll learn more later in this chapter).

What just happened?

We've just included an uploaded video into a Moodle web page. The advantage of this, over simply providing a link from the course front page, is that we can:

◆ Compliment the video with explanatory text and supporting images

◆ Avoid the problem of the student not knowing how to use the video player they have installed on their computer (which could be one of many)

- It keeps the student inside the course and focused on learning (rather than being tempted to start watching other videos)

- ...And they can read and watch at the same time

Did the video play correctly? Did the video player give you just a black box, rather than playing you your video? Computers can be a bit fussy over video file formats and to that end some formats are sometimes better to use than others. In the next section, we investigate video file format options.

Choosing a video file format

It's best to convert your videos in to one of the common video file formats—formats that are usually distinguishable by their file extensions. Those are the three letters that appear after the period in the file name. If you choose one of these common types then:

- Moodle will recognize the file and give it an appropriate icon when you upload it to your My private files area. This may not be particularly important at the moment, but it is if you have lots of files in there and you want to find particular types of files at a glance.

- The video will play on most modern computers without any special effort.

- Moodle will allow you to embed files of this type into Moodle web pages, as we shall soon see in the following sections.

If your video file isn't in one of these formats (for example they could be in MP4) then try out one of the free online file conversion tools, for example zamzar.com.

Moodle video troubleshooting

Are you seeing a link to your video but no video player? You might be seeing this:

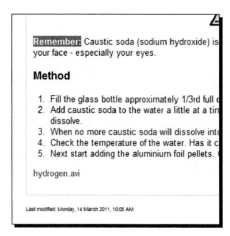

That is, a link but no player, when you want to see this:

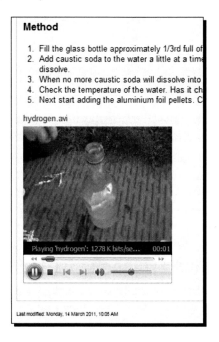

Let's run through the troubleshooting steps. Put a tick next to each one as you run through them.

Time for action – getting your videos to play in Moodle

1. Ensure you are using one of the common video file formats (see previous discussion).

2. Ensure your link is set up correctly. Try clicking on the link to ensure that your computer's video player can play your video. Links can be accidentally broken as you are editing text, so we can try re-linking the video. To break a link before you start again, press the Editor's Remove link button:

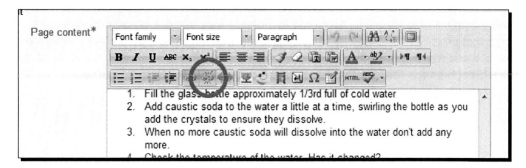

3. Once the old link has been removed (the text will revert to its default color and formatting); follow the steps outlined in *Turning text into a web link* to put the link back in.

4. If you have reached this final step and the video player still isn't being displayed then it looks like Moodle isn't configured the way we need it to be. Check out *Ask the Admin* section at the end of this chapter.

Have a go hero – do more with your videos

You could obviously have a Moodle web page with just a video in it, but that isn't very exciting. In the previous example, I've included a video as part of a page of instructions. I've also included a few pictures in there as well, to try and brighten things up a bit. Now our course is starting to become a truly multimedia experience—making things much more exciting for students.

Embedding a video from a video sharing website

That's not the only way to embed videos into your courses. Like me, you may well have found videos on YouTube that you use in your teaching that you would want included in your course. Or if you want to embed a video, and can't persuade the admin to turn on multimedia filters (or increase the maximum file size), then TeacherTube can provide the answer. TeacherTube works a lot like YouTube, but is entirely focused on educational content. Because of this you can usually access it from within schools—making it a great place to put your teaching videos. Why bother uploading videos to YouTube or TeacherTube? If a lot of students want to view the video at the same time in school then they could well bring the computer that Moodle is running off—and/or the network supplying the IT suite—to a grinding halt. If space on the computer running Moodle (the 'Moodle server') is an issue then uploading them to YouTube or TeacherTube is worthwhile.

 Remember: you may not have consent to upload images and videos of students onto third-party computer systems. Check your institution's policy on the use of images and videos of students.

Both YouTube and TeacherTube allow you to embed a special video player into your web pages that plays the video directly from their respective websites. If we embed a video from YouTube and we have the entire class each with a computer attempt to play the video at the same time, then it is YouTube that has to take the strain, not the Moodle machine.

Remember: before you think about embedding a video from YouTube or TeacherTube in your course, ensure that students can access these websites from within your institution. They could be filtered out. Also remember that YouTube videos can be taken down at any time. If they are then your link won't work.

Let's start by looking at how we can include videos from YouTube.

Including videos from YouTube

We've basically got four options if we want to include videos from YouTube in our courses:

* Embed the video directly from YouTube, using YouTube's special player.

* If YouTube is blocked, then extract the video from YouTube and upload it to our course, then embed the video just as we did in the previous section (remember that you should contact the author of the video before doing this).

* If we don't want to put too much strain on the computer running Moodle then we can extract the video from YouTube and then upload it to TeacherTube. But you'll need to create a TeacherTube account for yourself in order to do this (again, remember to check with the creator of the original video before doing this—unless, of course, that's you).

* Type in the direct link to the YouTube video and let Moodle's multimedia filter turn the link into an embedded player (which means you must make sure your admin has Multimedia filters turned on and configured correctly).

Let's look at embedding the YouTube video player into our course. Why explain a process in detail that may not work? Because the process of embedding a video from TeacherTube is exactly the same.

Time for action – embedding the YouTube player into your course

The first task is to search for a video that you want to include. A good idea here is to have Moodle and YouTube open at the same time. If your web browser supports tabs then you can tab between them. If not, then have Moodle open in one browser and open YouTube in a second browser.

Here's a video I've found in YouTube on firing a match rocket:

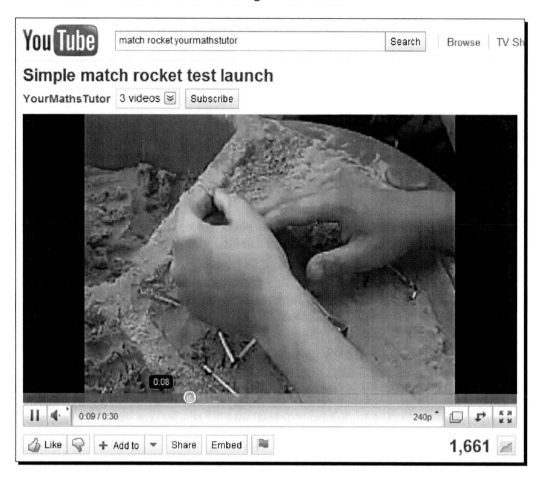

And here are the steps you need to take to embed it into a Moodle web page.

1. Choose the topic you want to include the video in and click on **Add a resource...** and choose Page.

2. Add a small piece of introductory text. I'm just going to write "Watch this video from YouTube showing a match rocket test launch".

3. Then, click on the Editor's special **Edit HTML Source** button:

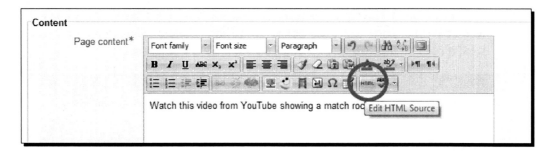

4. Web pages are written in a special code called HTML and this button allows you to switch between the code for the page (which the Editor is creating for us) and what the page actually looks like (What You See Is What You Get—or WYSIWYG for short). An **HTML Source Editor** is displayed:

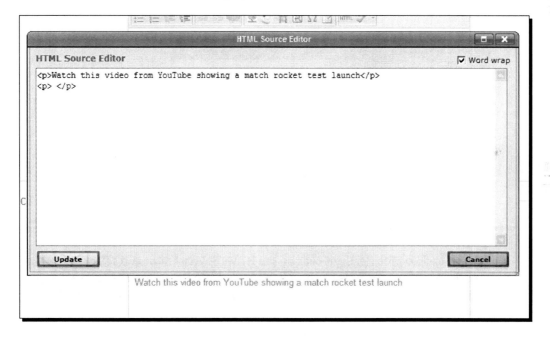

5. Now switch to YouTube and the video you want to include. Look for the word **Embed** on the page. Click on it, and the text you need to copy over to Moodle is highlighted. As you can see, the text looks almost incomprehensible. It is, in fact, a fragment of web page code. Don't worry: we don't have to bother about what it looks like, or what it does, to that extent. Right-click on this code and select copy:

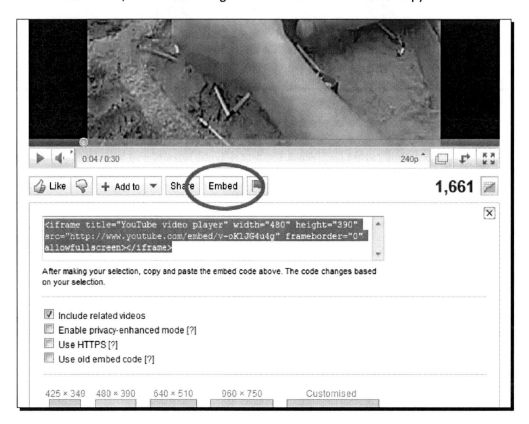

6. Switch back to Moodle. Right-click on the **HTML Source Editor** and select paste. The special code from YouTube has now been copied into the Editor. The code we've just copied looks horrible, but, again, we don't have to worry about what it looks like at this stage:

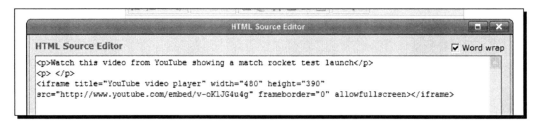

7. Now press the **Update** button on the HTML Source Editor to switch us back to what the web page actually looks like, rather than the code it is written in. You will now see the YouTube video embedded into your Moodle web page:

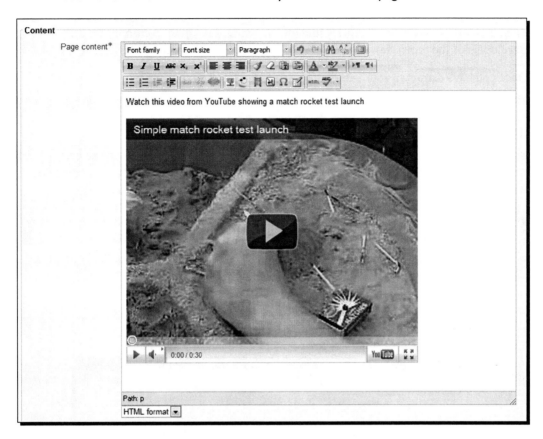

What just happened?

We have just seen how easy it is to take the code provided by YouTube and embed a special YouTube video player into a Moodle web page. That's great, because if we want all students to watch the video at the same time then YouTube is geared to handle lots of people viewing the same video simultaneously. The problem is that YouTube is very often blocked to students.

Let's overcome this problem by extracting the video from YouTube. Note that you might require permission from the author of the video before doing this.

Extracting a video from YouTube

There are a number of websites dedicated to extracting videos from YouTube—`zamzar.com` and `keepvid.com` are two good examples. Rather than explain in detail how to use these websites, a better idea is to direct you back to YouTube and to carry out a search for videos on zamzar and keepvid. You'll quickly find lots of instruction videos (often by the actual developers of the tools) showing you how to extract videos from YouTube.

Once you have extracted your video, simply follow the instructions on embedding a video (see *Time for Action – embedding a video into a Moodle Page*).

Including videos from TeacherTube

Both Vimeo and TeacherTube provide a special code to allow you to embed their own respective video players and the process is exactly the same. As it's dedicated to education, let's quickly run through the process of embedding a video from TeacherTube.

Time for action – embedding a video from TeacherTube

It is easier to have both Moodle and TeacherTube open at the same time, just as we did when working with YouTube. Have a look for a video that takes your fancy. Here's the match rocket test launch video again:

1. In Moodle, return to your course front page, click on **Add a resource...** and select **Page**.

2. Type in some introductory text, just to introduce your video to your students, and then press the **Edit HTML Source** button.

3. Switch to TeacherTube and look for **Embeddable Player**:

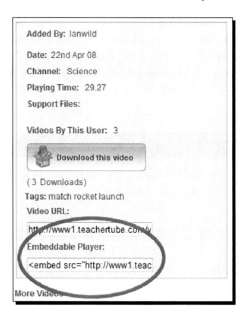

4. Right-click on the web code (as we did with YouTube) and click on **Copy**.

5. Now return to Moodle, ensure the Edit HTML Source editor is still open, and paste in the code from TeacherTube we have just copied:

Now we have the same video included in our course, but now being played from TeacherTube instead.

What just happened?

Embedding a video from TeacherTube is very simple—and pretty much the same process we used to embed a video from YouTube. The advantage with using TeacherTube is that students, more often than not, can't get access to YouTube.

If YouTube is blocked then one of the options open to us is to extract the video from YouTube and then upload it to TeacherTube or Vimeo (a site dedicated to collaboration and sharing). This is ideal if we don't want to keep the computer running Moodle under any strain, especially if we want to have our students all view the video on their own computers at the same time. It is also a good solution if you don't have that much space on the computer running Moodle (your Moodle admin might start complaining if you fill up the Moodle server with videos). Before you start uploading videos to TeacherTube, you will need to get yourself a TeacherTube account.

Pop quiz

Can you outline the advantages and disadvantages of having all your videos stored on a file sharing site on the Internet (for example, YouTube)?

Playing audio

There are three ways to include audio in Moodle, just as there are three ways to include video:

1. Include a link to the audio file in your course front page.

2. Embed the audio file in a Moodle web page—which, just as with video, requires multimedia filters to be enabled by your administrator.

3. Upload the audio to an audio sharing website and stream the file from there.

 You have possibly found, as you experimented with including videos in your course, that not all school and college computers, for understandable reasons, have got audio enabled (some schools even go so far as to snip the wires to the headphone socket). As you work through the following guide to embedding audio, remember that if there isn't any sound coming out of the speaker holes or the headphone socket speak to your technician or help desk. That your computer is silent may well be intentional.

Choosing an audio file format

Always convert to one of the common audio file formats. As with video file formats (see the discussion *Choosing a video file format*) these formats are distinguishable by their file extensions. However, when it comes to audio choose MP3 or, at a push, OGG. If you choose MP3, then:

- ◆ Moodle will recognize the file and give it an appropriate icon when you upload it to your course files area. As with videos, this may not be particularly important at the moment, but it is if you have lots of files in there and you want to find particular types of files at a glance.

- ◆ The file will play on most modern computers, phones, and portable players without any special effort.

- ◆ As with videos, Moodle will allow you to embed files of this type into Moodle web pages, as we shall soon see in the following sections.

If your audio file isn't in MP3 format then try out one of the free online file conversion tools, for example zamzar.com, Audacity, or even iTunes, if you use it.

Letting Moodle handle your sounds

Many of the processes used to embed audio, either by uploading an audio file, or by using an audio sharing website, are very similar to those used to include videos, so this section is much shorter than the last simply because a lot of the techniques are the same. Let's start by seeing how Moodle can embed its own audio player into a Moodle web page.

Time for action – embedding an audio clip

1. Choose a topic you want to add your audio file to and from the **Add a resource...** list choose Page.

2. I've got an audio file all about the history of rockets that I'd like to include. Firstly, I'm going to add a short piece of introductory text "Listen to this program all about rockets...".

3. Then, I'm going to use the **Moodle Media** button to insert my audio file. See *Time For Action – Embed a video into a Moodle Page* for details on how to use the Insert/ edit embedded media dialog. I'm going to use the File picker to upload my audio file and then select it. When you are done. click on the **Insert** button.

4. Scroll down to the bottom of the Editing Resource page and press the **Save and return to course** button.

5. Click on the link to the new Moodle web page from your course front page. Moodle will have embedded an audio player into your web page:

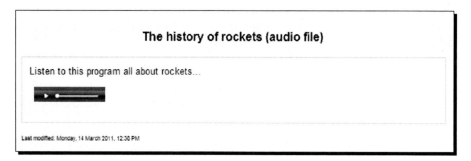

What Just happened?

Embedding an audio file is much the same as embedding a video file. Again, as with video, having Moodle embed an audio player means you don't have to worry about your students knowing how to use the audio player they have installed.

Troubleshooting audio—what if Moodle doesn't embed a player

What if you just saw the link to your audio, instead of the link and the little player? Then, you need to speak to your administrator about reconfiguring Moodle. Check out the *Ask the Admin* section at the end of this chapter for details.

Embedding audio from an audio sharing website

Why use an audio sharing website? Here are some good reasons...

◆ If the audio file is large then you might well be putting your Moodle computer under a lot of strain if more than a few students are trying to listen to it at the same time

◆ You might be limited with space in your course (this issue applies to videos, too)

◆ Your admin doesn't want to enable multimedia plugins

Audio sharing sites worth looking at include SoundCloud (`http://www.soundcloud.com`), Soundboard (`http://www.soundboard.com/`), and FindSounds (`http://www.findsounds.com/`). Certainly, Soundboard provides an embeddable audio player that you can include in your Moodle pages. For more information on using SoundCloud, Soundboard, and FindSounds check out YouTube. You'll find plenty of instructional videos on there.

> If you choose to use an audio sharing website, remember to check that students can access it on your institution's computers. Often, they can be blocked.

Have a go hero – start a podcast

There are many sites on the Internet that let you create podcasts, for example Huffduffer (`http://huffduffer.com/`). You could record your lessons or lectures as you give them and create a dedicated lesson podcast. Remember, as with video, you might need to check whether you have consent to upload any audio where your students can be distinctly heard. If you are particularly keen on experimenting with podcasts then there are special podcast modules that your Admin can install into your Moodle.

More on embedding

In this chapter, we have been investigating embedding video and audio. When it comes to multimedia, we can certainly upload PowerPoints or Photostory (`www.microsoft.com/windowsxp/using/digitalphotography/PhotoStory/default.mspx`) files. But these are Microsoft-specific, and Moodle users need the correct viewers installed on their computers. To overcome this problem, there are plenty of video and audio sharing websites to choose from—but remember to check that they are available to your students (and haven't been filtered out as being 'unsuitable' by your institution's web filtering software). A popular photo sharing website (and alternative to Photostory) is Slide.com, which you can use to create an embeddable photo montage from uploaded images. Let's take a look at doing that now.

Picture shows using Slide.com

Multimedia everywhere!

So far we have embedded multimedia in 'page' resources only. As you may have guessed, you can embed multimedia anywhere that uses the HTML editor—including topic summaries.

I'm going to take another look at my instructions for making a match rocket. At the top of the page I want to include a photo montage—a sequence of photographs with a caption underneath showing the actual process of making a rocket—a bit like a PowerPoint presentation but centered solely on images.

Slide.com is a photo-sharing service that will allow me to create a photographic slideshow of the flavor I would like. There are many designs of montage to choose from (and I can include music as well, if I want to!). Once I've created the show the service provides, just like many of the services we looked at in this chapter, a small fragment of web page code that we can embed into our Moodle pages. And, as with all the other sharing services we have investigated, you don't have to make your photo montage public if you don't want to. Let's look at including a slide show using Slide.com...

Time for action – adding a slide show

If you're going to use Slide.com, then you will need a Slide.com account (note that there are many sites of this type but once you've used one then you'll be able to use the others with ease). Registration is free and the service comes with comprehensive online help. As we found previously, it is easier if you have two instances of the browser open for the following task or, if your browser supports them, have your Moodle course open in one tab and Slide. com open in another.

1. Create your photo montage in Slide.com. Simply follow the instructions given in Slide.com's online help.

2. Your slide show comes with its own embeddable code:

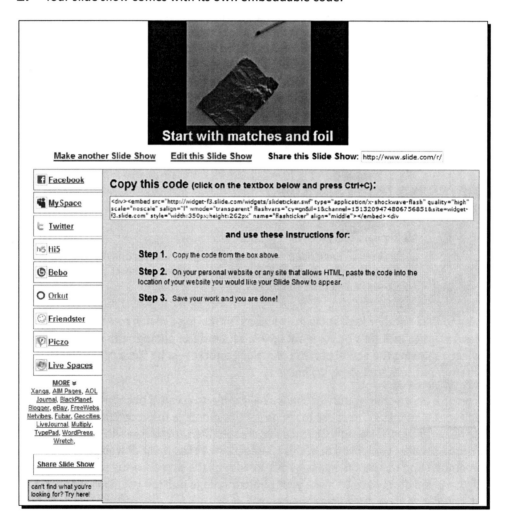

3. Right-click on the code and click on Select All. Right-click again and choose Copy.

4. Return to your Moodle course and to the place where you want to include the photo montage. I want mine at the top of the Moodle web page that contains the instructions for making match rockets. I want to update this resource so I need to click on the Update icon:

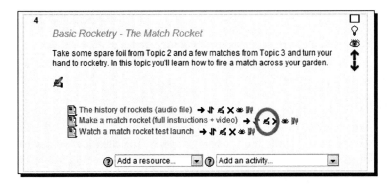

5. Click on the **Edit HTML Source** button to open the HTML Source Editor.

6. Right-click on the Editor and click on Paste, to paste in the code provided by Slide.com.

7. Click on the **Update** button to close the HTML Source Editor and return to normal viewing mode and the photo montage is now embedded in your Moodle page:

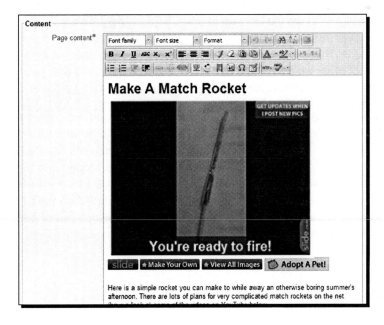

What just happened?

I wanted to include a photo montage in my instructions on how to make a match rocket. I've done this using Slide.com, a free online service that allows me to upload photographs, including captions, and create a slideshow. Using Slide.com, we can employ lots of engaging visual effects to dissolve from one photograph to another. Slide.com also allows you to play music while your photo montage is displayed.

Don't want advertisements at the bottom of your slidecast? Select the images in the editor and press the *Delete* key.

Ask the Admin

In this chapter, we included multimedia files in our course and it is very important that Moodle has been set up to handle multimedia properly. The next few sentences probably won't mean a lot to you, but if Moodle didn't play your audio or video for you then you need to speak to your administrator about enabling what is called the 'Multimedia Plugins' filter, and ensuring that everything—including playing Flash animations (again, just repeat this to your administrator even if you aren't sure what it means)—is enabled. There isn't any good reason why it shouldn't—that's just how it comes out of the box.

What happens if you don't enable multimedia plugins

You can certainly include multimedia files in your course by simply uploading them, just as we did in *Chapter 3, Adding Documents and Handouts* and then including links to them on the course front page—as we did later on in that Chapter. The problem is that there needs to be a media player installed on the student's PC in order for them to see or hear what, exactly, is in the file. That could be Windows Media Player, RealPlayer, or Apple QuickTime, or a whole host of other media players out there in multimedia-land that your students, their parents, or your school's technician may have installed.

Don't allow Moodle to play your files and you will get bombarded with issues regarding whatever player a student is trying to use. And that's nothing to do with Moodle. Convincing your Moodle admin to enable multimedia plugins means Moodle will handle the media player for us. Not only that, but the actual video or audio is embedded into the web page, rather than playing in a separate player. That means we don't get lots of students not knowing how to use the media player they happen to have installed on their computer. Currently, Moodle ships with multimedia plugins for the following types of files (use this list as a guide for the types of files you can upload to Moodle):

- MP3 (audio files)
- SWF (Flash animations)
- MOV (movie files)

- WMV (Windows movie files)
- MPG (mpeg video files)
- AVI (video files)
- FLV (Flash videos)
- RAM (real audio clips or sequence of clips)
- RPM (audio files)
- RM (audio files)
- YouTube links (Moodle can recognise a link to a YouTube page and automatically embed the video)
- OGG (audio files)
- OGV (video files)
- Enables auto-embedding of linked images (Moodle recognises a link to an image and embeds the image automatically)

Summary

In this chapter, we turned our courses into a truly multimedia experience:

- It was easy to include multimedia in our courses. Moodle can even embed audio and video into web pages for us, as long as our Admin has got that set properly.
- Embedding videos from YouTube and TeacherTube was simple, using the fragments of web page code they provide you'll have to make sure that your students will also have access to any websites that you embed videos from, though.
- Multimedia doesn't just stop at videos and audio. We ended the chapter by including a fantastic free photo montage in the course using Slide.com. I even had music playing in the background as my montage played—but you'll have to take my word for that!

There has been a lot of discussion in this chapter about teachers using the Internet to store content. It is worthwhile mentioning that there are pros and cons to doing this. You will need to keep track of where you put your resources on the Internet. You may find it better to place as much as possible inside Moodle, where you can ensure students will be able to get access and view content and that the content they are viewing is safe.

If you upload audio or video to Moodle then students can download the files from Moodle if they want to. This might help you determine how you place video/audio into Moodle.

Now we've reached the half-way stage for this book and I think you'll agree that our courses are looking pretty good. In *Chapter 5, Moodle Makeover* we'll be taking a look at tips and techniques that'll take our courses from looking good to looking great.

5

Moodle Makeover

We have come a long way over the first five chapters. We've got all of our resources uploaded into Moodle, and in the previous chapter we saw just how easy it is to move from static, text, and image-based resources to turning our courses into a complete multimedia experience. In fact, you could almost invite students in now and I'm sure they would be impressed with the results of our work so far.

Because we've been working so hard, and before we move on to the second half of the book and look at converting our quizzes and student projects, let's take a break to look at techniques that build on what we have learned and achieved so far, techniques to make a Moodle course even more absorbing and fun. Reworking and rearranging the resources and improving the presentation will definitely improve the functionality and ease of use. In this chapter we shall:

◆ Do more than make each topic a long list of resources. Use the label resource and Moodle's indenting tool to change this:

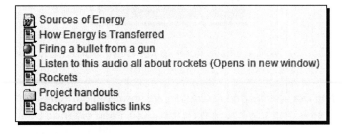

to this:

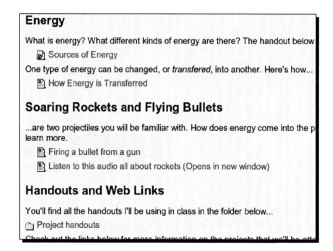

- Find out where we can get lots of free images for our courses
- Explore different ways to use HTML to make our courses even more engaging
- Include a talking character, an animated avatar, using `Voki.com`:

- Back up all of the work we have done so far. There would be nothing worse than to lose all of our hard work to a computer glitch!

In *Chapter 3, Adding Documents and Handouts*, we imported our documents and handouts to our Private files area, and saw how easy it was to sort and organize them. And so far I've been adding links to resources on the course main page without much thought as to how the links themselves are organized on the page. Let's get that sorted now!

Arranging your resources

Why is it important to spend a little time arranging resources in a topic? Isn't it all eye candy? Let's take a look at my Topic 1:

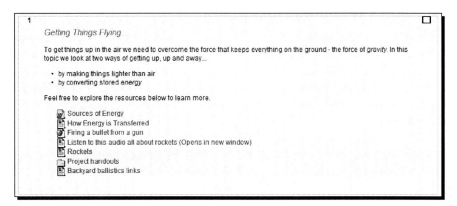

I've got a nice colorful title, some text to introduce the topic, and then a long list of resources which, quite honestly, looks just like the list of files in the shared drive I already use to distribute my documents and handouts to students. What if the topic looked like the following screenshot:

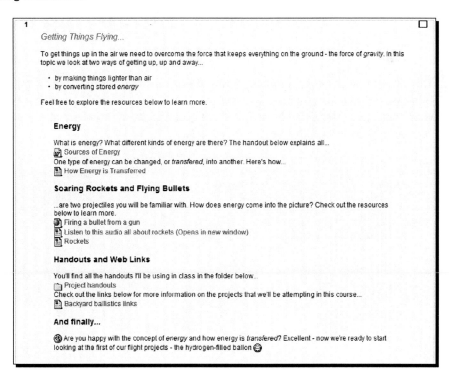

This is much more the effect we need. I've reordered my resources and included some labels, so that it is much easier for students to find a resource. In this section we're going to learn how to bring some order into our topics.

Putting your resources in order

One obvious difference between a shared drive and Moodle is that in Moodle you can put the resources in the order you want, not the order the computer insists on (usually numerical/alphabetical). However, in Moodle any new resources you add are simply queued on to the end of the topic. This has meant that resources in my **Getting Things Flying** topic aren't exactly ordered in a sensible way, just the way I added them. I'm going to take action to remedy that now.

Time for action – arranging your resources

1. Remember that you need editing turned on before you start.

2. Choose the resource you want to move. I'm going to move my Backyard Ballistics links resource to the end of the topic. To start the process I need to "pick up" the resource. I click on the move icon:

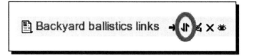

3. This causes two things to happen. Firstly, the resource I want to move disappears. Don't worry, imagine you have it in your hand and you are ready to place it back into your course. Secondly, the boxes that have now appeared represent all the places you can move the resource you are holding to:

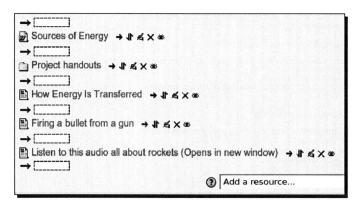

4. Choose where you want to move the resource to. I want my list of links at the end so I'm going to click on the box at the bottom. The boxes disappear and my resources have been shuffled:

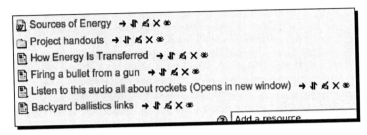

What just happened?

A list of resources in Moodle isn't simply a list of files, such as you would find on a shared drive. One obvious difference is that in Moodle you can arrange your resources to be listed in the order you want, and we've just seen how easy it is to achieve this.

You can't find the move icon?

Your site may be configured so that you can drag and drop resources. In that case, instead of the move icon you will see crosshairs next to your resource.

To move the resource, click on the crosshairs and, keeping your finger pressed down on the left mouse button, drag the resource to its new location. Look for the line in the background, this tells you where your resource is going to be dropped into, then let go of the mouse button when you have found the spot.

Now I've got my resources in the order I wanted, I have to say that my topic looks like just another resource dump which is what I am trying to avoid.

Remember the screenshots in the *Arrange your resources* section? My resources would be much easier to use if I could introduce each of them with a short piece of text:

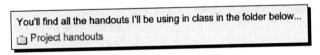

Introducing a resource with a short introduction is a great way of improving the visual appeal of your course. The tool to achieve this is called a Label resource, and here's how to use it.

Time for action – inserting a label

I'm going to start the process of arranging my resources by having a short piece of text to introduce the **Backyard Ballistics** links resource:

1. Make sure editing is turned on, click on **Add a resource** and choose **Label**.

2. In the **Adding a New Label** page, enter your label text. When you are done, press the **Save and return to course** button.

3. The new label is added to the end of the list of resources, which is obviously the wrong place for it. Click on the move icon, next to the label you have just added:

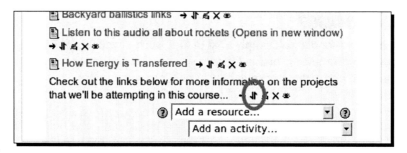

4. The page is redisplayed. Your new label disappears and lots of boxes have appeared. These boxes represent the places where your new label can go:

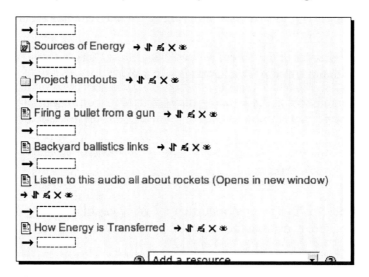

5. Click on the relevant box to place your label. You're done!

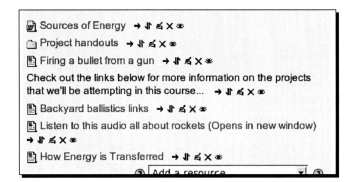

 If you don't have a move icon you'll have crosshairs next to the label that you can click on to drag it to the right place.

What just happened?

After all the experience we have had with Moodle so far, using the label resource will be fairly straightforward. Judicious use of labels means our course topics don't have to be simply a long list of resources. Remember to treat labels as a way of leading the student towards and into a resource. Labels are not designed for content, so try to keep labels short, perhaps two or three sentences at the most. Labels are like the glue that holds topics together. You don't want your glue to be too thick.

It's looking better, but my topic is still looking a little flat. You can indent your resources by clicking on the move right icon next to the resource:

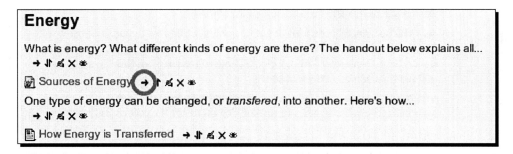

The following screenshot shows how things now look with a little indenting:

1

Getting Things Flying...

To get things up in the air we need to overcome the force that keeps everything on the ground - the force of *gravity*. In this topic we look at two ways of getting up, up and away...

- by making things lighter than air
- by converting stored *energy*

Feel free to explore the resources below to learn more.

Energy

What is energy? What different kinds of energy are there? The handout below explains all...
🔗 Sources of Energy
One type of energy can be changed, or *transfered*, into another. Here's how...
📄 How Energy is Transferred

Soaring Rockets and Flying Bullets

...are two projectiles you will be familiar with. How does energy come into the picture? Check out the resources below to learn more.
📄 Firing a bullet from a gun
📄 Listen to this audio all about rockets (Opens in new window)
📄 Rockets

Handouts and Web Links

You'll find all the handouts I'll be using in class in the folder below...
📁 Project handouts
Check out the links below for more information on the projects that we'll be attempting in this course...
📄 Backyard ballistics links

And finally...

🌐 Are you happy with the concept of *energy* and how energy is *transfered*? Excellent - now we're ready to start looking at the first of our flight projects - the hydrogen-filled balloon 😊

Seeing the course from a student's point of view

As a teacher, you will see a lot of options on the screen that your students won't. To get a clear idea of how a student will see the course, use the **Switch role to...** option from the course **Settings** block. Choose **Student** from this list, and you will see the course as students see it.

When you're done, click **Return to my normal role** and you'll get your normal view back. You will also need to turn editing on to get the edit controls back.

Hypnotic HTML: Finessing your web pages and descriptions

You can see that my **Getting Things Flying** topic is still mostly words. The only pictures I have in there are the Moodle icons, used to indicate the resource or activity type. I really want to liven it up with pictures and animations, but where can I get the graphics from and what's the best way of including them?

Finding decorative images

The Internet has some fantastic resources for free images to include in our courses. Here are just a few of the more popular ones.

Google image search

It is great for finding a picture on just about anything. Be careful about copyright (more on that later). The pictures are of mixed quality and you have to be prepared to hunt around. But they are good fun and wonderful for livening up an otherwise dry course.

Visit `http://images.google.com/` for the Google image search main page.

I'm going to look for a picture of a do-it-yourself rocket. I type in the words "`DIY Rocket`" into the search box and hit the **Search Images** button. I'm presented with a page full of miniature versions of the original pictures Google has found:

Next, if you want to, you go to the web page containing the full-sized version. Then right click on the image to save it (if you're happy with the thumbnail then you can save that instead). Internet Explorer has a nasty habit of occasionally only allowing you to save an image either in the format it is already, or as a BMP (bitmap) which is why, sometimes, Firefox can have the slight edge if you're saving images from a web page. It is a good idea to speak to your technician or IT help desk about converting any images you save in this way to a JPEG (if it isn't already) or PNG (see the discussion about image file formats under the *Images* section in *Chapter 3, Adding Documents and Handouts*, for more information).

Once you've saved the image on your computer and converted it to a suitable format (JPEG or PNG) then you need to upload it to, and include it in, your course. Check out *Uploading Files* section in *Chapter 3, Adding Documents and Handouts*, for details.

Of course, other image search websites are available. AltaVista (`www.altavista.com/image/`) is another good search tool for images because it also allows you to search for images that are a specific size.

Flickr

Flickr holds quality original photography, and you can restrict your search to creative commons so you don't have to worry about copyright issues. You're relying on someone else posting a picture of something you are interested in, but if you find one, the quality is usually excellent. For example, there are plenty of rocket images taken by many amateur enthusiasts who are also enthusiastic photographers. Once you've found your image then you can right click on it to save it. Sites are available that allow you to search for creative commons-licensed Flickr images, for example `http://compfight.com`.

General clip art libraries

Line drawings, stick figures, and more. Usually good quality but you often find yourself trawling through a good many unimaginative images before you find a good one. A free and frequently used clip art resource is from Discovery Education (`http://school.discoveryeducation.com`). The Discovery Education site contains a comprehensive clip art gallery, all from the pen of illustrator *Mark A. Hicks* (I'm specifically citing Mark's work because it is where the image of the rocket in the topic outline (**Summary of General**) at the top of my course came from).

`www.alamy.com` and `www.openclipart.org` are two more huge resources of "royalty free" images that are well worth a visit.

Microsoft Office clip art library

Microsoft has packed a fantastic range of clip art images into Office. So in Word 2003, for example, click on **Insert** in the main menu, slide down to **Picture** and then slide across to **Clip Art...** to open the **Clip Art** side bar. My search in there for "rocket" found me a myriad of clip art images, actual pictures, and animations. You can limit your search to specific types of media. To add the clip art to your document simply double-click on the thumbnail. This way we can put together a single document just containing the clip art images we need for our course.

Now we've got our clip art gathered together in a Word document, what's the best way of grabbing the images? You've got the same problem if you already have a document, or a PowerPoint presentation, that contains an image (including animated pictures) you want to grab.

Time for action – grabbing an image from a Word document

In *Chapter 4, Handing in Work through Moodle*, we learned how to convert Microsoft Word and PowerPoint presentations to web pages as a way of overcoming the problem that your students might not have Office installed on their computers at home, and so might not be able to view your document. If you save a document as a web page, grabbing an image is easy:

1. In Word 2003, select **File** from the main menu and slide down to **Save As...** The **Save As** dialog is displayed.

2. At the bottom of the **Save As** dialog, click on the **Save as type** drop-down list. Select **Web Page, Filtered (*.htm; *.html)**.

3. Make sure you are happy that Word is about to save your document to the right folder and that you are happy with the name. Press the **Save** button.

4. Don't worry about what the next dialog says. Click **Yes**.

5. Go to the folder you just saved your document to. In there you should find a folder ending with "_files". In there will be your images:

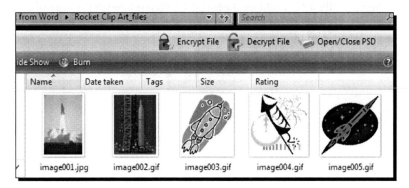

What just happened?

Often you'll already have a Word document or a PowerPoint presentation containing an image that you want to include in your course. We've just created a new Word document, collected images from the Office clip art library, and then we've seen how easy it is to grab images by saving the document as a web page. You can easily do the same for PowerPoint presentations.

Copyright caution

We have already encountered a problem with copyright in the previous chapter (*Is it legal to extract videos from YouTube or TeacherTube?*). Let's take another look at the issues.

Because we are working in the education sector, and as long as we aren't planning on making money out of someone else's pictures, copyright shouldn't be that much of a problem. In fact I've never had a problem with copyright; if it isn't obvious what you can and can't copy off a website then all you have to do is ask the copyright holder. In my experience, asking for images from the larger corporations often prompts them to send you even more images. If you still aren't sure, and are fortunate enough to have a librarian working in your establishment, then they should be aware of what you can and can't copy and how it can be used.

Another issue to think about is that of including photographs of staff and students (or just people generally). Will you need their permission to include their likeness in your course?

HTML Editor tips and tricks: Smilies and other gimmicks

If you really want to set your course apart from the crowd and you are looking for the right tool to do it then look no further than the HTML Editor we have been using all along. The Editor does a good job of making it very easy for us to improve the look and feel of our courses, and in helping us to create engaging Moodle pages. Let's spend the rest of this section spending a little time exploring some new ideas.

Smilies

Have you checked out the **Insert Smiley** button yet? It's a really simple way of putting a little bit of expression in your text. Want to be sarcastic but you don't want students to get the wrong end of the stick? Add a:

Want to show how happy you are? Insert a:

No smiley button?

If your HTML Editor doesn't have a smiley button this means your Moodle admin hasn't turned on this feature. Ask them to take a look at `http://docs.moodle.org/en/Display_emoticons_as_images`.

Just by the inclusion of a few little graphics such as this helps to give our courses a much more friendly face, because, let's face it, often students are put off by seeing too many words. Here's one way of remedying that problem.

Creating imaginary dialog

Turn your course into a story and have a dialog between the characters. Imagine that there's an emergency in space:

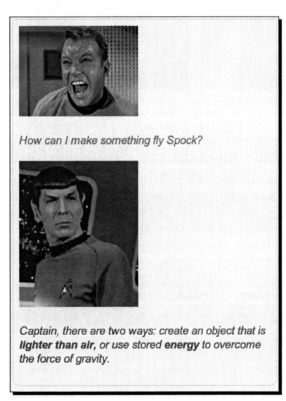

How can I make something fly Spock?

*Captain, there are two ways: create an object that is **lighter than air,** or use stored **energy** to overcome the force of gravity.*

Arranging your HTML

While I've been busy sorting and arranging, the thought struck me that up to now I haven't given much thought as to how text and pictures are arranged on a page (although that thought may well have struck you). At the moment I've got text then pictures, text then pictures, one under the other. It doesn't have to be so, because I can also arrange my pictures side by side using borderless tables:

Here are two ways to get things flying...

1) Be *lighter than air.*   2) Use *stored energy* to overcome the force of gravity.

Time for action – displaying things side by side

Let's try this by adding a new web page to a topic. Make sure you've got a couple of images that you can display side by side:

1. After you have created a new web page, we first need to insert a table. Click on the **Insert Table** button to display the **Insert Table** dialog:

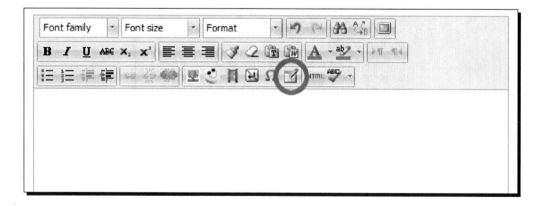

2. You can now specify the number of columns and rows your table will have. Don't worry if you aren't exactly sure how many you will need as you can always change things later on. I'm going to have two pictures side by side, each with a fragment of text underneath. That means two rows and two columns. When you first insert a table, the border has a thickness of 1. If you want a borderless table then you must set the border to be 0.

3. Insert an image into each of the two cells in the top row of the new table:

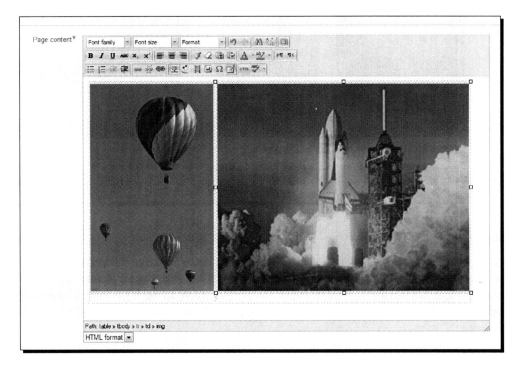

4. If you want a full view of the page so that you can position the images then remember you can drag on the bottom right-hand corner of the Editor or, alternatively, click on the `Toggle fullscreen view` button to open the fullscreen view:

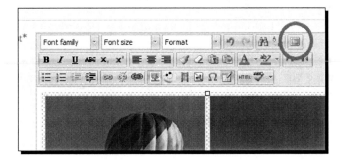

5. I'm then going to enter some text into the cells underneath each picture, give the page a title, and that's it! I'm done:

Get things flying by making them *lighter than air*...

...or use *stored energy* to overcome the force of gravity

What just happened?

By using borderless tables to arrange our HTML we can vastly improve the visual appeal of our web pages. Rather than having text, then a picture, then text, then a picture repeated down the page, we can arrange items in cells in a table which, as we have seen, is very easy to add in. It's also easy to reconfigure the table later on if you find that your content needs to change.

Remember: if you want a borderless table then you must set the border to be 0.

Getting animated: Add a talking character

Multimedia these days isn't just limited to audio and video. How about having your own custom-designed animated character included in your course? Not for everyone but a good deal of fun is the free online service Voki (at time of writing there is now a special "Voki for Education" area in the Voki website)

Voki characters are animated, onscreen avatars that can talk either using computer generated speech, or from a recording or uploaded file. Check out `http://voki.com` for more information.

You will ultimately need to create a `Voki.com` account, but if you visit `Voki.com` you can start creating an animated character straight away. Remember when we were embedding multimedia content in *Chapter 4, Sound and Vision—Including Multimedia Content*. Again, Voki provides you with a fragment of web page code, and we can embed that code into any HTML we add to our course.

Showing you how to create a Voki character is beyond the scope of this book, but the Voki website contains lots of guidance on how to do this.

In the following screenshot I've edited the course summary and added in a Voki of me (kind of!) giving out an important safety warning:

HTML blocks: A bit on the side

We've come a long way since we first looked at all the components that make up a Moodle page back in *Chapter 2, Setting up your Courses*. Remember at the beginning we talked about blocks, those small boxes down the left and right-hand sides of the page? I mentioned you could add your own blocks and position them how you wanted. Let's take a look at doing that now, because one of the blocks you can add is an HTML block.

Let's use an HTML block to create a welcome message for our students.

Time for action – adding a welcome message

1. Making sure you've got editing turned on, scroll down the course main page and look for the **Add a block** block, usually under the last block on the right-hand side of the page:

2. Click on **Add...** and select **HTML** from the list. Moodle will add a new HTML block to the page:

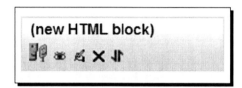

3. To configure the new HTML block, click on the configuration icon:

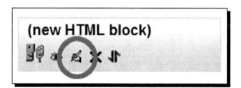

4. And you're taken to the **Configuring a (new HTML block) block** page. Give your new block a title and then add in your content. When you're done, press the **Save changes** button, Here's my new welcome message (including an animated GIF):

5. But a welcome message is no good hiding down in the bottom right-hand corner of my course main page. Click on the configuration icon once more and scroll down to the **On this page** section. To position the welcome message at the top-left of the page I need to specify the region to be on the left and a weight of -10 (that is, as light as a feather, rather than the elephantine +10):

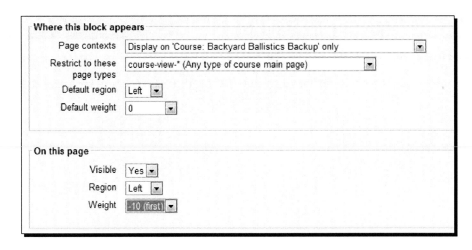

_6._   I can now get my message positioned just where I want it:

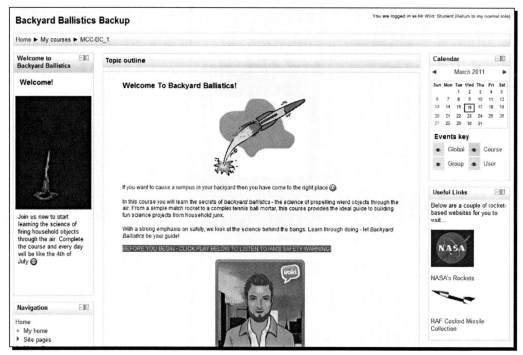

What just happened?

We've added a new HTML block to the course main page to provide a welcome message to our students. Any HTML can be added in there. What's great is that you can add as many HTML blocks to your course front page as you like.

Have a go hero – doing more with HTML blocks

If you're happy with HTML blocks then here are some more ideas for you to try:

 ◆   Move your list of useful links into an HTML block. It makes them far easier to find:

◆ Have you added a Voki to your course? Move your Voki character into an HTML block. Students can hide the character by clicking on the hide icon in the corner of the block:

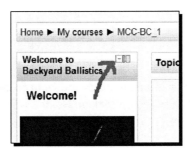

◆ If you don't see a hide icon speak to your Moodle administrator. Your Moodle might not support them.

◆ If your students are viewing your course on a notebook with a small screen they can dock blocks to the dock bar:

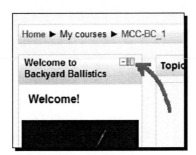

◆ Try investigating the other types of block that are available in the **Add a block** list. You won't break anything and you can easily delete a block by clicking on the delete icon. (I'm going to resist recommending any and let you have a play. The types of blocks you will find useful will all depend on your subject area and your teaching style).

Backing up your course

Before we end this chapter and this section, now is a good time to back up the work we have done so far. There is a lot you can do with the backup and restore functionality in Moodle, and I'm going to be returning to it more fully in *Chapter 9, Putting it All Together*. For now, return to your course front page and look down the options in the course **Settings** block. Two options listed are **Backup** and **Restore**. Choose **Backup** and let's get all the hard work we've done so far backed up quickly; it's better to be safe than sorry.

Time for action – backing up your course

You'll find many, many options you can choose as we run through the backup procedure. At this stage it's best just to stick with the defaults and back up everything.

Once you've selected **Backup** from the **Settings** block you are taken to your **Course Backup** page. Simply leave the defaults as they are (where most options will be selected), scroll down to the bottom of the page and click on **Next**.

The next page allows you to choose which topics you want to include in your backup. Again, scroll down to the bottom of the page and click on **Next**.

Now we can choose a name for our backup file. Moodle automatically creates a name for you, based on the time, date, and the course short name. You can leave it as it is, if you want to. This page also allows us to confirm all that we have specified so far. Assuming all is well, we can scroll to the bottom of the page and press the **Perform backup** button.

Moodle will now have created the course backup for you (scroll down to the bottom of the page and check you have the message "**Backup completed successfully**"). If all is well, click on the **Continue** button at the bottom of the page. Moodle now takes you to your course and user private backup areas:

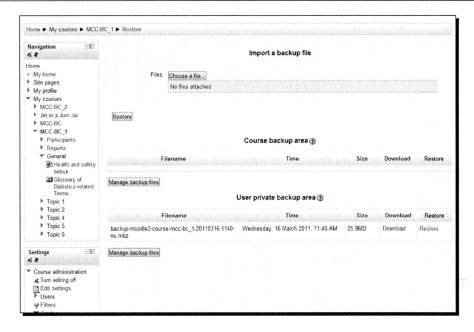

You can see that Moodle has backed up your entire course into a single file and put it in your private backup files area. That's fine, but if something goes wrong with the computer Moodle is running on, that isn't much help. Click on the **Download** link. You are given the option to either open it or save it. Click **Save** and save the file to your computer, USB memory stick, or portable hard drive. Keep it safe:

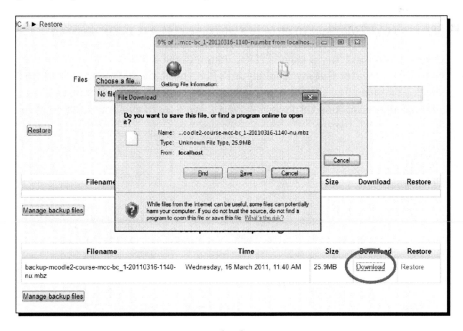

What just happened?

I think I would probably burst into tears if I'd have lost all of the work that I've done so far. Thank goodness that backing up my course is easy. I simply select **Backup** from the course **Settings** block and follow the instructions. There are lots of settings allowing me to choose what I actually back up, but at the moment I'm just wanting to back up everything, there really isn't any harm in doing that. Remember: we'll be looking again at what you can do with backup and restore later in this book.

Summary

We have spent the first half of this book learning about Moodle and seeing how we can take the resources we've been using and importing them into our Moodle course. We've come across many different techniques we can use to achieve this, and we've used this chapter to spend a little extra time practicing and reinforcing the ideas we have learned in this book so far.

Specifically, we covered:

- Arranging resources within topics to make topics look more visually appealing. We used the Label resource as the glue to hold resources together.
- We took a comprehensive look at tips and tricks we can use to make our courses more engaging for students.
- We included an animated character using `Voki.com`, and gained more practice at using embeddable code. Other free, animated characters are available (for example, `http://digimi.com`).
- We used an HTML block to provide a welcome message to our students.

We've covered converting the so called "static" elements of a taught course from the classroom to the computer. But my teaching isn't just about giving PowerPoint presentations and handing out information sheets. I set my students projects and assignments. I give them little quizzes as we are working through the course. We'll learn all about managing student work online in the next chapter.

6
Managing Student Work

I think you'll agree that we've come a long way in the first half of this book. We've got all of our documents, handouts, videos, and sound files uploaded. In the previous chapter, we investigated lots of ways we can make our courses more engaging and entertaining for students. Have you checked out the free Moodle 2.0 Course Conversion sample chapter download on the Packt Publishing website? This sample chapter looks very briefly at how students can hand in their work through Moodle. In this chapter we expand on that theme to learn how to fully manage online work that students need to hand in to me.

Currently, in my Backyard Ballistics course, I set two major end-of-course projects:

◆ A poster on energy sources
◆ A PowerPoint presentation to the group on how energy is transferred when objects are sent flying through the air

Both tasks are graded separately.

There are a number of headaches associated with assignment submissions: files (such as PowerPoint presentations) go missing. Students claim they have e-mailed files that never reach you. The school technician is wary of students bringing in work on memory sticks because of the threat of viruses. There's no quick way of knowing which students have yet to hand in their work. Marking might involve having to make notes on paper, and having a system to associate those notes with digital photographs of work stored elsewhere. We need a system that allows us to manage student submissions in one self-contained tool—one that can be used to exchange files between our students and us without having to resort to other, far less reliable, means. As well, wouldn't it be good to have a tool that allows us to comment (and include photographs, videos—in fact, any digital file we liked) and grade work all under one umbrella?

Added to that, you might be required to grade students on key skills: numeracy, literacy, and the use of ICT. And that's not something you might specifically set a project for. In that case, we would need a way of grading students on those aspects of their work separately from any specific project. That's yet another headache!

By converting to Moodle we can easily find answers to all of these issues, and more.

In this chapter, we shall:

- Demonstrate how to manage projects and assignments online
- Learn how to mark student projects online, including specifying your own custom grades
- Learn how to manage student grades, including grading them on their key skills
- Show how work can be passed between students and teachers online without resorting to e-mail, burning CDs/DVDs, or students having to bring in work on a memory stick

So let's get on with it, and make a start with converting my poster project and PowerPoint assignments to Moodle...

Converting projects and assignments

Earlier in this book, I introduced you to the four ways an out-of-the-box Moodle provides for managing student work online. Recall that there are four types of assignment activity, and they will match any kind of project that you are likely to set your students. As we did in that *Chapter 5, Moodle Makeover*, turn editing on, go to any topic and click on the **Add an activity** list. In this list, you will see the four different assignment types Moodle supports. They are:

- **Offline activity**: If your student projects can't be uploaded into Moodle because the student submission isn't electronic (just like my poster project) then you can manage grades and your notes on the students' work using this kind of assignment type.
- **Online text**: Students are going to be creating the assignment submission using the text editor built into Moodle. That's the one we've been using to create our course so far.
- **Upload a single file**: Students can only upload one file. That's the activity we used to allow our students to hand in their homework to us earlier in this book.

- ◆ **Advanced uploading of files**: Students can upload more than one file. As a teacher, you can also use Moodle as a mechanism for exchanging files between students, instead of using e-mail (unreliable), or a memory stick (virus risk).

Take a look at these assignment types now. With editing turned on, click on **Add an activity...** and select any of the assignment types. That way you can get a feel for the kinds of settings we'll be dealing with before we start.

 Remember: if, while you are trying out different assignment types, you mistakenly add an assignment to your course, you can easily delete it by clicking on the delete icon next to the assignment name.

Structuring converted projects and assignments online

For larger projects or assignments, it is often preferable to have a self-contained topic containing the actual assignment itself, together with any supporting materials. You could include exemplars (for example, examples of work from previous years) and give students the opportunity to discuss them together. There's more on using Moodle to discuss exemplars online later in this book. By having the assignment, and all of the supporting materials, in a single topic means I can hide the assignment from students until it is time for them to attempt it.

To demonstrate how this would be done, firstly we need to add a new topic to our course, and then we can add in an assignment activity.

Adding a new topic to a course

I'm going to add a new topic to my course specifically for my student projects. Then I'm going to hide that topic until we have covered the course. Remember how we hid a "teacher's only" topic in the course earlier in this book? I'm going to do the same with my projects and the support materials associated with them. You don't have to treat assignments in this way: as you work through the settings for a Moodle assignment you'll notice that you can specify a time period that those assignments are available for (it's a setting we'll talk about shortly). I've decided that I want to ensure that my students focus on the preliminary work before they start attempting any assignments so I will completely hide this element from them.

Time for action – adding a topic and hiding it

1. Return to your course front page and choose **Edit settings** from the **Settings** block.

2. Scroll down to the number of weeks/topics setting and change the number in the drop-down list to add another topic to your course:

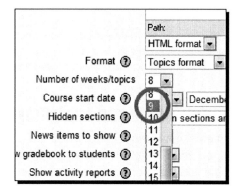

3. At the bottom of the page, press the **Save changes** button. That's it, we're done—and now there's a new empty topic at the end of your course.

4. For the moment, I want to hide this topic from students. Click on the eye icon on the right-hand side to hide the topic:

5. It depends on your theme but, to show that a topic is hidden, two gray bars are shown on the left- and right-hand side of the topic:

What just happened?

We've now got a new, empty topic added to our course. I don't want students to be able to view the assignment until we are all ready, so I've hidden this topic from them for now.

Which assignment type

For the purpose of my project, I'm only going to be looking at two different assignment activity types—but by looking at those two now and from having looked at the Single File assignment earlier on in this book, we'll gain the skills and confidence to be able to use all the available types quite happily. It's worth noting that because Moodle is modular, software authors have provided other assignment types: a popular addition (especially among language teachers) to any Moodle is the Nanogong assignment (`http://gong.ust.hk/nanogong/index.html`). Again, with the experience gained here you'll soon be able to get to grips with any custom assignment module you find installed in your Moodle.

Converting a project to Moodle using an Offline assignment

The first project—the poster project—is going to be converted to use the Offline activity assignment type. I'm going to use Moodle to manage student grades and to organize my notes and comments on their work. Let's see how easy it is to add an Offline activity.

Time for action – adding an Offline activity assignment

1. Make sure you still have editing turned on. In the topic you want to add your new assignment to (in my case my new, hidden topic) click on **Add an activity...** and choose **Offline activity** from the list. You're now taken to the **Editing assignment** page.

2. Give your assignment a name. Enter in a brief description of the task in the Description box. Don't worry if the box looks a bit small. We can include all of the supporting materials in the topic together with the assignment activity itself on the course front page:

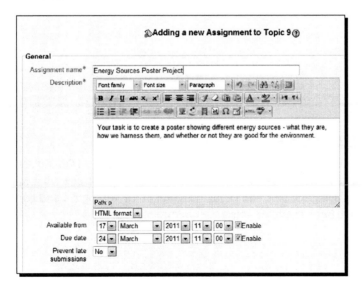

3. Use the **Grade** setting to specify the maximum grade you are going to give for this assignment. I'm going to leave the Grade setting at 100 (meaning I can grade this assignment out of 100). Maybe your assignment forms part of an overall mark and you need to mark it out of less. You could choose to mark your assignment. You can even choose to create your own custom grades (for example, A, B, C, D, E, or F), which we learn how to do later on in this chapter.

4. Choose when you want the assignment to be available. I want to hide both the assignment and the supporting resources and materials, so this option is redundant. I do have the option of disabling this setting so this is what I'm going to do, in this instance. If you aren't hiding the assignment, the **Available from** and **Due date** settings are a useful way of preventing students handing work to you before you are ready:

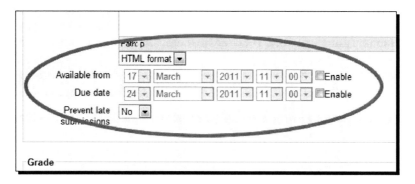

5. That's it! We're done. Press the **Save and return to course** button. A new assignment has just been added to the course:

What just happened?

Converting my poster project to Moodle was as easy as adding an Offline assignment activity to my Backyard Ballistics course. Click on the assignment now to see what happens. You'll see a screen displaying the task you've just set, and in the top right-hand corner you'll see a **No attempts have been made on this assignment** link:

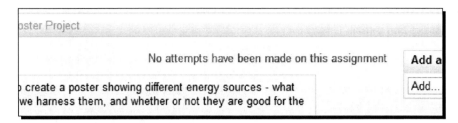

Click on that link now. You'll be taken to a list of students who are enrolled on your course. If you don't have any students enrolled on your course then this is what you will see:

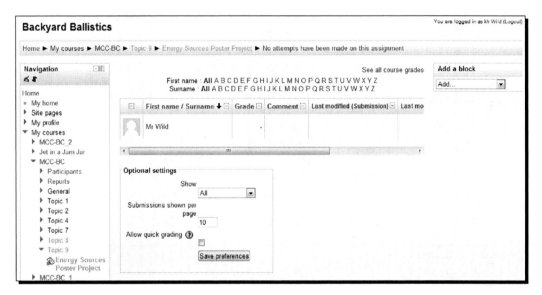

I'm the only person "enrolled" on my course (as teacher). I don't yet want students enrolled on my course until I know it is set up to be how I want it. In the free bonus chapter from the Packt Publishing website I demonstrate how to introduce a 'control student' on a Moodle course. I'm going to do the same again to test out my new included assignments. But before we do that, I'm going to think about the second assignment I need to convert—where students are required to produce a PowerPoint presentation.

Converting a project to Moodle using an Advanced uploading of files assignment

I'm going to get students to submit their PowerPoint file using an **Advanced uploading of files assignment** type. Why not upload a single file? Here are the advantages of using an advanced uploading of files assignment:

◆ Students can upload more than one file (the total number is controlled by me)

◆ My students and I can exchange work online, without us having to resort to memory sticks and e-mail

Let's run through the process of adding an Advanced uploading of files assignment now...

Time for action – adding an Advanced uploading of files assignment

With editing turned on, in the topic you want to add your new assignment to, click on **Add an activity** and choose **Advanced uploading of files**. Now you are at the **Editing assignment** page. There are many more configuration options for this activity compared to an Offline assignment, but for now I'm just going to worry about the important ones. Remember, for more information on specific settings, check out the Moodle docs for this page link at the bottom of the page—and you can always come back and change settings later on if you need to.

1. Give your assignment a name and fill out the description.

2. Use the **Grade** setting to specify the maximum grade you are going to give for this assignment. I'm going to leave the Grade setting at 100 (meaning I can grade this assignment out of 100). Maybe your assignment forms part of an overall mark and you need to mark it out of less. You can even choose to create your own custom grades (for example, A, B, C, D, E or F), which we learn how to do later on in this chapter.

3. Scroll down to the **Advanced uploading of files** options box:

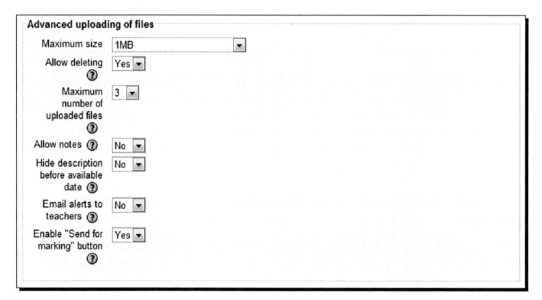

4. Because it is a PowerPoint presentation, I'm expecting students to upload it. I'm going to set the maximum file size accordingly. And I'm going to allow students to delete what they have uploaded (in case they accidentally upload the wrong thing).

5. If you want to allow students to include a short note with their submission then make sure **Allow notes** is set to **Yes**:

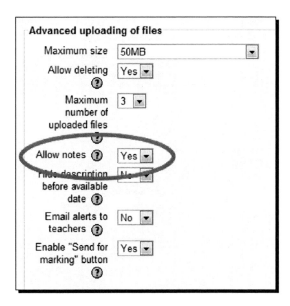

6. Because I'm hiding both of these projects until I'm ready, I can leave the **Hide description before available date** as **No**. If, instead of hiding the entire assignment as I am, you are employing the **Available from** and **Due date** settings then set **Hide description** to **Yes**. Students will know they've got an assignment coming but the description is only revealed when the **Available from** date is reached.

7. Set **Email alerts to teachers** to **Yes** so that you know when a student has submitted their work. Use this setting with caution: if you are a teacher on a course who isn't interested in the submission of pieces of work then receiving dozens of e-mails saying student work has been submitted will become tiresome (as well as annoying).

8. Scroll down to the bottom of the page and press **Save and display**. Your new assignment is now configured:

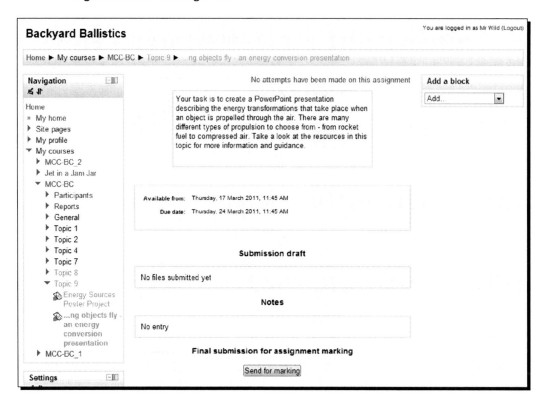

What just happened?

We've just completed adding two types of assignment, an Offline activity and an Advanced uploading of files assignment. We haven't covered the Online text assignment type but with the skills and experience you've gained so far you will be able to use those types with ease. Before we learn how assignments are marked in Moodle, why not spend a little time having a look at the Online text assignment now?

Introducing a student on your course

You've seen how easy it is for us to add assignments and project work to our courses. However, we do need to have a feel for how it is to be a student using Moodle to hand in work using assignments—and check our grades and teacher feedback after we have handed our work in. As with earlier in this book, what we need at this stage isn't one of our actual students. We need a 'control student' and, luckily, my Moodle admin has already created one for me (see the Moodle 2.0 Course Conversion free bonus chapter download on the Packt Publishing website). This lets me log in as a test student.

Enrolling a student

My Moodle admin has created a test student for me and previously enrolled that student on my course. Assuming you have permission to enroll students (you can check with your Moodle admin if you're not sure), here's how to enroll your own students:

Time for action – enrolling a student on your course

1. In the **Settings** block, under **Course administration**, look for the **Users** link and click on it—then click on **Enrolled users**:

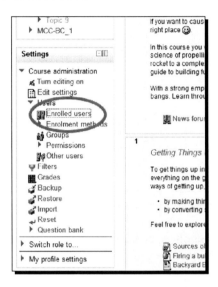

2. The Enrolled users screen is displayed. To enroll a new user, click on either of the **Enrol users** buttons:

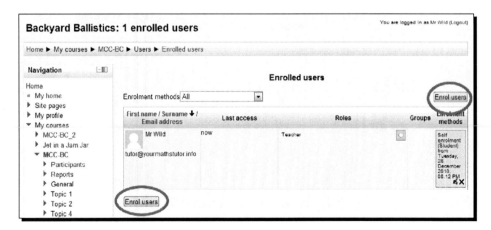

3. The **Enrol users** pop-up dialog is displayed. We are going to enroll a student so make sure you have **Student** selected in the **Assign roles** drop-down menu at the top of the pop up:

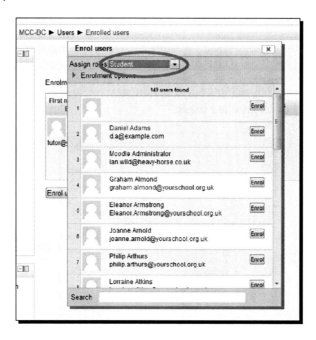

4. The search box at the bottom of this popup allows me to search for the test student my Moodle admin created for me:

5. Press the **Enrol** button to the right of the student's name to enroll the user as a student. Their name is then indented and the **Enrol** button disappears:

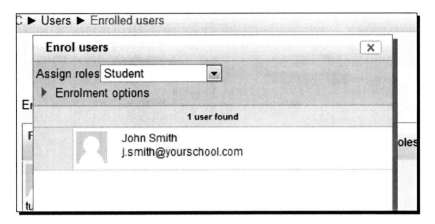

6. Click on the close icon in the top right-hand corner of the popup to both close the dialog and to actually enroll the student. You'll then see the student listed on the **Enrolled users** page:

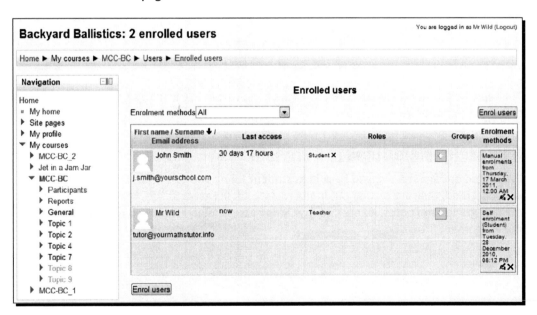

7. That's it! We're done.

What just happened?

Rather than bothering my Moodle admin to enroll the test student on my course, I've enrolled the user as a student myself. Armed with this knowledge, I could enroll my entire class on to my course if I wanted to. But there are various ways of managing enrollment (including having my students enroll themselves using a password selected by me), which we will be investigating in later chapters.

Remember: before I log in as a student, I need to reveal the assignment topic. If I don't and I'm a student, then I'll see this:

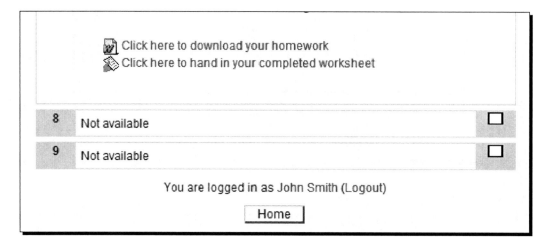

The topic isn't available. Make sure you click on the closed eye icon to open the eye and reveal the topic before you log out.

How assignments look to a student

I've logged out and then logged back in as student John Smith. As far as Offline assignments are concerned, they are carried out in the real world. In that instance, Moodle is used to manage grades and notes. If I click on my Offline assignment, I just see a description of the assignment:

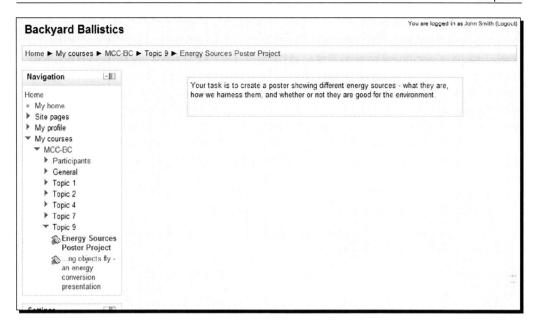

My second assignment requires students to upload a file. In the next section, we experience a little of what life is like as a Moodle student when we try uploading a project submission to Moodle.

Taking the Student's point of view – Uploading a project file

It is a very good idea to see what we are expecting our students to do when we ask them to upload their project work to us online. At the very least, when we ask students to upload their project work to Moodle, we need to know what we are talking about in case they have any questions. If you don't have a student login or you are still logged in as yourself and have asked a colleague to check that your assignment is working correctly, it's a good idea to take a good look over their shoulder while they are running through the following steps. Together, let's run though what a student must do to upload a file to us.

Time for action – uploading a file to an assignment

I only have one computer to work from, so the first thing to do is for me to log out and log back in as my pretend student "John Smith". If you have the luxury of having two computers next to each other then you can log in as yourself on one and your pretend student on the other at the same time. You might have two different browsers (for example, Firefox and Internet Explorer) installed on the same computer. If so, you can log into one as a teacher and the other as a student. Don't try to log in as two different people on the same computer using the same browser—it doesn't work. Now that you are logged in as a student.

1. Return to the course main page and click on the **Advanced uploading of files** assignment you added earlier. You will be presented with the following page:

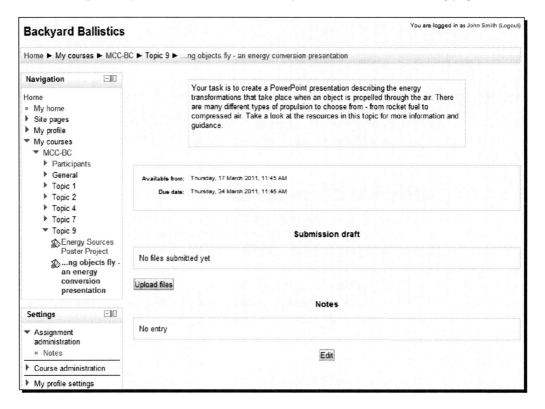

The top half of the page is our description of the assignment. The second half allows us to upload a file and, because I configured the activity such that students could include comments with their submission, an area allowing us to add a note. Students can browse for files and upload them in exactly the same way as we upload our teaching materials to the course files area. If they want to add a note then they need to press on the **Edit** button (at the bottom of the previous screenshot).

2. Click on the **Upload files** button now. On the following screen, press the **Add..** button to display the File picker dialog. This allows us to select a file to upload. You can choose any for now, just to prove the point. I've quickly created a text file using Notepad called `example_submission.txt`. Select the file you want to upload using the File picker (via the **Upload a file** link on the left-hand side):

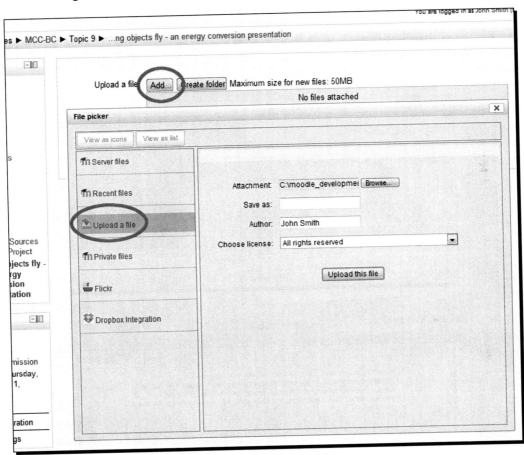

3. Press the **Upload this file** button. Then, press the **Save changes** button. You will now see the file listed in the **Submission draft** box:

As you may have spotted, you can use the File picker to upload more than one file if you need to.

4. To add a note to go along with the submission, I can press the **Edit** button towards the bottom of the page. Try leaving a note now. (If your assignment has been configured so that students are prevented from leaving a note, you won't have this option).

5. If I am happy that this is the final version of the project and I want to send it for marking then I can press the **Send for marking** button at the bottom of the page. Pressing this stops me from uploading any more files:

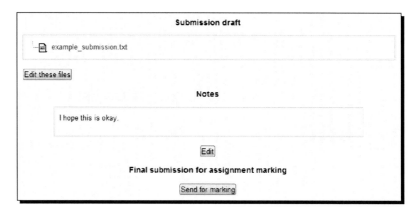

6. That's it. We're done:

What just happened?

It was easy for us to convert our assignments to Moodle. Now we've seen how easy it is for students to convert to using Moodle to hand in their assignment submissions. We've also actually got a piece of work to mark (albeit a pretend piece) and I am ready to start marking.

Before moving on to the next section, make sure you are logged in as yourself rather than as a student.

Marking assignments

Managing student grades and the paperwork associated with student submissions is one of my biggest headaches. By converting to Moodle I can avoid all of these problems. Let's see how easy it is to mark assignments in Moodle.

Marking Offline assignments

My Offline assignment, the poster project, is being carried out in the real world. Currently, I take a digital photograph of the poster and record my comments and grades on separate pieces of paper. Let's see how I can convert this to Moodle...

Time for action – marking an Offline assignment

1. From the course front page, click on your **Offline assignment**.

2. Click on the **No attempts have been made on this assignment/View 0 submitted assignments** link in the top right-hand corner of the page. You are now taken to the Submissions page. I've only got one student enrolled on my course—the pretend student my admin created and I enrolled on my course for me—so this is what I see:

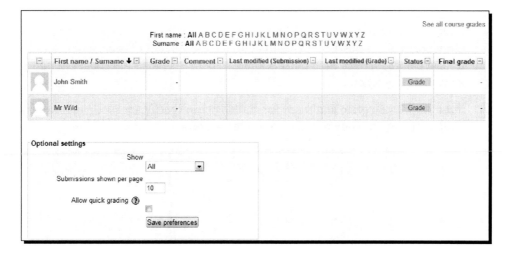

3. To grade John Smith's work I need to click on the **Grade** link, found in the **Status** column. The Feedback page is displayed:

4. I can use this screen to comment on the student's work. At this point I can include a photograph of the poster in the comment, if I wanted to (or I could get the students to take photographs of their posters and get them to upload the images as part of an online submission).

5. If the work is complete and ready for marking I can specify a mark (in my case out of 100) using the drop-down list in the Grades section:

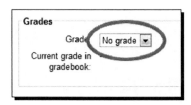

6. When you have finished commenting and/or grading, press the **Save changes** button. The Submissions table is updated accordingly:

	First name / Surname ↓	Grade	Comment	Last modified (Submission)	Last modified (Grade)	Status	Final grade
	John Smith	95 / 100	Excellent ...	Thursday, 17 March 2011, 03:02 PM	Thursday, 17 March 2011, 03:03 PM	Update	95.00
	Mr Wild	.				Grade	.

What happens after you press **Save changes**? From the teacher's point of view, the **No attempts have been made on this assignment** link changes to **View 1 submitted assignments**. If you are a student then you may have been sent an e-mail advising you that you have received feedback on your assignment (depending on how your Moodle has been set up).

What just happened?

We have seen how easy it is to convert to using Moodle to manage student grades and my comments on student work for my "Offline" poster project. Remember that, as with anything else in Moodle, if you need to change a comment or even a grade later on then you can come back and make the relevant changes very easily.

Let's move on now to looking at our Advanced uploading of files assignment. The first issue to understand is how to handle student submissions from a teacher's point of view.

Handling student submissions

Return to your course front page and click on your **Advanced uploading of files assignment**. When enrolled as a student, I submitted an assignment to this activity. Now look for the link in the top right-hand corner of the page:

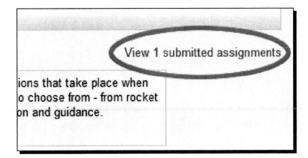

Click on the **View 1 submitted assignments** link. You are taken to the Submissions page for this assignment. You will see the submission we made previously now listed:

In the **Last modified (Submission)** column, click on the **Notes** link to display the comments we left when we made our submission (when we were logged in as a test student). You won't see this link if you have the Allow notes option turned off. If I click on `example_` `submission.txt` I am asked whether I want to open or save the file. Let's save it, make some comments, and see how these are fed back to the student. How do we provide feedback on project submissions using Moodle?

Time for action – providing feedback on student submissions

I'm going to add a comment to `example_submission.txt` and then save the file locally as `example_submission_v2.txt`. I'm then going to provide this slightly modified file back to the student by way of feedback on their work so far.

1. Click on the **Grade** link in the **Status** column, along from the student's name. The **Feedback** screen is displayed:

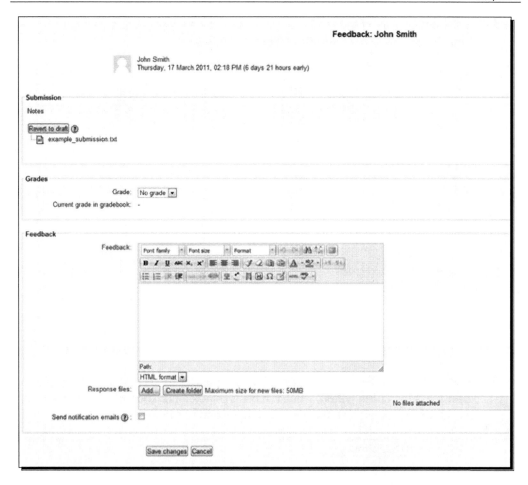

2. At the top of the page will be a list of the files the student has uploaded (in this instance, just the one). Recall that when I was logged in as a student I pressed the **Send for marking** button. This was to confirm that I thought I had finished the assignment, and it also prevented me from uploading or modifying files. Because I don't think this particular student has actually finished I can press the **Revert to draft** button to allow the student to modify and submit files again. If it is displayed, press the **Revert to draft** button:

3. In the bottom half of the Feedback screen is an area allowing me to provide feedback (in the form of Response files) to the student:

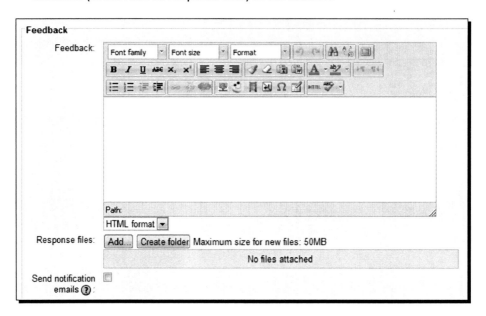

4. Next to **Response files:** click on the **Add...** button. Use the File picker dialog to select **example_submission_v2.txt**. Once the file is selected (via the **Upload a file** link on the left of the File picker), the file is now uploaded to Moodle:

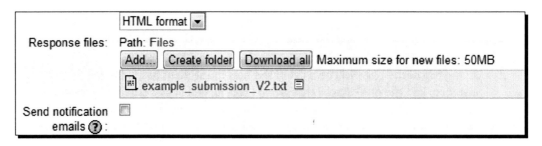

5. Enter your comments on this work in the editor. When you are finished, press the **Save changes** button (at the bottom of the page).

6. The Submissions page is updated accordingly and we're done:

What just happened?

Providing feedback on student submissions is easy when you convert to Moodle for course assignments. We don't have to worry about sending out e-mails (depending on how Moodle is set up, students are sent an e-mail advising them that you have provided some feedback) or worry about spreading viruses by using memory sticks. Everything is kept contained online within Moodle. But what does it look like for students when we provide feedback to them?

Confirming that our feedback has been received

It is a good idea at this stage to log in as a student again, so we can experience what it is like to be a student receiving teacher feedback.

Logging back on to Moodle as a student and clicking on my **Advanced uploading of files assignment** I see the following page:

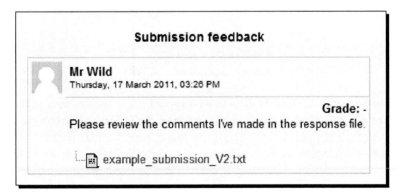

My note is displayed, and the student has the opportunity to download the corrected file I uploaded.

Marking student submissions

The process of marking student submissions to an Advanced uploading of files activity is much the same as that for marking Offline activities. From the submissions page, click on the **Grade** link along from the student's name. The Feedback dialog is displayed. For more details on setting the final grade, follow the instructions in *Time for action – Marking an Offline assignment*.

Specifying custom grades

Currently, I'm marking my projects out of 100 but, as I mentioned previously, that's not how they are graded. According to the syllabus, I can only give students one of four grades: Distinction, Merit, Pass, and Referral. So how do you specify your own grades? Let's learn how to do that now.

Time for action – creating a custom grade scale

Return to your course front page and look for Grades in the **Settings** block:

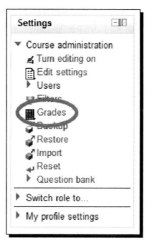

Click on **Grades** and you'll be taken to the **Grader report** page. We are now in the Moodle grade book. I'm not going to worry too much about all of the features in the grade book for the moment—but while you are there you might like to spend a little time having a look. As with anything else in Moodle, you can't do any damage by doing something by mistake.

At the top of the **Grader report** page, you will find a drop-down list of view options:

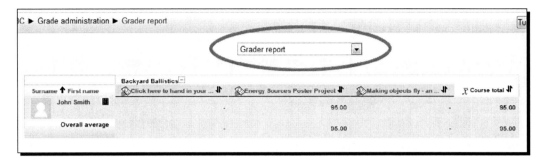

From the View list, select **View** under **Scales**. You're now taken to the scales page. We need to add a new scale, so press the **Add a new scale** button in the centre of the page.

On the following page, give your new scale a name and in the Scale box you can specify the possible grades contained in your new scale. This may sound counter-intuitive but make sure you specify your grades in order of increasing value because that's the way Moodle expects it. For example, if your scale is A, B, C, D, E, F, and U then you will need to specify them as U, F, E, D, C, B, A. Separate the grades with commas—no spaces:

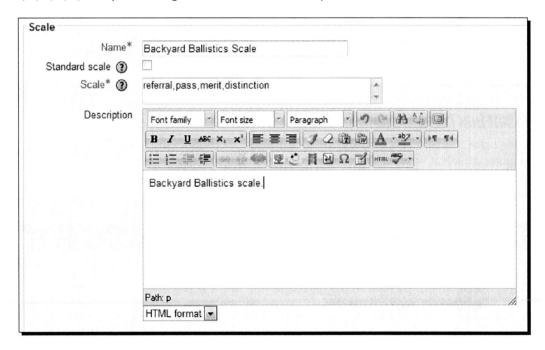

Although I've specified one, you don't have to worry about a description if you don't want to—it's optional. Are the grades you are specifying here used for grading in other courses? If you tick the **Standard scale** box then your scale will be made available to teachers on all courses.

When you are done, press the **Save changes** button. Your new scale is listed on the scales page. Because I didn't make my new scale a standard scale, it's listed as a custom scale:

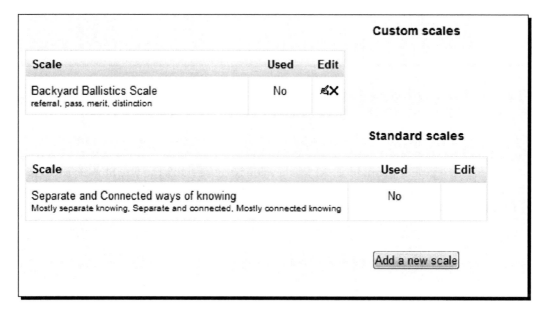

What just happened?

I don't give students a numerical grade for the Backyard Ballistics projects. The syllabus requires a qualitative grade, but luckily the system makes it easy to create my own custom grade scales. All I need to do now is modify my two assignment activities to use the new scale. That only involves a few clicks, so let's do that now...

Time for action – grading using a custom scale

1. Return to your course front page and click on the update icon next to the assignment you want to change to use your new custom scale. The Editing assignment page is displayed.

2. Scroll down to the **Grade** drop-down list. Click on the list. Scroll up if you need to, because the custom scale we want to use will be towards the very top:

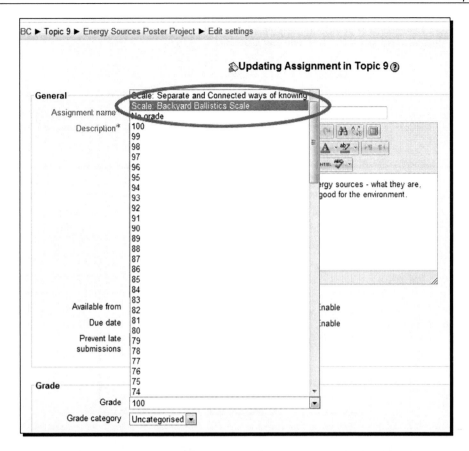

3. With the new grading scale selected, scroll down to the bottom of the page and press the **Save and return to course** button.

4. That's it. You will now be able to grade your project using your new scale.

What just happened?

We've just modified the assignment to use our new grading scale. All that remains now is to demonstrate how you use it. Now that we are back at the course front page, click on the link to the assignment itself to display the assignment's main page (displaying the description of the task we've set). Click on the **View submitted assignments** link in the top right-hand corner of the page to take you to the Submissions page.

Choose a student and, down in the Status column, click on the **Grade** link. If you've already marked that student then the link will say **Update**:

Click on the link to open the **Feedback** page. Click on the **Grade:** drop-down list in the **Grades** section to display the grades you can give to this piece of work. The grades listed are the ones from our new custom grade scale:

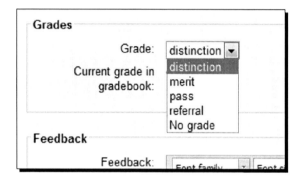

More uses for Moodle assignments

We aren't limited to using the four assignment activities just for major projects. Here are some more ideas on using the assignment activity to convert your current teaching over to Moodle.

- Include an online text assignment to support tasks for which students can use Moodle's text editor to write their submissions, for example writing a short story or for short essay homework tasks

- If you're able to display the Submissions page of a single file assignment to the class during teaching time, keep refreshing the page as homework is submitted. You'll quickly find that there'll be a race on to be the first to hand their homework in. You could easily turn that into a game for younger students.

- Use an Offline activity to manage the grades of any task you set your students— homework handed in on paper, for example. You don't have to confine yourself to just projects.

On that last point, there is another way of managing grades directly. We've already been briefly into the Moodle grader report when we set up our custom scale. Let's revisit that page to see how we can set up custom grading items.

Grading students on core competencies

Often as educators we need to grade assignments on core competencies, otherwise known as key skills or goals. That certainly applies to my syllabus: a percentage of the final grade for my course includes marks for numeracy, literacy, and the use of ICT. Because we are converting to Moodle, and in Moodle-speak the competencies that I am grading are called "outcomes", in this final section we learn how to specify the core competencies we need to grade, and how we can then grade students on them. There are pros and cons of converting to Moodle, specifically: I can choose to enable outcomes on a per assignment basis, but you can't use the default numeric grading scale to grade outcomes, only standard and custom grading scales (such as my custom Backyard Ballistics scale that I created in *Time for action – Creating a custom grade scale*.

Configuring outcomes

Let's start by seeing how easy it is to specify learning outcomes for an assignment.

Time for action – creating a custom grade item in the grader report

1. Return to your course front page and click on the **Outcomes** link in the **Settings** block:

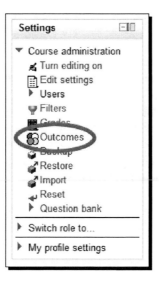

Don't see the Outcomes link?

If you can't see the Outcomes link, then you need to speak to your administrator to get this enabled. Check out the *Ask the admin* section at the end of this chapter.

2. You are now taken to the **Outcomes used in course** page. If the outcomes you need to grade aren't listed in the Standard outcomes box then we need to add them. Assuming that is the case, click on the **Outcomes used in course** drop-down list and select **Edit outcomes**:

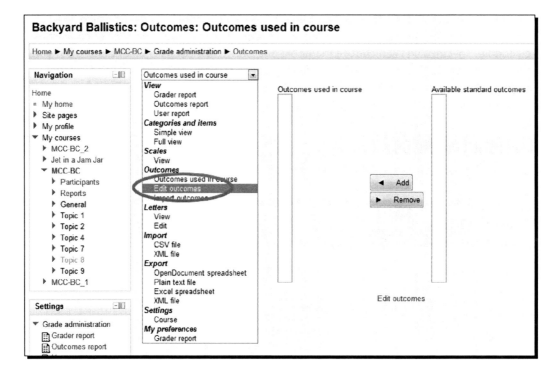

3. Press the **Add a new outcome** button. Give your outcome a name, a short name, and choose the scale that you want to use to grade this outcome. Remember: you can create your own custom scales to judge outcomes if you need to. When you are finished, press the **Save changes** button at the bottom of the page and, as you add more, you'll start to build up a list of outcomes:

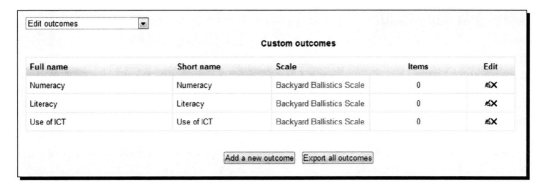

4. When you are done, click on the **Edit outcomes** drop-down list and select **Outcomes used in course** and you will see your new outcomes listed:

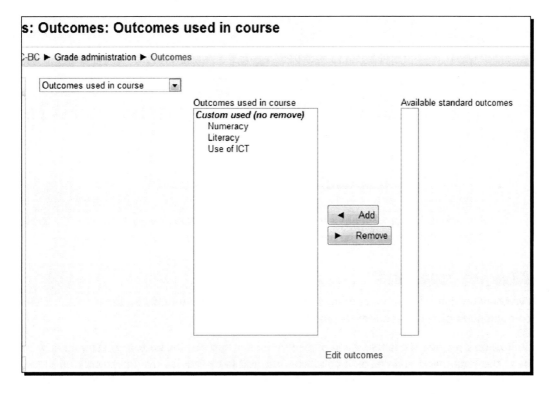

What just happened?

We've just seen how easy it is to define outcomes (core competencies) for our course. Now the outcomes are defined, we need to specify which outcomes we are going to grade, on a per assignment basis.

I'm going to alter my poster project assignment. It's an Offline assignment activity, but this can be any type of assignment activity...

Time for action – grading core competencies in assignments

1. Return to your course front page and click on the Update icon next to the assignment you want to change to open the **Editing assignment** page.

2. Scroll down the page and look for the **Outcomes** box. If you needed to ask your admin to turn outcomes on for you then this box is a new addition to the Editing assignments page:

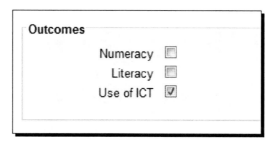

3. I've ticked the competencies that I want to grade students on (just Use of ICT). Scroll down to the bottom of the page and press the **Save and display** button.

What just happened?

I've configured my Offline assignment so that I can now grade students on the three core competencies of numeracy, literacy, and ICT.

So how do we grade students? If you pressed the **Save and display** button you should now be at the assignment main page. If you have returned to the course front page click on the assignment you just reconfigured now. Click on the **View submitted assignments** link in the top right-hand corner of the page.

The table showing student submissions now contains a new column, **Outcomes**. If you grade a student, you will see new options in the **Grades** section to grade the outcomes you have ticked. Have a look at these new options now, for example:

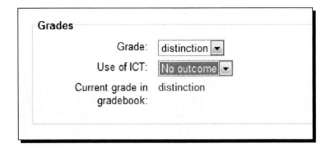

Ask the admin

Before we can specify core competencies, we need to make sure Moodle Outcomes are enabled—and this is a job only our Moodle administrator can do. The setting we need is accessed via the **Settings** block under **Site administration**, then click on **Advanced features**. Your admin needs to ensure that the **Enable outcomes** option is ticked.

Summary

We learned a lot in this chapter about managing student work in Moodle.

Specifically, we covered:

- How to structure converted projects and assignments online using Moodle. We discussed how to add a new topic to a course, and how doing so allows us to hide an assignment, and its supporting reference materials, until students are ready to begin their project work.
- Matching one of the four Moodle assignment activities to your course assignment or project. We discussed how each activity can be used to move homework tasks online, as well as more substantial projects.
- How an assignment looks from the student's point of view. We discussed the importance of knowing how students submit assignments, so that you are ready to give help and guidance as students begin to work online.
- How to mark assignments online. We saw how easy it is to manage project grades in Moodle.

We also discussed how Moodle can be used to grade core competencies—showing how this can be configured on a perassignment basis.

Now that we've learned about managing student work, we're ready to move on to learning how to discuss work with students online—which is the topic of the next chapter.

7
Communicating Online

In the previous chapter we saw how to convert projects and assignments to Moodle, but that's only part of the story. When we set an assignment it's rare that we just hand out the work and tell our students to get on with it. Assignment work is supported by discussions, both discussions with us as teachers and constructive (we hope) talk among the students themselves. If we are going to move project work online then not only does it make sense to move those kinds of discussions online, but there are distinct advantages to doing so. In this chapter we will cover:

- *Forums*
- *Online chat rooms*
- *Moodle messaging*

Communicating in Moodle

Two-way communication in Moodle comes in three flavors:

◆ **Real-time, synchronous chat**: Moodle's very own built-in instant messaging system (such as MSN), allowing us to talk to students when they (or we) are out of the classroom:

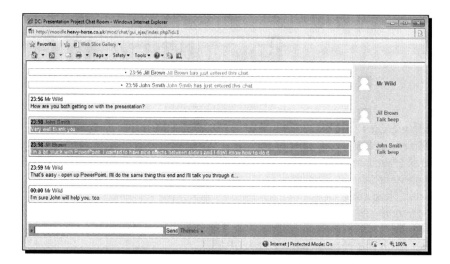

◆ **Forums**: Just like old-fashioned message boards. You post a question or comment and later on someone posts a response:

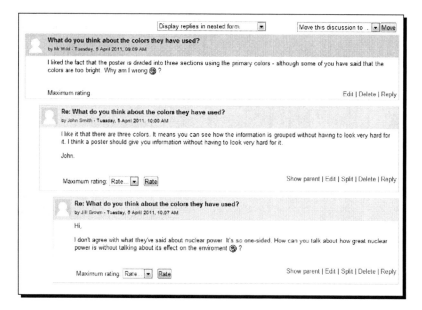

◆ **Messaging**: Don't be confused by the name; the Moodle messaging service allows you to send a message to any other Moodle user. This is different from chat in that it's more like e-mail messaging, rather than being instant messaging. The Moodle messaging system is the online replacement for your staff and student pigeonholes:

In this chapter we will not only learn how to set them up, but also the best practice for each in a teaching context. Specifically, in this chapter you will:

◆ Create a Moodle forum and explore the various ways it can be used.

◆ Open a chat room, allowing students to talk online in real time. We'll explore the pros and cons of this tool.

◆ Learn how to push a Moodle message into your students' pigeonholes.

◆ See that all student comments are fully recorded and traceable to the students who make them. Moodle provides all the tools necessary to support your establishment's Data Protection or e-Safety policy.

In the previous chapter we converted our assignments to Moodle, so let's build on that by seeing how a forum can support and encourage students to do well in their project work.

Forums

In *Chapter 6, Managing Student Work* you worked with me in creating a new, hidden topic for my course project work. I thought it would be great to upload to Moodle a project exemplar and allow students to discuss what they thought were the strengths in that work. It's something I already do in the class, but doing this online means:

- Students can take their time to study the example work and formulate an answer without the pressure of being sat in a classroom. Students who can be shy in the classroom don't always feel the same social pressure online.

- Forum posts can be kept as long as you wish (even when the student who posted has left) so student responses are always available for reference. A good argument or idea is kept online for students to refer back to.

- We can hold more than one discussion at a time online. When we are online we can cover more topics more easily.

- Forum posts can be edited or deleted for only a relatively short period after they are made (which is somewhat different from typical online forums), which reinforces the idea of engaging in a Moodle forum being similar to an online conversation.

After a short time you'll find that when a student posts a problem it is other students that are helping them out. That's certainly been my experience.

Adding a forum to your course

Let's see how easy it is to create a forum in a Moodle course. There are actually four different types of forum supported by Moodle, but I'll talk about those later. Let's get a forum added to our course. To add a simple forum there are only a couple of settings we need to worry about.

The first thing I did was upload the exemplar, following the instructions in the *Time for action – uploading a file* section in *Chapter 3, Adding Documents and Handouts*. Then I provided a brief introduction using both the topic summary (*Time for action – defining each week / topic* section in *Chapter 2, Setting up your Courses*) and a label (*Time for action – inserting a label* section in *Chapter 5, Moodle Makeover*). So, here is my starting point:

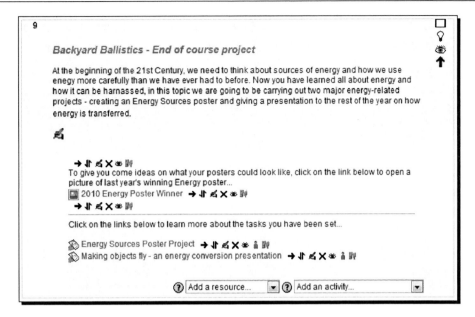

Now, to allow the students to discuss last year's poster winner, let's add a forum.

Time for action – adding a forum

1. In the topic you want to add a forum to, click on the **Add an activity...** list (if you don't see this option then check that you have editing turned on). Select **Forum** from the list:

2. Leave the **Forum type** as **Standard forum for general use**. There's more on the different types of forum later in this chapter.

3. Give your new forum a name and a brief introduction:

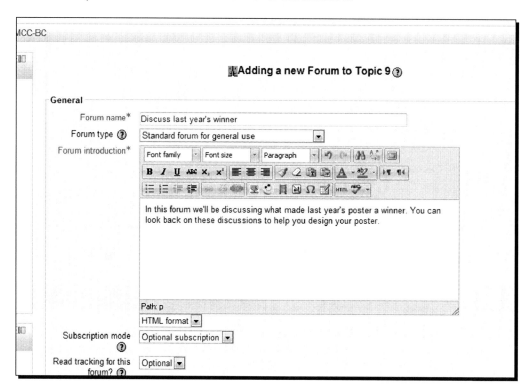

4. Scroll down to the bottom of the page and press the **Save and display** button. And that's it, we're done:

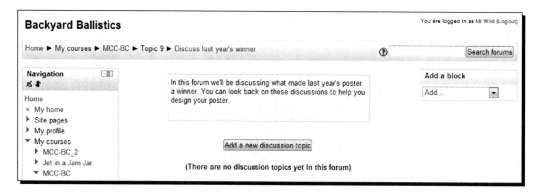

What just happened?

Following these simple instructions we now have a new forum in our course, where students can discuss what they think made last year's poster project such a winner. I appreciate that there are a few configuration options I've missed out, but remember that our task is to get our course up and running with the minimum of fuss.

Subscribing to forums

I'm expecting my forum to be quite active but I don't want to have to remember to log into Moodle to check to see whether there are any posts I need to respond to. Fortunately Moodle can e-mail you every time a message is posted. Let's look at how to set this up now.

Time for action – subscribing users to a forum

1. Return to your course front page and, with editing turned on, click on the update icon next to the forum:

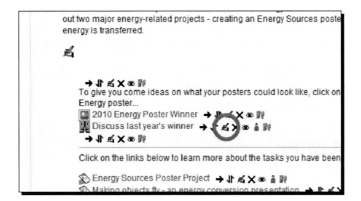

2. Scroll down to the **Subscription mode** setting. Click on the drop-down menu to reveal your options:

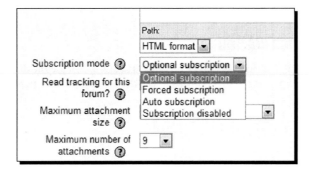

3. The options are fairly self-explanatory, but to force everyone to always receive an e-mail every time someone makes a post, choose **Forced subscription**. If you want to allow your students to unsubscribe (they may complain about getting too many e-mails) then select **Auto subscription**. Make your subscription selection from the list, scroll down the page and press the **Save and return to course** button.

4. That's it. You're done!

What just happened?

We've just configured our forum so that students will receive an e-mail every time a new discussion thread is started. I've forced this so that there should be no excuse from my students for missing an important discussion taking place in the forum. At the start of your course you could force users to be subscribed to a News forum. If it is coming up to exam time you could force users to be subscribed to a dedicated "Exams FAQ" forum (note that this will only work if your students have an active e-mail address enabled in Moodle).

Before we move on to the next section I'll just make a quick point about terminology. "Subscribing" students to a forum doesn't mean that you are making everybody join the forum, they are already members of the forum by virtue of being on your course. Subscribing users to a forum means they will receive e-mails every time there is new activity.

Our next task is to encourage students to start posting, and if we are going to encourage and manage debate then we need to take on the role of moderator, or chairperson, a "forum moderator" in Moodle-speak. In the next section we take a look at what is involved.

Moderating a forum

The forum moderator needs to:

◆ Get a discussion started

◆ Ensure discussions stay focused

◆ Make sure that discussions are easy to follow

Let's look at each of these aspects now.

Getting a discussion started

The easiest way to start a conversation is to ask a question. I'm going to make an initial post to my forum asking students to comment on the colors used in the example poster that I've uploaded:

Time for action – starting a discussion

1. Press the **Add a new discussion topic** button:

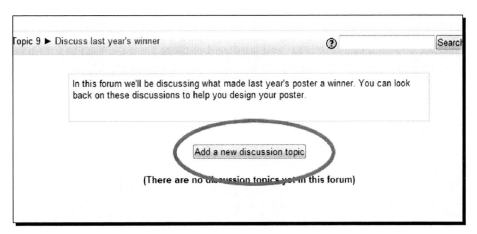

2. You're now taken to the **Add a new discussion topic** page. Your new forum post needs a subject line and there is a box for you to create your message. Here's mine:

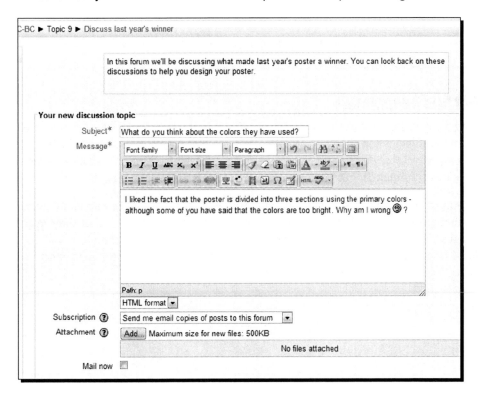

3. At the bottom of the page you'll see that there is an option to include an attachment with your post. This is very useful: students can scan in work they are stuck on and attach the scanned image to a post. While we are experimenting with forum posts, you could try attaching a file (anything will do, Moodle isn't fussy). Remember, you won't break anything.

4. Once you're happy with what you are about to post, press the **Post to forum** button. After the confirmation message (reminding you that you have only a short time frame in which to change your mind about what you've just written), you're taken back to the forum where your new post is listed:

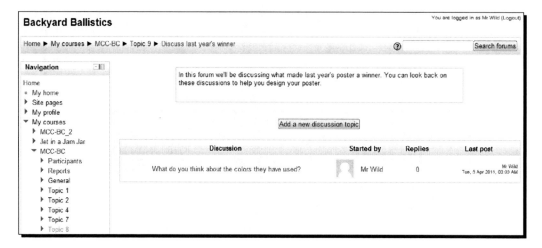

What just happened?

Getting a conversation started can often be difficult in the classroom and sometimes you've the same problem when you convert to teaching online. It's a sure bet that a forum that starts empty will stay empty, so I always start the ball rolling with a question (or sometimes a contentious statement!) that I know will get my students responding back.

Once you've got the discussion started, you often find that there will be an initial flurry of posts that quickly dies away as everyone decides that they have said all that they've got to say. If students can see that it has been a while since the last post then they will be less inclined to post themselves. Also, as forums grow, discussions can sometimes venture off-topic. Let's look at a few techniques to keep discussions focused.

Keeping discussions focused – Managing the discussion

Moderating a forum takes much less effort than you would at first imagine. Here are some tips and tricks to help you tackle some of the issues you might encounter:

- The frequency of posts can fall away if students think that no one is going to respond to them. It is a good idea to state how often you visit the forum and when you intend answering posts, especially if you've added a forum to support work that is being done over a weekend or a holiday.
- Respond to posts with positive feedback. Thank your students for posting, it encourages them to post some more.

When it comes to moderation you need to decide how much you are going to exercise. As a teacher you can edit or even remove posts but too much moderation might stifle debate and alienate students who are familiar with forums. Too little might allow certain students to dominate and alienate those students who aren't familiar with forums. There is always the option to set a post threshold to limit your more enthusiastic students. Perhaps you want students to take some level of ownership of the forum much as you want them to take ownership of their own work. In that case, too much moderation might be seen as interfering.

Coping with the rude and unruly

It is rarely a problem, but some students can say things on a forum that they would never think of saying in person. If you've a fear that your forum may get out of hand then lay down a set of rules before you start. Make the rules for student conduct clear in your course. Use rating scales, these can moderate student behavior, especially if their final grade depends on getting good ratings from teachers or other students.

 If you decide you would rather check the suitability of messages before they are posted then take a look at `Moodle.org` and search for "`approve forum post`" or similar. There are a variety of solutions available, although you will have to speak to your Moodle admin about implementing them.

One out of the box solution is to rate a post. If it is totally unsuitable then obviously you will need to delete it completely.

Time for action – rating forum posts

1. We need to reconfigure our forum to allow us to rate posts. If you have returned to the course front page then click on the update icon next to your new forum:

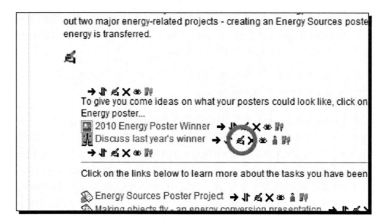

2. If you haven't left your forum main page then, in the **Settings** block, click on **Edit settings** under **Forum administration**:

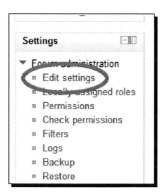

3. On the **Editing forum** page, scroll down to the **Grade** box. Select how you want posts to be graded from the aggregate type list. Grades given to posts are used to give students an overall grade for the forum activity. The options should be self-explanatory.

4. Select the grading scale you want to use. You can use a custom grading method if you want to (see the *Time for action – create a custom grade scale* section in *Chapter 6, Managing Student Work*). I'm going to allow a rating out of 10.

5. Finally, if you want to keep students focused on the particular posts, you can restrict grading to a certain date range. You'll find these settings at the bottom of the **Grade** box.

6. And that's it. We're done! Now, depending on the date range you restricted grading to, you are given the option to grade posts:

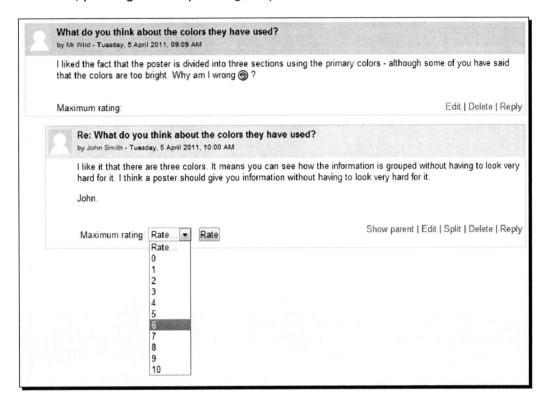

What just happened?

The great thing about converting our courses to Moodle is that you can grade student's input into the discussion much more easily than you can in a classroom or lecture theater. Knowing that their posts are likely to be rated prevents discussions getting out of hand. But what if a discussion ventures off onto another topic but the new topic is still one that needs to be discussed? We'll look at this issue in the next section.

Ensuring discussions are easy to follow

I've already promoted forums as a great way of discussing topics because with a forum it is easy to look back on a discussion to find a point well argued or a case well made. But that only works if threads of discussion are kept organized. It's something that happens often in forums. For example, one of the discussions in my poster forum changed from being about colors to nuclear power:

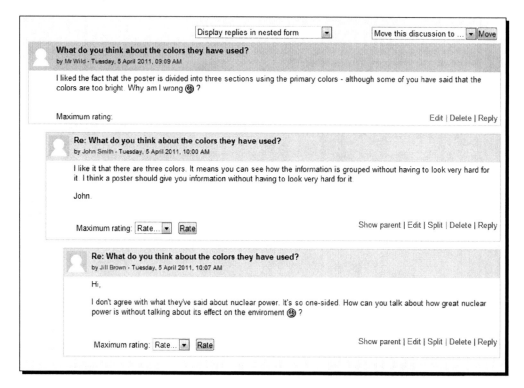

Time for action – splitting a discussion

1.   Choose the topic you want to split the discussion at and click on **Split**:

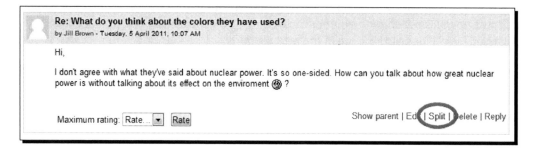

2. Choose a new name for the discussion thread; I'm going to call mine "**Nuclear power: Is the poster balanced?**". When you've chosen a new title press the **Split** button.

3. You've now created a new discussion thread, and both discussions are now much easier to follow:

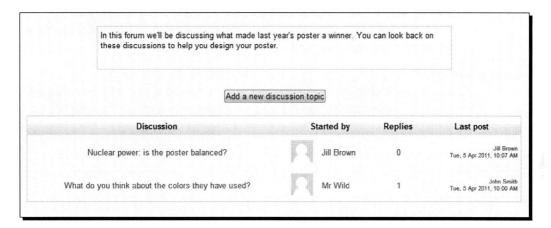

What just happened?

Managing forums in Moodle is all about making discussions easy to follow, and easy to refer back to later on. But we've just seen how managing discussions is very easy. It's one of the advantages of moving your courses online.

Now we've learned pretty much all there is to know about Moodle's Standard forum for general use. But that kind of forum doesn't fit every kind of discussion or debate you might want to hold online. But that's no problem because Moodle provides four different flavors of forum.

Types of forum

So far we've been using a Standard forum for general use, and most of the time that will suit your needs. But there are four other types to choose from:

- A single simple discussion, where only one discussion thread is allowed. If you want to keep the discussion brief and to the point, then this is the type of forum to choose.

- Each person posts one discussion, where each student is only allowed to start one discussion each but can reply as freely as they like in any other discussions. It is used when students are only allowed to make a single statement or comment, for example online debates.

- Standard forum displayed in a blog-like format, which displays a discussion thread as you would see the comments at the bottom of a blog, or possibly more familiar to your students, on a Facebook wall.

- Q and A forum, where students are prevented from seeing other posts until they themselves have posted something. Used often in situations where you don't want students copying each other's work (language teaching), or thoughts and ideas. It can also be used in the online equivalent of a "round robin" teaching exercise, where I ask a question that the first student answers. They then ask a question that the next student answers. And so on.

When we first added a forum to the course at the very start of this chapter (*Time for action – Adding a forum to your course* section), I said to leave the **Forum type** setting as **Standard forum for general use**. It's this setting (on the forum configuration page) that allows you to specify the forum type.

As you can see, converting to Moodle opens up new possibilities for discussion, and remember that Moodle easily allows you to carry the discussion on beyond the classroom.

What about different ways you can use forums to support your teaching? Let's take a look at a few forum tips and tricks in the next section.

Forum tips and tricks

Forums are a great way of managing discussion and debate. Here are just a few ideas on how you can use a Moodle forum in your teaching:

- Do you have project work that needs to be carried out over the weekend or a holiday period? Use forums to support your students outside of the classroom or lecture theater.

- If your students spend very little time together as a group then create a social forum, allowing your students to get to know each other better online.

- Remember that there are many different types of course format to choose from. If you choose the Social format then your course is simply one big forum. For more information on specifying course formats see the *Time for action – setting up the course format* section in *Chapter 2, Setting up your Courses*.

- If you are teaching a foreign language and you don't want students to copy each other's posts then try using a Q and A forum; they can't see other posts until they have made a post themselves.

- For short, focused group work create a forum and display posts on the interactive white board. Use these posts to support verbal discussions in the classroom or lecture theater.

- To make discussion threads easier to follow you can change the way they are displayed on the screen using the display replies drop-down menu. Note that this is a personal setting rather than something that can be changed for others:

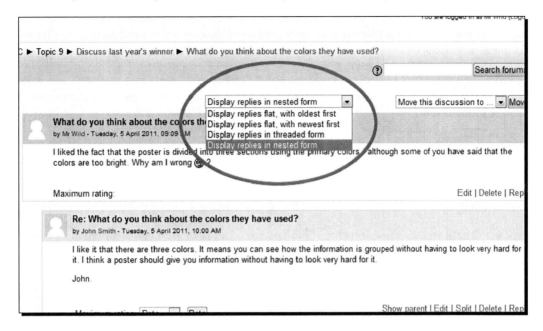

- Create a Frequently Asked Questions forum to support major project work. Save this forum for subsequent years. You'll be able to see the areas students struggle with more easily.

- Students working in groups can have their own discussion forum so they can communicate and collaborate together (there's more on setting up student groups later in this book).

- Prevent over-keen students from making too many posts by using the **Post threshold for blocking** settings on the **Editing Forum** page.

- Remember that forum posts are time and date stamped. Students will get to know your sleeping habits if they see you posting to forums at 4.00am. Likewise, you'll get to know your student's work habits if they do the same!

Have a go hero – creating a school leavers book

Create a forum for school leavers to post their farewell messages and photographs. These forums always prove very popular. Some schools even copy the messages and photographs and have them printed for students to take away with them when they leave.

The News forum is not really a forum

Every course has a News forum, but that name is misleading. The News forum is actually a notice board for teachers, a place for you to post the latest course news. The important point is that only teachers can post to it, so don't expect students to respond to you in there. Any posts you post to the News forum appear in the **Latest News** block, so you can use the News forum to announce changes to the course, project deadlines, exam dates.

Forums are a great tool to support discussion and debate. However, there are times when you need to provide a real-time chat environment for your students. In the next section we look at Moodle chat.

Online chat rooms

If you need to support learners who aren't in the classroom then chat rooms are the ideal way of doing so:

- ◆ Create an exam revision chat room and spend an hour with your students the night or morning before an exam.
- ◆ Support learners who are away ill. If they have access to a computer they can still join in with class discussions.
- ◆ Support project work over the weekend or holiday period with chat sessions. They will cut down on the amount of catch-up work you have to do when you return to work on Monday morning.
- ◆ Hold online tutorial sessions if you and your students are finding it difficult to arrange a time and a place when you can all be together in person.
- ◆ Invite a guest speaker into your chat room. By inviting them to join your class online you can dramatically cut your expenses bill!
- ◆ Moodle chat rooms are safe and only open to those enrolled in your course.

And using a chat room within Moodle means that users don't have to learn how to use yet another "chat client", as they are called.

But chat rooms have their downsides:

- ◆ Because chatting online lacks hand gestures and verbal cues, it is very easy for misunderstandings to take place. Using emoticons (or smileys) can help prevent this problem.
- ◆ Chat rooms are always open, 24/7. Misbehavior may take place without you being aware of it.

◆ Young learners can be very used to chat, and can often start trite conversations along the lines of "sup? who u lovin?". Chat sessions are recorded and can be displayed to the class on the interactive white board if necessary. As with forums, it's best to set the rules for good behavior before you let the rabble in.

The other feature of chat rooms is that hiding a chat room renders it closed.

We'll look at all of these issues as we learn more about Moodle chat. Let's start by spending the next section learning how to add a chat room to your course.

Adding a chat room to your course

Adding a chat room to your course is easy. All you need to do is choose the topic you want to add the chat room to, click on **Add an activity...** and choose **Chat**.

I want to include a chat room to allow students to discuss the presentation they have to make. It is something they all get quite worried about, and it is good when they work together to overcome any difficulties they might be having. Rather than using a forum for this, students have said that forums can seem quite isolating when they are waiting for a response to be posted, I am going to use a Moodle chat.

Time for action – adding a Moodle chat

1. Decide on the topic in which you want to include a chat room. With editing turned on click on **Add an activity** and choose **Chat**.

2. Give the chat room a name and provide a short piece of introductory text:

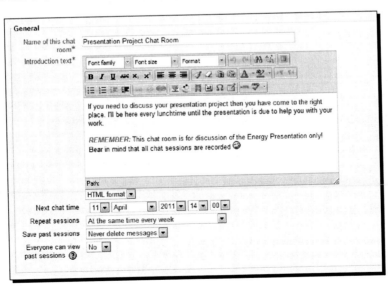

3. For now the default settings will do. Simply scroll down to the bottom of the page and press the **Save and display** button:

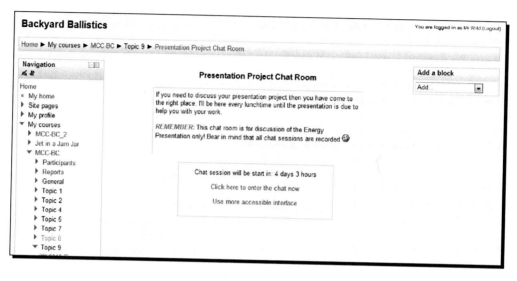

What just happened?

We've just added a chat room to our course! It was very easy, just a few clicks and we're done. To enter the chat room simply click on the **Click here to enter the chat now** link. Ask a student or colleague to join you. You can see whether there's anyone else with you in the chat room on the right-hand side of the screen:

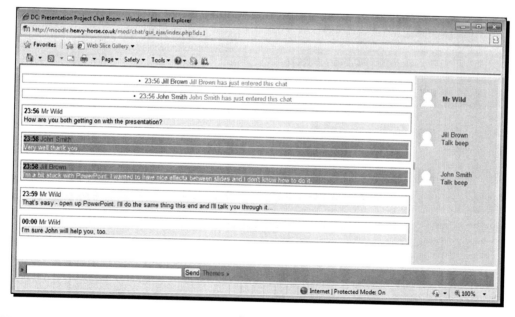

Being understood – Using emoticons

As we have already mentioned, without visual cues, facial, and hand gestures, it is very easy to be misunderstood in a chat room. For that reason emoticons, or smileys, were invented. Have you tried inserting smileys using the HTML editor:

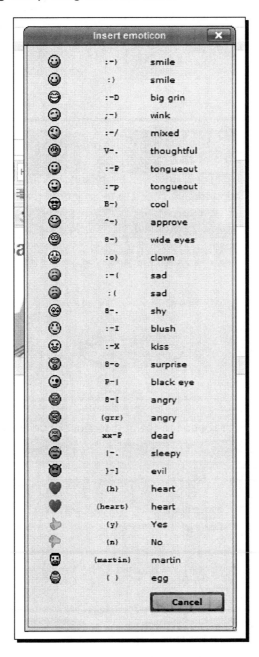

That dialog isn't present in Moodle chat, but you can use the keyboard shortcuts shown next to each picture in the HTML editor dialog to use that smiley when you are chatting. For example, type in this:

And it gets displayed as:

Viewing past chat sessions

Chats can happen at lightning speed. However, by default they are always logged, so if there is an element of that discussion that you need to refer back to then simply click on **View past chat sessions** to see the chat:

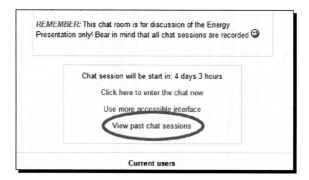

As a teacher, you now have the option to see past sessions or delete them if they are no longer relevant:

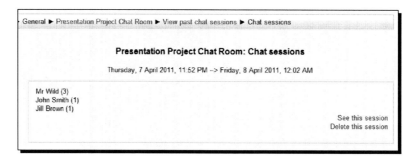

Click on **See this session** to view the chat.

Have a go hero – doing more with chats and forums

If an important point is made in a chat that needs elaborating, perhaps vital to a particular learning goal, then use a forum to discuss the issue further. You could even copy the chat from the past chat session to a forum post. You can edit out the names to protect the innocent!

Letting students know when you are available

Chat rooms are always open, but you can indicate when you are going to be around to talk to your students, as you've probably guessed and as I did previously, using the **Next chat time** settings. Let's update our chat room now.

Time for action – telling students when we're around

1. If you are on the course front page then click on the update icon next to your chat room. If you are on the chat room page then select **Edit settings** under **Chat administration** in the **Settings** block.

2. Scroll down the **Editing chat** page until you see the chat time settings (in the **General** box):

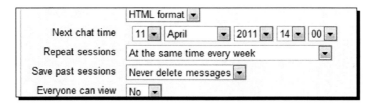

3. I initially configured the chat room to publish chat times (you can see the effect in previous screenshots). I want to have the same chat time every Monday at lunchtime, so:

4. Scroll down to the bottom of the page and press the **Save and return to course** button. And that's it. We're done.

What just happened?

We've just specified when we are going to be around for a chat, but how are students going to know? One way is to check out the **Upcoming events** block on the course front page (usually on the right-hand side of the course main page):

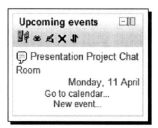

Try clicking on the **Go to calendar...** link in the block. The course calendar is displayed:

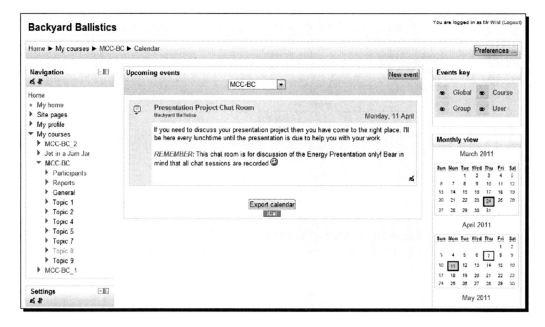

You can see what a great tool the course calendar is. You can add new events, either reminders to yourself or course events, where you can let students know about upcoming exams. For the truly adventurous, the calendar can be exported and uploaded to your mobile phone, iPad, or PDA/tablet device of choice.

You can even display a mini-calendar on your course front page. I appreciate this chapter is about communication, but because I want to let my students know when I am going to be available for a chat, now is the time I want to include an events calendar in my course. Let's see how to do that now.

Adding a calendar to your course front page

Adding the calendar onto your course front page is all a matter of adding the **Calendar** block:

Time for action – adding the calendar

1. Return to your course front page and with editing turned on, click on **Add...** in the **Blocks** block. Then select **Calendar**:

2. A calendar is now added to your course front page. You can reposition it either by using the move icon:

Or, if instead of the arrows you see crosshairs, then by clicking on the block and dragging it.

3. Once you've got the calendar where you want it (I like to have the **Calendar** block and the **Upcoming events** block next to each other) then you're done.

What just happened?

Calendars are great tools for letting students know what's about to happen on your course, and we've just learned how to add a mini-calendar onto our course front pages.

The course event shown on the calendar previously (I can tell it's a course event because the background is pink) is to indicate that I am going to be in the Poster Presentation chat room at 1:00 pm. If I hover the mouse pointer over the 7th July, I see this:

Have a go hero – calendar events

In *Chapter 5, Moodle Makeover*, we saw how to convert our projects and assignments to Moodle. Remember that you can also specify when a Moodle assignment is available. Configure the Available from and Due date. The assignment will be added to your calendar.

Chat room tips and tricks

Before we leave chat rooms, here are some ideas for using chat rooms on your courses:

- Let students join the chat room to allow them to get to know each other and you before they meet.

- Hold meetings with colleagues about your course using a hidden chat room.

- Invite guests into your chat room, perhaps specialists from your local college or university.

- Is your school "twinned"? That is, does it have a special link with another school (perhaps even one in another country)? Hold chats with the twinned school using Moodle. We've used chats to share Backyard Ballistics anecdotes!

We'll spend the rest of this chapter looking at Moodle messaging, Moodle's own built-in e-mail system.

Moodle messaging

Forums and chats are primarily a teaching tool. Moodle messages, on the other hand, are the ideal course admin tool when you want to send out messages to your students. As we will find as we work through this section, students can also message each other, further supporting collaborative working, especially as we continue converting our courses to run online.

Note that I've left discussion of this topic to the end of this chapter because often Moodle messaging is turned off. Before reading on, it's certainly worth checking that messaging is enabled in your Moodle.

Sending a welcome message

I figured it would be good to send all of my new students a welcome message, thanking them for joining me on the Backyard Ballistics course. Let's see how easy that is now:

Time for action – sending a message to your students

1. In the **Navigation** block, under your course, click on **Participants**:

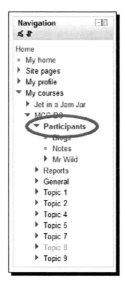

2. Under the list of participants, press the **Select All** button.

3. Click on the **With selected users...** drop-down menu and select **Send a message** from the list:

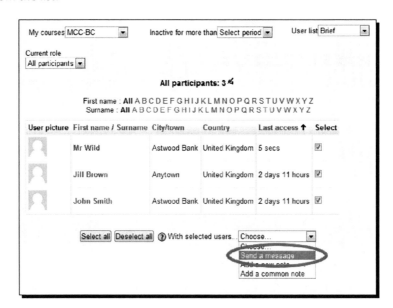

4. Type your message into the message box:

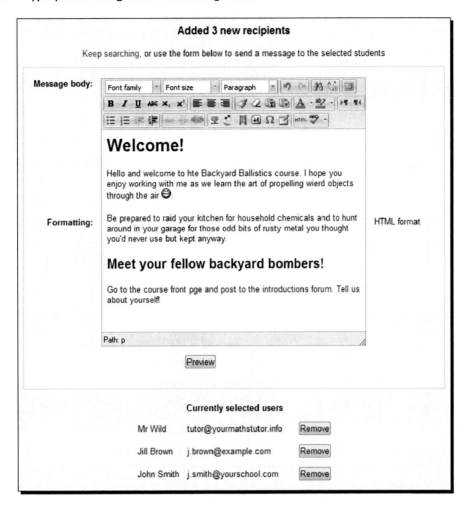

5. Take a look at the currently selected users list at the bottom of the page. You can remove users you accidentally selected on the previous screen by pressing the **Remove** button next to their name. Note that I'm purposefully sending the message to myself. If one of my students claims they haven't received it and I have, then I know it's not a problem with Moodle.

6. When you are happy with your message, press the **Preview** button.

7. If you want to make changes, press the **Update** button. If you are happy then press **Send**.

8. That's it. We're done!

What just happened?

We've just sent out a message to all of our students welcoming them to our courses. Sending a message to students is easy, you simply choose the students you want to message from the list of course participants.

Are you getting the message

How do I know when I have a message? If someone sends me a message then a pop-up messages dialog appears either when I first log on or, if I'm already logged on, whenever a new message is received:

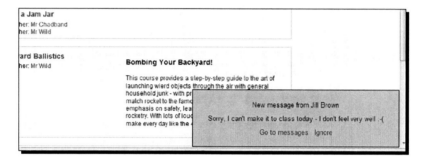

If you can, ask a colleague or one of your students to message you before reading on.

Been sent a message but don't see the message dialog?
Then the chances are that pop ups are blocked. Speak to your IT help desk or technician for help.

I've just received a message from Jill Brown. If I click on the **Go to messages** link I can see I have an incoming contact in the **Messages** screen. I am going to click on Jill's name in the **Incoming contacts** list:

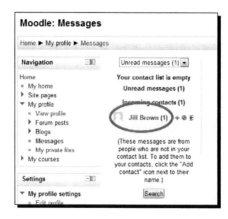

On the next screen there is a box for me to message Jill back with a response:

If you receive a message when you are logged off then you may also receive an e-mail as well. The default setting is for Moodle to send you an e-mail if you're offline for more than 10 minutes. You can alter this behavior by clicking on **Messaging** in the **Settings** block. The next time you receive a message, or use the messaging, take a look at the settings to get a feel for how messaging can be configured. You'll see that you can also:

- Enter an e-mail address specifically for Moodle messages.

- Use a Jabber chat client to receive messages, for example, on your cell phone you'll need a Jabber (nowadays renamed to XMPP) server installed and your Moodle configured to talk to it, so you'll probably also need to speak to your Moodle admin. Ask them to take a look at Prosody IM (see `http://prosody.im` for details) as this is the most compact and easiest to install.

- Block messages from users not on your contact list and many other settings besides these.

One way of making messaging between participants easier is to add the **Messages** block to your course front page. Let's take a look at how that's done:

Time for action – adding and using the Messages block

1. Remember to make sure that editing is turned on. Click **Add...** in the **Blocks** block. Select **Messages** from the list. The **Messages** block is now added to your course front page:

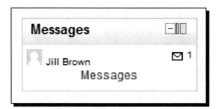

2. I've got a message from Jill Brown. Clicking on the envelope displays the message dialog, where I can view her message and respond to it if I want to (clicking on her name only displays Jill's profile).

3. If I want to send a message then click on **Messages...** The messages screen is displayed listing my incoming messages. Click on the name of the sender to view the message:

What just happened?

We've just added the **Messages** block to the course front page to make messaging between participants much easier. Students may not want to post to a forum or join in a chat room, but now we are converting our courses to Moodle, we want communication between learners to be as straightforward as possible.

Managing your contacts

In this last section we look at how you can manage your contacts, especially if you've configured your messaging to block messages from users not on your contact list. If you've added the **Messages** block to your course front page then click on **Messages...** now.

Time for action – adding a contact

1. In the **Navigation** block, click on the **Messages** link under **My profile**:

2. You can either search for a user or you can list the participants in the courses you are enrolled in. I'm going to type in the name of the person I want to add to my contacts list using the **Search people and messages** option:

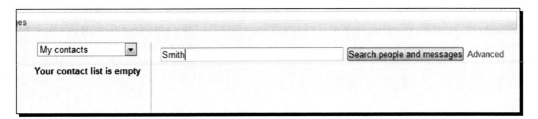

For further search options click on the **Advanced** link.

3. Press the **Search people and messages** button. If a user is found they will be listed. To add that user to your list of contacts click on the **Add contact** icon:

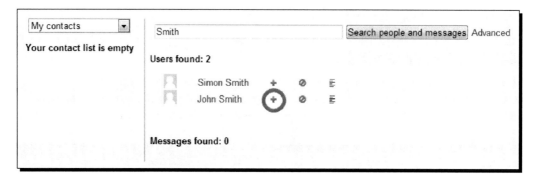

4. You've now got a new contact added to your contacts list:

What just happened?

Adding a contact is straightforward, simply search for a user and click on the **Add contact** icon. You can also block contacts by clicking on the **Block contact** icon:

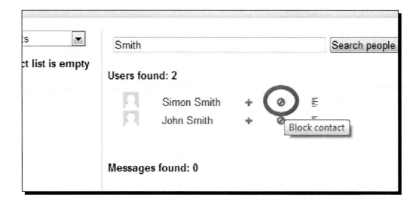

Summary

We learned a lot in this chapter about communicating online. If we are going to convert our courses to Moodle then communication and communicating well is more vital than ever. You wont be able to use the kinds of gestures, expressions, and verbal clues that you would normally use to talk to people in the real world. We saw how you could use forums and chat rooms as teaching tools, and Moodle messages as a course administration tool.

Specifically, we covered:

- How to add a chat room to a Moodle course using Moodle's very own built-in instant messaging system (such as MSN). A Moodle chat room allows students to talk in real time when they (or we) are out of the classroom. We explored the pros and the cons of using this activity.

- You can announce when you are going to be available for a chat, and we learned how to add a mini-calendar onto our course front pages to make it easy for students to see what course-related events are about to happen.

- How debates and discussions could be had online using a forum. We saw that there were four different kinds of forum and how each could be used to support different kinds of discussion.

- How to convert the staff and student pigeonholes over to Moodle using Moodle messaging, and how to send out a welcome message to our students.

We also discussed how to make yourself more easily understood, looking specifically at how you can use emoticons to show how you mean what you type.

Now that we've learned about communication we're ready to look closely at enhancing our teaching using other Moodle activities, such as quizzes and wikis. We'll cover these and more in the next chapter.

8
Enhancing your Teaching

At this stage, I'm sure you're itching to experiment with some of the more advanced Moodle activities, and in this chapter that's just what we're going to do.

In this chapter, we shall:

- Learn how to create a Moodle quiz. Convert your tests to Moodle and have them returned to you already marked!
- Convert role-play and scenarios into a Moodle lesson.
- Encourage peer review and help develop skills in providing constructive criticism using the workshop activity.
- Have students collaborate on project work online using a Moodle wiki.
- Create an online multimedia dictionary using a Moodle glossary.
- Convert quick-fire quizzes and straw polls to Moodle using the choice activity.

Do you want to prevent your students from accessing an activity or resource until they've completed some prior task? For example, I need all of my students to agree to a health and safety disclaimer (to keep my insurance company happy) before they can start the course proper. We can achieve this using Moodle's "conditional activities" feature and in this chapter we'll learn how.

We've got some exciting and interesting work to do in this chapter. We'll come across lots of configurations settings we can play with—remember: if you aren't sure what a setting does then click on the yellow circle with the question mark in it next to that setting. If you are feeling doubtful about pressing a button or choosing an option, remember: you can't break anything. Go ahead and see what happens!

Let's get straight on with learning all about Moodle quizzes...

Quiz

When I'm teaching my Backyard Ballistics course, I often bombard students with questions as I am going along—to gauge understanding, to re-enforce topics specific to particular learning goals, or simply as entertainment. Then I set a final test, to ensure that what I have been teaching has sunk in.

So why should I convert my quick-fire quizzes and final tests to Moodle? Because by doing so I can address two problems:

- Managing my questions:

  I keep a bank of questions I've thought of in Word documents, one for each subject I teach. I also have other documents containing questions my students have written themselves for my class competitions: I often split the class into two teams and get each team to quiz the other—and often student's questions are much more challenging and incisive than mine!

- Marking tests: marking quizzes and tests takes up a lot of my valuable time.

Converting quizzes to Moodle is a two-step process. The first task is to upload my questions to Moodle. Then, once questions are in the question bank, you need to add questions from the question bank to your quiz.

Using Moodle's built-in question editors

Why does including a quiz take two steps? There are many advantages to having the questions kept in a separate question bank:

- Reusing questions is easy. Choosing questions from a question bank means I can repeat a question throughout my course if there are questions I want to ask in order to reinforce a particular point.

- Having a bank of questions makes it far easier to share questions with my colleagues.

Let's start by adding a simple question to the course question Bank. The very simplest is a True/False question...

Time for action – adding a question to the question bank

1. On the course front page, click on **Question bank** in the **Settings** block. Your course Question bank is displayed.

2. Click on the **Create a new question** button and on the Choose a question type to add dialog select **True/False** and press **Next**.

3. Give the question a name.

Be careful naming your question...

This question is going into a question bank. Don't call it '1', or 'a' because we aren't adding this question to a quiz just yet, and we don't know where in the quiz it will be. We need to give the question a name that's meaningful to us—and to our colleagues if we choose to share our questions later on.

4. In the **Question** textbox, you need to write the question you are going to ask. See that we are using the HTML editor to edit the question. That means that we can include all of the ideas and techniques that we've learned so far to make the text of a question just that little bit more interesting:

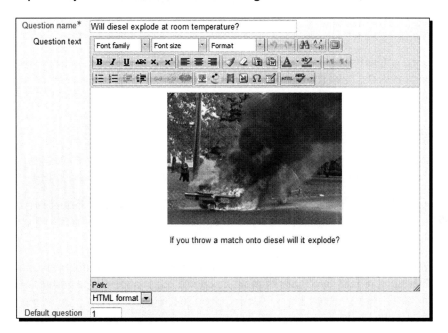

5. Scroll down to the **Correct answer** setting and specify whether the correct answer to your question is true or false.

That is enough to configure a True/False question. We could ignore the rest of the settings on this page, scroll down to the bottom and press the **Save changes** button. But I probably won't be there when my students are answering this question so I want to give them encouragement and guidance, depending on how well they did answering the question. Let's add in some feedback.

6. Scroll back to the **General feedback** box. If there is a learning goal or a particular point you need to stress regardless of whether the student got the answer right or wrong, then state it in here:

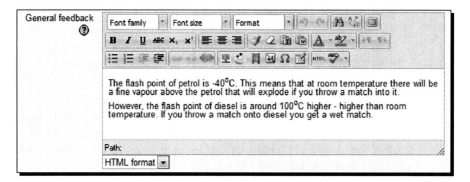

7. You can also specify feedback for a correct or an incorrect answer.

8. Once you're happy with your feedback, scroll down to the bottom of the page and press the **Save changes** button. Your new question will now be listed in the question bank.

What just happened?

We've just seen how easy it is to add questions to the question bank. However, you can imagine that adding lots of questions to your question bank could take some time.

Let's have a look now at the other types of questions you can add to your question bank. A True/False question is the possibly the most straightforward (in terms of settings) you can ask a student. You also have available:

- **Multiple Choice**: Students select their answer from one of a number of options. There are, in fact, two types of multiple choice questions—single answer and multiple answer (see `http://docs.moodle.org/en/question/type/multichoice`).

- **Short Answer**: Students respond with a word or phrase. You will need to specify the correct answers using wildcards, so that Moodle can pick the correct answers out of the responses students have typed. Take a look at Moodle docs for more information (`http://docs.moodle.org/en/question/type/shortanswer`).

- **Numerical**: If you are asking a question that expects a number as a response (even including units) then choose this question type. You can also specify an acceptable error in that number. There's more information at `http://docs.moodle.org/en/question/type/numerical`.

- **Description**: Not actually a question but a way of breaking up questions—perhaps providing some text/graphics or maybe a video presentation before a student attempts a set of questions.

- **Calculated** (including Calculated Multichoice and Calculated Simple): Calculated questions use wildcards that Moodle replaces with "random" numbers (although you will need to specify the numbers that Moodle chooses from). More details can be found at `http://docs.moodle.org/en/question/type/calculated`.

- **Essay**: The student's answer is in essay format. If you are setting your students an assignment, then (obviously) use the assignment activity—see *Chapter 5, Managing student work*. Note that answers to these questions will need to be manually graded. For more information on assignments, see `http://docs.moodle.org/en/question/type/essay`.

- **Matching**: The student is presented with questions, each of which has a drop-down list of possible answers. The student must match the correct answers to each question. For more details see `http://docs.moodle.org/20/en/Matching_question_type`.

- **Random Short-Answer Matching**: You choose how many "sub-questions" are chosen (randomly) from the short answer questions that are available. See `http://docs.moodle.org/en/question/type/randomsamatch` for details.

- **Embedded Answers (Cloze)**: This is a fill-the-gaps exercise, but greatly enhanced by virtue of being "computerized". Moodle presents the user with a passage of text that has questions embedded in it. The learner completes the text with their answers (see `http://docs.moodle.org/en/question/type/multianswer` for details).

Since this is a beginner's guide, I haven't included all the configurations. However, more details are given in Moodle docs (check out the links previously provided and at `http://docs.moodle.org/20/en/ Question_types`). A YouTube search also yields lots of instructional videos demonstrating how to configure Moodle questions. It is far better to experiment with the question types you think might be useful.

If you have a lot of questions you need to convert to Moodle, then there are ways to help along the conversion:

- **Import questions**: these could be questions that someone else has created for you, or questions that you have created using other tools that you are more used to.

- **Sharing questions**: again using questions written by someone else, but shared from other parts of your Moodle site.

Let's spend the rest of this sub-section looking at these alternatives.

Importing questions

Entering one question at a time into the question bank can be a slow process. Luckily, we can import questions from other sources.

How do we know which types of files can be imported? The answer is to click on the **Import** link under **Question bank** in the **Settings** block.

On the Import page, you can immediately see a variety of sources of questions you can convert to Moodle:

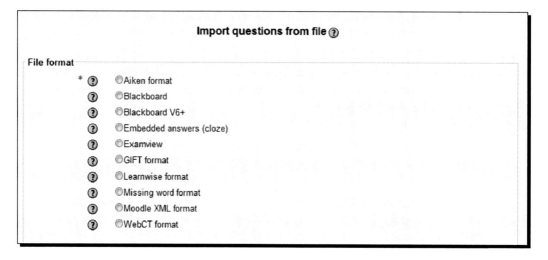

You can see from the list that if you want to convert questions from another learning management system (for example, Blackboard or WebCT) you can do so using the Import function. See `http://docs.moodle.org/en/question/import` in the Moodle docs for more details.

Managing questions

Now, we've started to convert our questions to Moodle then we need to mention briefly how to manage them. Moodle allows you to categorize questions. What is the benefit of this? There are questions that my science colleagues are writing on chemical reactions and energy transformations that I would love to use on my course. The mathematics department have a collection of questions on trajectories that I don't want to reinvent. Likewise, the mathematics and science departments want to use my questions in their courses. Now, we are all converting to Moodle, we can all share our questions very easily, and that's the benefit of categorizing questions. Let's see how easy this is:

Time for action – categorizing questions

First task is to create a new category:

1. Return to your course Settings block and under **Question bank** click on the **Categories** link.

2. Let's create a new category for questions related to burning fossil fuels—I know the science department is interested in those. Give your new category a name.

3. Select the **Parent** category (you might not need to worry about this just yet). For example, energy questions might be categorized under Physics, which in turn is under Science.

4. Although you don't have to, give your category a meaningful description. It will make your new category friendlier to your colleagues if you decide to share it with them.

5. When you are happy with the settings of your new category, press the **Add category** button. The **Edit categories** page will be updated to show your new category, and how it fits into the hierarchy of other categories. For example, the parent of my new category is my course, basically:

Edit categories ⑦

Question categories for 'Course: Backyard Ballistics Backup'

- Default for CF101 (0) The default category for questions shared in context 'CF101'. ✗ ✎

  - Backyard Ballistics - fossil fuels-related questions (2) A set of questions on the subject of burning fossil fuels. ✗ ✎ ←

---

6. The numbers in brackets indicate how many questions are in that category.

7. Click on the **Questions** link under **Question bank** in the course **Settings** block to return to the question bank. To move a question into a category, you first need to select the category containing the question from the **Category** drop-down list.

8. Click on the tick box next to the question you want to move to select it.

9. With the selected question, we want to move to the new category. Select the category you want to move the question to from the **Move to** drop-down list:

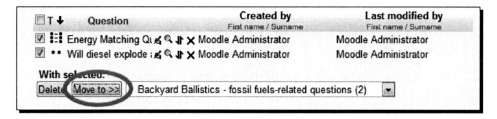

10. Press the **Move to >>** button to move the selected question (or questions) to the chosen category.

What just happened?

We've just seen how to manage questions in your question bank. You can organize your question bank using categories. But how do you share categories with other courses?

By default, teachers can only see questions from the question bank in their course. They can't see the question banks from other courses, and they can't share questions between courses, either. If that's what you want to do then you first need to speak to your admin and ask them for question categories shared outside a course. For more information see the *Ask the admin* section at the end of this chapter.

Here is where the Backyard Ballistics course is, in relation to the structure of courses and course categories on my Moodle site:

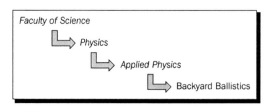

Here are the categories available to me before my admin makes the change:

> **Question Categories for 'Course: Backyard Ballistics'**
>
> • Default for CF101 (0) The default category for questions shared in context 'CF101'. ✗ ✎
>   ○ Backyard Ballistics - fossil fuels-related questions (2) A set of questions on the subject of burning fossil fuels. ✗ ✎ ←

And here's what it looks like after:

Question Categories for 'Course: Backyard Ballistics'

- Default for CF101 (0) The default category for questions shared in context 'CF101'. ✗ ✎
  - ○ Backyard Ballistics - fossil fuels-related questions (2) A set of questions on the subject of burning fossil fuels. ✗ ✎ ←

Question Categories for 'Category: Applied Physics'

- Default for Applied Physics (0) The default category for questions shared in context 'Applied Physics'. ✎

Question Categories for 'Category: Physics'

- Default for Physics (0) The default category for questions shared in context 'Physics'. ✎

Question Categories for 'Category: Faculty of Science'

- Default for Faculty of Science (0) The default category for questions shared in context 'Faculty of Science'. ✎

You can see that I can now get access to questions from the entire faculty of science.

Now, we've added questions to the question bank we can now include a Moodle quiz in our course and start setting students online tests.

Setting a test

Once you've got a question or two in your question bank, or perhaps you can get access to questions written by one of your colleagues, then setting a test is easy. Here's how:

Time for action – adding a quiz to the course

1. Choose the topic you want to add a new quiz to. Making sure editing is turned on, click on **Add an activity...** and select **Quiz** from the list.

2. Give your quiz a name and, if you want to, you can write a brief introduction.

3. If you want a timed quiz, then check the Time limit setting in the **General** box. If you are interested in setting a timed quiz but you are unsure about any setting then remember that you can click on the yellow circle with a question mark in it if you need extra help.

4. Press the **Editing quiz** button.

5. There are a lot of settings we could investigate. To get us started, scroll down to the bottom of the page and press the **Save and display** button.

6. You are now presented with, essentially, a split screen view with the (empty) quiz on the left-hand side and a link to the course question bank in the top right.

7. Click on the [**Show**] link next to **Question bank contents**. The question bank is displayed:

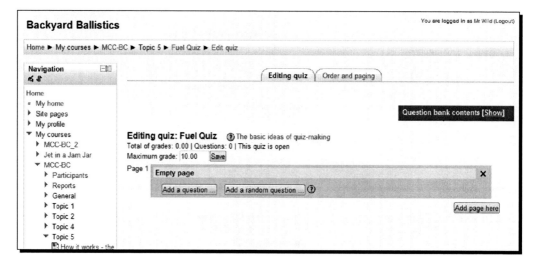

8. Select the category containing the questions you want to add from the **Select a category** drop-down list.

9. Select the questions you want to add to your quiz by ticking them, then click on the **Add to quiz** button:

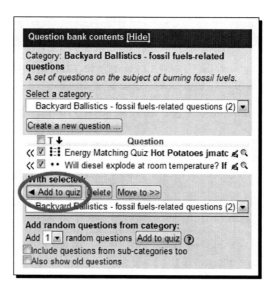

10. You will see the question now included in the quiz, listed on the left-hand side of the page:

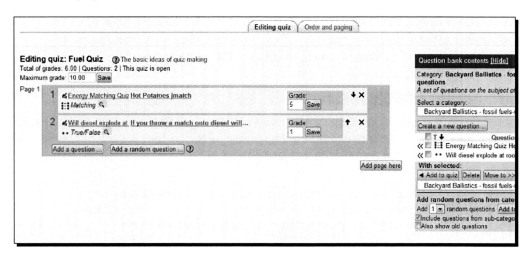

11. Once you've added questions to your quiz, you can preview it using the **Preview** link, under **Quiz administration** in the **Settings** block.

12. That's it, we're done!

What just happened?

We've just seen how easy it is to add a quiz to our course and to include questions in it from the course question bank. If your admin has allowed you access to your colleague's questions, then you can easily add their questions to your quiz, too.

If you want to view the results of a quiz, then click the **Results** link in your **Navigation** block. You'll see all of the attempts listed there.

Lesson activity

Teachers often assume this activity is some kind of lesson planning tool. A Moodle lesson is actually a tool for creating action mazes: the ideal device for exploring scenarios and decision trees, posing quandaries, and for interactive case studies.

Think of a lesson rather like a text-based adventure game, or the Choose Your Own Adventure books popular in the 1980s and 90s, where you find yourself in a certain situation and you need to decide what to do next: You are in a dark dungeon. Do you go through the door on the left? Do you pick up the bloodied axe? Do you take the bag of gold coins from the sleeping troll?

You'll often find these kinds of scenarios in health and safety training. Imagine you are shown a video of someone working in a storeroom and her colleague knocks a box on her head, knocking her out cold. Then, you are asked: who is responsible for this accident—the employee or employer? Your choice then leads you on to, perhaps, another video and another set of decisions or questions. As a user, I can take one of many paths, or "branches"/"answers" in Moodle-speak, as I explore the scenario.

Structuring Moodle lessons

Moodle lessons are basically made up of a series of web pages. At the bottom of each page, you can have either buttons or a question. Depending on the button pressed, or how you answer the question, you are taken to another web page.

 We've been learning how we can use graphics and multimedia to make content engaging and entertaining for students. There is nothing stopping us using these skills in the pages of a Moodle lesson.

Why include a lesson

There are many ways that lessons have been used successfully in the classroom. Here are just a few examples that I've come across of classroom activities that have successfully been converted to Moodle lessons:

- "Guess Who?" games. Ask your students to choose one from a number of characters from a story. The computer poses a series of questions to determine who that character must be.

- Exploring scenarios. As we have already described, lessons are the ideal way to explore specific scenarios: legal, scientific, health and safety, and more.

- Role-play. You are Charles I and the period of personal rule has begun. Gentlemen are writing pamphlets speaking out against your choice for Archbishop of Canterbury. Do you a) Give in to their demands and change the Archbishop? b) Get really annoyed and cut their ears off? c) Ignore them because you're in charge so it doesn't matter? (in fact, Charles cut their ears off).

- Medical diagnosis. Given a set of symptoms, can you diagnose an illness correctly? As a practitioner, can you ask the right questions?

- Virtual tours. Together with your students, create a virtual tour of a battlefield or a medieval village. Working together with the class to create Moodle lessons shares the effort required to put them together.

Supporting classroom-based teaching with lessons

Unless you get the class to help you (see the virtual tour example given previously), a meaningful lesson activity can take a while to set up. If you've spent your evening constructing a detailed scenario, it can be a little disheartening when you see your charges rattle through it in a couple of minutes.

However, think about using a lesson to explore ideas with a class as a group activity. If you've a projector or an interactive white board in your class, work through the lesson together with your students. It is one of the easier ways to ensure that no learning goal is missed.

Including a lesson in your course

Don't think of lessons as purely a teaching tool. I'm sure you've got lots of great ideas for lesson activities. For me, I need my students to work their way through a series of health and safety notices and agree to certain "Terms and Conditions" before they are allowed to join me on my course. For the rest of this section, I'm going to convert this paperwork over to Moodle.

Configuring a lesson

I'm going to start by adding a lesson to the course front page and configuring the basic settings:

Time for action – configuring a lesson

1. Return to your course front page, choose a topic you want to add the lesson to, click on **Add an activity...** and select **Lesson** from the list.

2. Give your new lesson a name.

3. Scrolling down, you can see there are lots of options to choose from. I'm not going to worry about these now, and instead I'm going to scroll down and press the **Save and return to course** button.

4. That's it. We're done!

What just happened?

We've just configured a new lesson (which was pretty easy because the default options are more than enough to get us started). But now I have an empty lesson that I need to fill.

Adding a content page – A web page with buttons at the bottom

The first part of my health and safety notice is a set of three pages outlining the behavior I expect from my students. Let's begin at the beginning by converting the very first page.

Time for action – adding a content table

1. From the course front page, click on the name of your new lesson (don't click on the Update icon as this takes you back to the lesson configuration page). Moodle now asks me what I want to do first. The five choices are:

   - **Import questions**: This is importing questions into a lesson, not into the course question bank. The two are separate.

   - **Import PowerPoint**: At this stage, teachers get excited. However, importing PowerPoint presentations is a convoluted process: convert your presentation to a set of web pages, compress them into a ZIP file, upload them to Moodle, and a lesson is created for you. Then, you find that all of your impressive transitions and effects are missing. Great for converting a simple set of slides into a Moodle lesson, but not that advanced.

   - **Add a content page**: Another ill-named option. Rather it is add a web page with buttons at the bottom giving you the choice of which page you go to next.

   - **Add a cluster**: Moodle will randomly choose from a cluster of pages—a great way to ensure that your lesson is interesting and different every time your students explore it.

   - **Add a question page**: This does what it says. You add a web page and configure a question at the bottom.

   My health and safety notice is currently a Word document. It starts with an introduction page where I set the tone. Let's now convert that over to Moodle:

2. Click on **Add a content page**.

3. Give your new page a title and write in your page contents. I'm going to copy and paste from my original Word document. I've pasted via the **Paste from Word** button. Remember that you can easily include graphics and multimedia in the page.

4. This is the type of page with buttons at the bottom, and I now need to specify the buttons. Scroll down the page until you reach the list of **Content** boxes (under the **Add a content page** box). Here, we specify what buttons I want at the bottom of the page. And here we have another slightly misleading configuration option: If you specify a **Description** in the **Content 1** box, this in fact becomes the text on the first button at the bottom of the page. So:

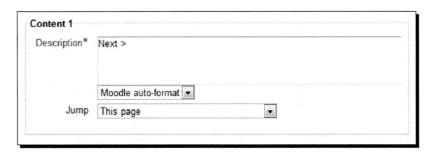

becomes:

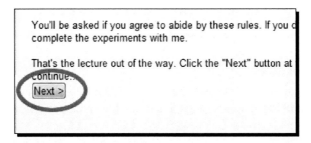

5. Don't worry about specifying which page the button jumps to (the "Jump" setting). It is better to add in all of your pages first and then join them together afterwards.

6. When you have specified all the buttons you need, press the **Add a content page** button at the bottom of the page.

7. Your new content page (that is, web page with buttons at the bottom) is now added to your lesson.

What just happened?

I've just added a content page—what Moodle calls a web page with buttons at the bottom. I converted the first page of a health and safety notice over to Moodle. To add another page, simply click on the **Add a page...** drop-down menu and select **Add a content page** from the list. Having converted the other two, this is what my lesson looks like, in outline:

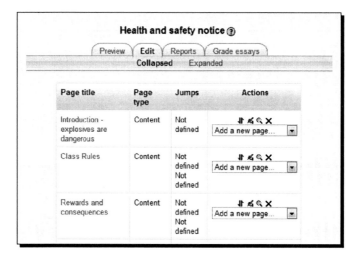

Adding a question page

The last page of my paperwork is where the students have to agree to the rules. For this final page, I am going to add in a question page. It's much the same process, so let's do that now.

Time for action – inserting a question page

1. Click on **Add a page...** and this time select **Question** at the bottom of the list.

2. Choose the type of question you want to add by selecting from the drop-down list. I want to add a **True/false** question so:

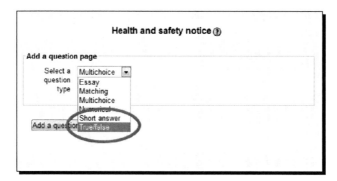

3. Regardless of question type, we need to give our page a title and provide some content.

4. That done, we need to configure the question that appears at the bottom of the page. For my **True/False** question, that entails providing two sets of answers and responses. Note that I've given the "I agree" response a score of 1. You can probably guess that this will be important later on:

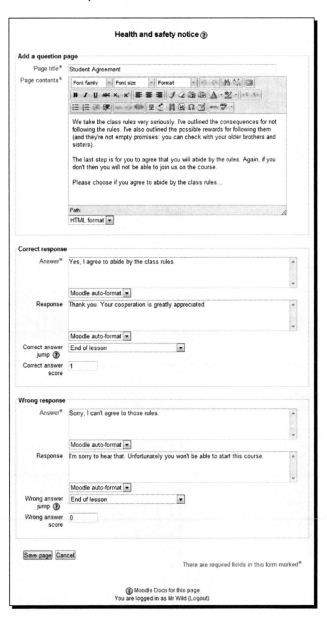

5. And that's it. You can see that you can jump to different pages depending on how the question was answered but, again, I'm not going to worry about that just yet. So we're done for now. Press the **Save page** button at the bottom of the page.

What just happened?

I've just added a simple question page to my lesson, a True/False question I'm asking my students to confirm that they agree to abide by the class rules.

So far, I've ignored linking the pages together. Let's learn how to do that now.

Putting it all together – Linking lesson pages

Let's return to the lesson editing page:

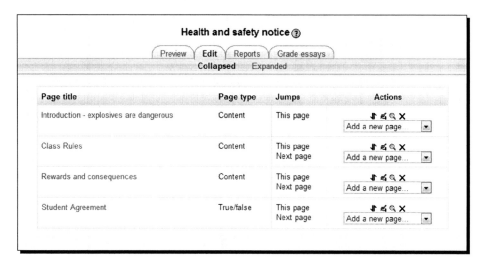

You can see in the table the types of page included in my lesson (the **Page Type** column) and the pages that they link to (**Jumps** column). Here's how I want my lesson to be arranged:

A basic, linear arrangement where you can move in either direction through the lesson pages. Pressing **Next** on the Class Rules page takes you to Rewards and Consequences. But clicking **Previous** takes you back to the Introduction. It's only when you reach the Student Agreement I want you to finally commit yourself (or otherwise) to my course. Let's now make these buttons jump.

Time for action – configuring page jumps

1. Return to the lesson **Edit** tab. Click on the first page's update icon:

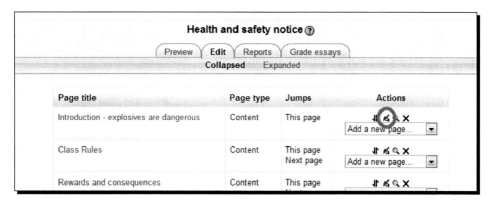

2. Scroll down the page to the **Content** boxes. I need to configure the **Next>** button to jump to the **Class Rules** page. I click on the **Jump** drop-down menu and select **Class Rules** from the list:

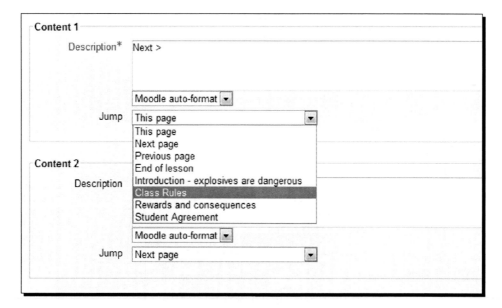

3. Scroll down to the bottom of the page and press the **Save page** button.

4. The lesson has been updated successfully:

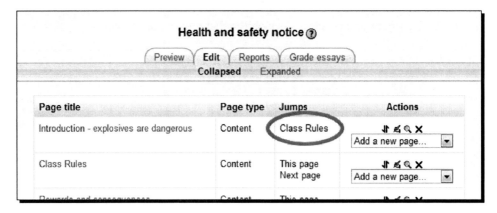

5. I need to repeat that process for the **Class Rules** page and the **Rewards and Consequences** page.

6. I don't need the final **Student Agreement** page to go anywhere. Select the **End of lesson** option from the list of **Jump** pages:

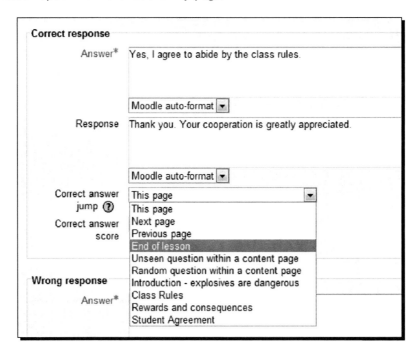

7. That's it. All my page jumps are now fully configured:

Health and safety notice ⑦

| Preview | **Edit** | Reports | Grade essays |

Collapsed   Expanded

Page title	Page type	Jumps	Actions
Introduction - explosives are dangerous	Content	Class Rules	⬇ ✎ 🔍 ✕ Add a new page... ▾
Class Rules	Content	Introduction - explosives are dangerous Rewards and consequences	⬇ ✎ 🔍 ✕ Add a new page... ▾
Rewards and consequences	Content	Class Rules Student Agreement	⬇ ✎ 🔍 ✕ Add a new page... ▾
Student Agreement	True/false	End of lesson End of lesson	⬇ ✎ 🔍 ✕ Add a new page... ▾

What just happened?

I've just configured all the page jumps that allow students to navigate through my newly converted student agreement. And that's it: I've finished converting my health and safety agreement over to Moodle and am ready to allow students to work their way through it and agree to abide by the rules (I hope).

 If you want to test whether your lesson is configured correctly, click on the **Preview** tab at the top of the lesson configuration page.

But how do I know whether the students have worked through this document, and have made the final agreement? Let's take a look at this next.

Monitoring student progress through a lesson

Converting my paperwork over to Moodle means I can check very easily whether students have agreed to the rules I've laid down. From the course front page, click on the link to your lesson. Click on the **Reports** tab.

You will see a breakdown of attempts made on the lesson. Immediately, I can see whether a student agreed to abide by my course rules (they score 100% in the lesson):

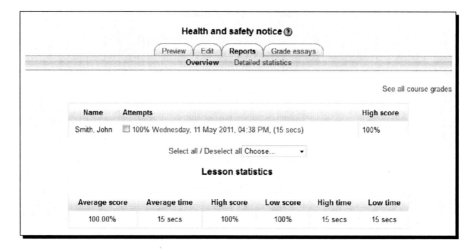

Planning your Moodle lessons carefully

A final word on lessons: I'm sure you can see that a good Moodle lesson is always one that was developed from a good plan. Always start by sketching out your lesson first, and don't try and develop a lesson organically. I've seen many try, only to fail and then conclude that Moodle lessons are too complicated to use when converting to teaching online. Plan well, try not to over-complicate, and ensure you keep the course learning goals in mind.

Workshop – Peer review and assessment

The workshop activity isn't new to Moodle—in versions prior to Moodle 2.x it was disabled by default. That said, if you are familiar with previous incarnations of the Moodle workshop then you'll notice quite a few enhancements to the look-and-feel. Let's spend this section taking a brief look.

What is a workshop? A Moodle workshop is a peer review activity. For example, I could have students submit their project work for peer review through Moodle and use Moodle to record all of the comments and suggestions class members make about each other's work. I could, if I wish, upload an exemplar and have the class comment on just that instead. I can upload examiner's comments on a project and students can then compare their review with those comments. As you can gather, it's a very powerful tool.

As we will see shortly, the Moodle workshop activity supports three types of review:

- ◆ **Reviewing uploaded exemplars**: Students can review the exemplar and compare their review with a reference review (for example, examiner's comments)

- **Peer review**: Students review each other's work. Note that students can be graded on the quality of their review as well as receiving a grade for the work they handed in

- **Self- assessment**: A user can review their own work and receive a grade for the quality of that review

 Note that these types of review aren't mutually exclusive. You can enable combinations (or all) of these options.

I am a big fan of students commenting on each other's work. It isn't part of the syllabus just yet, but peer review is becoming an important part of my teaching, generally—which, up to now, I've been supporting with forums.

Time for action – adding a workshop

1. Ensure you have editing turned on and, in the relevant section of your course, click on the **Add an activity...** drop-down menu and select **Workshop** from the list.

2. Give the activity a name and, if required, provide an introduction:

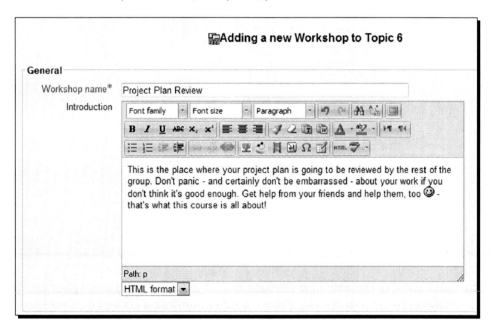

3. In the **Workshop settings** box, you can enable the relevant peer review features. I want my students to peer review each other's work so I'm only going to check the **Students may assess the work of others** option:

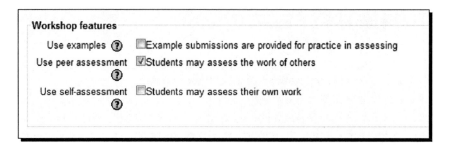

4. I now need to configure the submission and assessment options. This is where I specify the instructions I give both when students are uploading work for review and for then they are doing the reviewing:

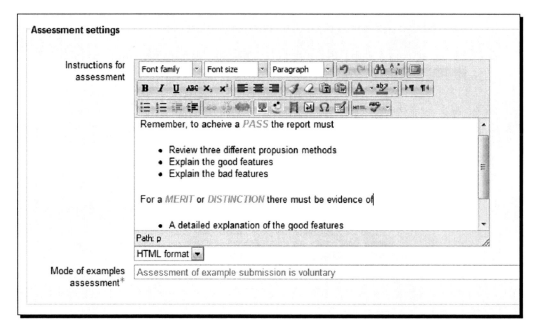

5. Scroll down to the bottom of the page and press the **Save and display** button. The **Project Plan Review** (for that's what I called it) workshop planner is displayed:

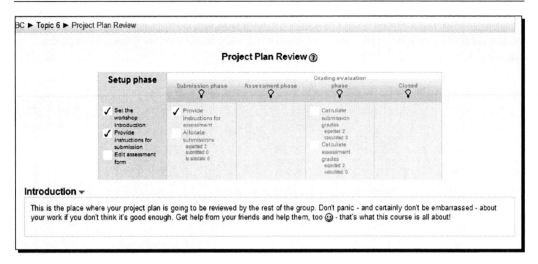

What just happened?

We've just configured a Moodle workshop for peer review. There were quite a few settings I ignored but they are all self-explanatory, for example the Grade settings—where you can specify the split between marks awarded for the quality of their review and the marks awarded for the work they uploaded—and the Access control options—where we configure time windows within which work can be uploaded, reviews must take place, and so on.

Now that the workshop planner is on-screen you can see what tasks I have already completed and what needs to be done. For example, I still haven't completed the Setup phase yet as I need to edit the assessment form:

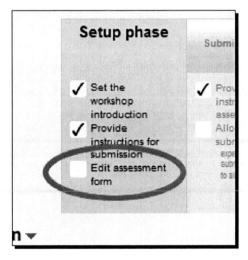

The words **Edit assessment form** are a link. Click on that link now. I can now create a form which students complete when they are reviewing each other's work. Once created, this page can be previewed:

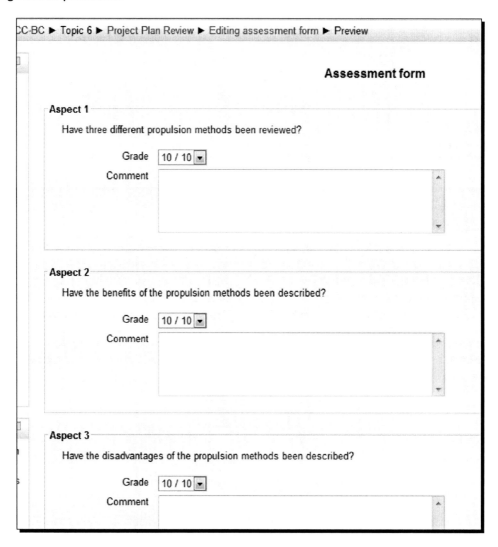

When you return to the workshop planner page, you'll find that the **Edit submission form** task is now checked:

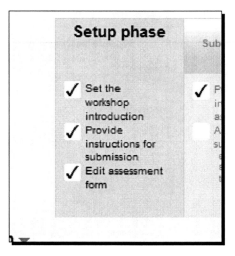

Meaning the Setup phase is now complete.

Now we're ready to move into the Submissions phase. We need to click on the Switch phase icon at the top of the **Submission phase** column:

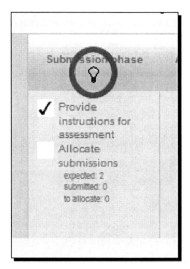

We are warned that we are about to move to the next phase—which is what we want to do so click on the **Continue** button. You are returned to the workshop planner page where the **Submission phase** column is now highlighted:

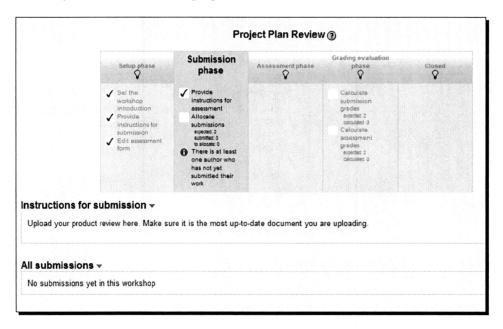

Not only does the workshop planner allow us to move through from one phase to another, the planner is also great for seeing, at a glance, which steps have and haven't been completed. For example, once students have started uploading work, I can allocate submissions. This is what a student will see when they upload their submission:

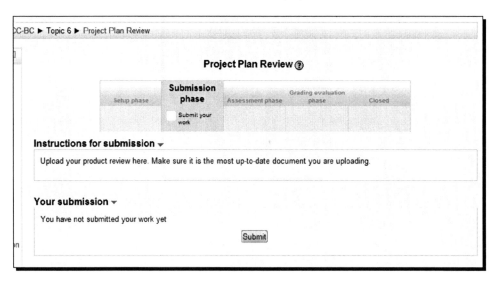

Once work has been uploaded, I can then distribute it for review. You'll need to click on the **Allocate submissions** link in the workshop planner:

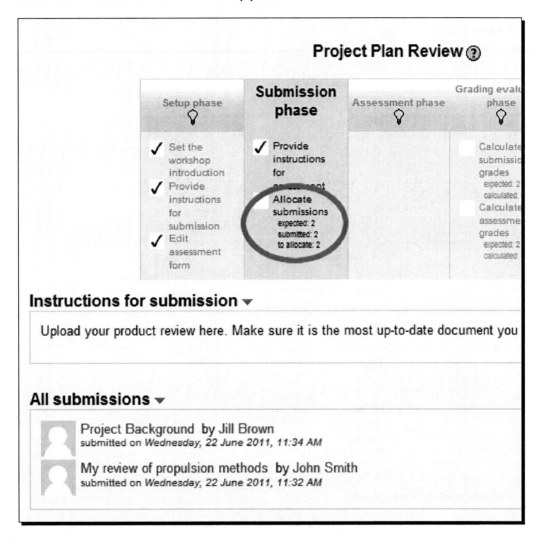

Allocation of work can either be manual or random. You just need to click on the relevant tab.

Once the Submission phase is complete (the work has been submitted and the reviewers allocated), we can move on to the Assessment phase. You'll need to return to the workshop planner and click on the Switch phase icon at the top of the Assessment phase column. The planner is updated:

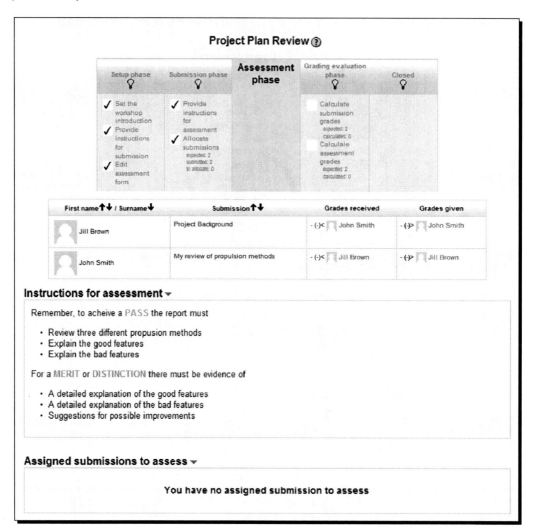

How does a student review a submission? They will need to click on the link to the **Workshop activity** and they will be presented with the Assessment page, including a list of submissions they need to assess:

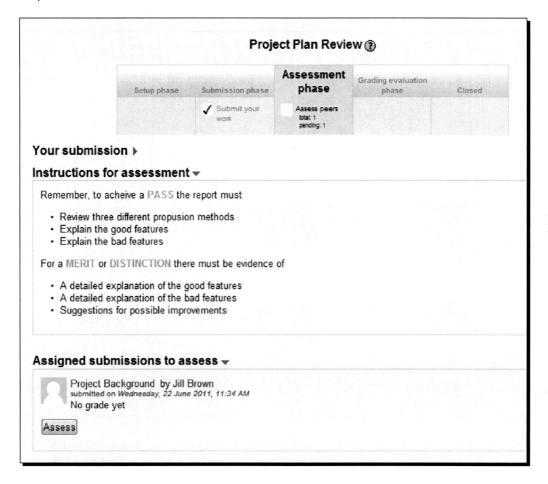

Pressing the **Assess** button allows them to perform the assessment using the criteria (the "Aspects") that we specified in the Setup phase.

Once the assessments have been made, we can move on to the Grading evaluation phase (remember you'll need to click on the Switch phase icon at the top of the **Grading evaluation phase** column in the workshop planner):

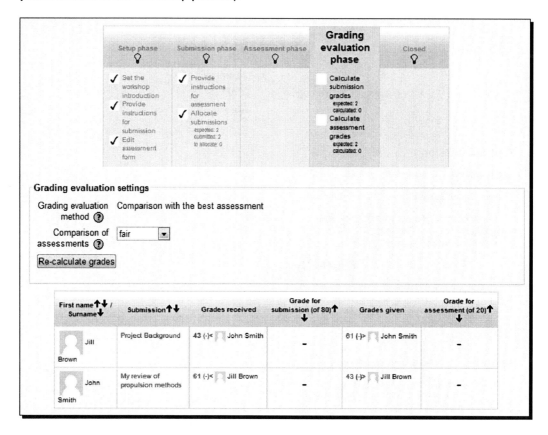

In the **Grades given** column, I can study the reviews each student has given (review the reviews, as it were) and, if I think they are comparable and fair, I can click on the **Re-calculate grades** button to complete the grading process:

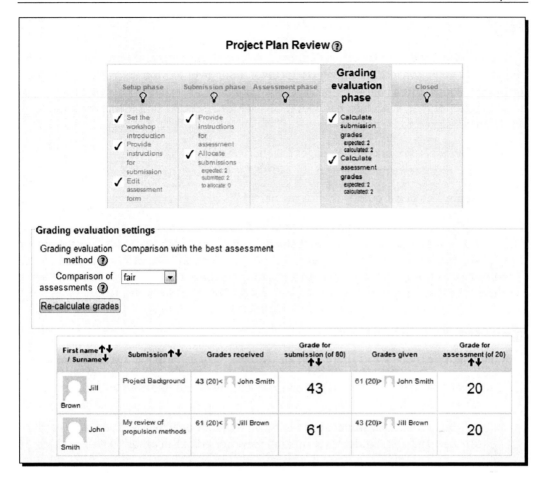

The final step—to indicate to all that the workshop is complete—is to click on the Switch phase icon just beneath the Closed column heading in the planner.

 You can switch from one phase to another at any time (including switching back to previous phases) by clicking on the relevant Switch phase icon in the workshop planner.

This section has given the briefest of overviews of a very powerful teaching tool. For more information on the Moodle workshop activity, please refer to the Moodle docs at `http://docs.moodle.org/20/en/Workshop_module`.

Wiki

I first showed you the Moodle wiki in *Chapter 3, Adding Documents and Handouts* when we saw that you could convert departmental documentation over to Moodle. Wiki is Hawaiian for "quick". People often hear the word wiki and think that a wiki has to be an online encyclopedia (for that, Wikipedia has a lot to answer for). But that simply isn't the case. Wikis were designed to:

◆ Allow users to work on web pages collaboratively

and

◆ Create web pages quickly (hence the name)

If you are going to collaborate with others on a web page then there must be some sort of audit trail, so you can tell who made what change and when. That's no problem: a system for doing so is already built into Moodle's wiki system. To allow you to create web pages quickly, Moodle's wiki system has it's own built-in formatting language for you to use. But don't let the thought of that put you off. As you'll see in this section, the formatting is very simple.

What are my wiki options

Even though there is one wiki system built into Moodle, you can use it in two different ways:

1. Collaborative wiki. You have just one wiki with all of you (teachers and students) working on it together.

2. Individual wiki. Each student has their own wiki that only they and you as a teacher can view and edit. Students can neither view nor edit each other's wikis.

What can you use a wiki for

Here are just a few examples of using wikis in a course:

◆ Collaborative project plans and project write-ups, using a Collaborative wiki.

◆ Student diaries, using an Individual wiki.

◆ Project write-ups, either using a Collaborative or Individual wiki.

◆ Lists of web links. Rather than having to maintain a text document (which would need uploading every time you made a change), have your list of web links kept in a wiki instead.

◆ Characters from a novel, a Group wiki developed by students in the class.

As far as managing a wiki is concerned, aside from making sure the content is suitable and students don't start making silly entries, the only issue we need to be aware of is the possibility of a tug of war ensuing between two students trying to edit a wiki page. It may happen that one student makes a change that the other doesn't like, and they repeatedly try to alter each other's work, back and forth. It sounds strange but it often happens.

On my course, when it comes to the final practical assignment, all of the students on my course have to complete their projects within two weeks and as they do so they need to fill out a student record. Handling that paperwork is awkward: unfortunately students often lose it, and if they don't manage to lose it then by the time they hand it in, the record sheets look like they have been savaged by wild dogs. I'm going to use a Student wiki to convert this component of my course over to Moodle. Let's spend the rest of this section learning how.

Adding a wiki

The first task is to add a wiki to our courses. Because I want each one of my pupils to have their own wiki (each has their own record card), I also know that this is going to be an Individual wiki:

Time for action – adding a wiki

1. Choose the topic you want to add your new wiki to, click on **Add an activity...** and select **Wiki** from the list.

2. The name of my new wiki is going to be "Student Diary". Enter a name for your wiki.

3. Write a brief summary of the wiki. This is shown above every page. Try to keep it short and descriptive.

4. I'm going to click on the **Type** option and select **Individual** from the list. Choose the type of wiki that best suits your needs.

5. Scroll to the bottom of the page and press the **Save and return to course** button. You'll see your new wiki listed on the course front page:

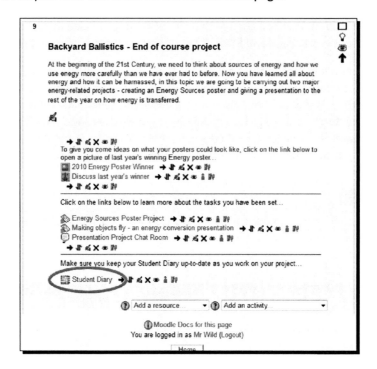

What just happened?

I now have a new wiki. If I click on the link to the wiki on the course front page, I am presented with an option to create a new empty page and give it a name:

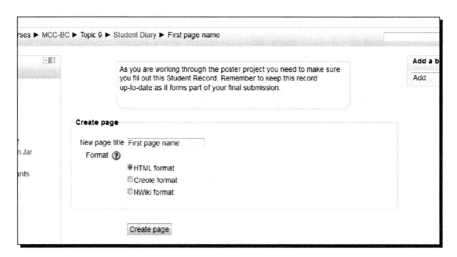

I'm going to call my new page "Student Diary Introduction" (rather than "First page name"), leave the **Format** as the default **HTML format**, and press the **Create page** button.

So how do you actually start editing a wiki?

Editing a wiki page

The page we have been presented with is basically the first page of the wiki. All pages will be linked from this "front page", as it were. Therefore, it is sometimes best to think of this initial page as a contents page, and perhaps even structure it as such. How do you edit it? Simply type in the text you want using the Editor in the usual way.

 Remember that because we are using the Moodle Editor to edit wiki pages, you can make wiki pages engaging and entertaining by using the skills and experience you have gained as you have been working through this book.

Creating a new page

Creating a new wiki page is easy—if you know how. Have you got a fragment of text that you want to turn into a link to a new page? Simply surround the word or text with double square brackets [[ ]], like so:

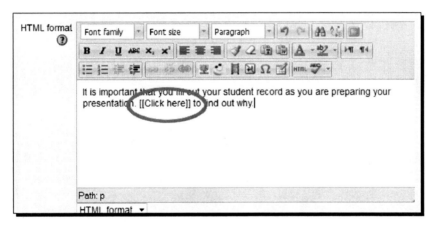

Then, click the **Save** button immediately below the editor:

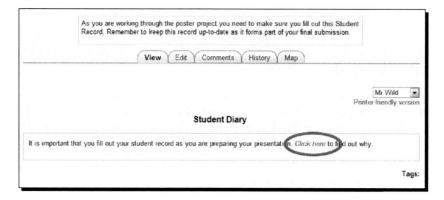

You can see that the phrase I surrounded in square brackets is now highlighted. That highlight is in fact a link (hover the mouse pointer over it to see what I mean). Click on that link now. You'll see that immediately a new page is about to be created. Press the **Create page** button and you are ready to start adding new content to it:

And that's how easy it is to create a new wiki page.

Viewing a page's history

If wiki pages are easy to change and we are brave enough to let our students start editing them, then we certainly want to know who has been changing them and when. Luckily that's no problem with the Moodle wiki system: simply click on the **History** tab at the top of the page to see a complete audit trail.

In the history page, you can:

◆ See at a glance who has been making changes to a page—and when they made them

◆ Compare different versions of a page (to see what has been changed)

◆ Revert back to a specific version

We've learned how easy it is to use a wiki, and that's great, but I still have to convert my student record sheets over to Moodle and to do that I need to specify a template that my students can fill in using a Moodle wiki. I've got the original document in Word format, so let's convert that to a Moodle wiki template now.

Have a go hero – there's more to a wiki than just teaching

See *Chapter 3, Adding Document and Handouts*, for another wiki idea. At the end of that chapter, we saw how you could convert your departmental documentation into a Moodle wiki. By doing so, not only is it far easier to make the document available to staff when it is online, being a wiki makes it easier to modify the document. And when you do modify the document each page has its own audit trail, so you can easily see who modified the document and when.

Glossary activity

I've got a glossary of ballistics-related terms that I currently give to students as part of their welcome pack. It's basically a sheet of paper I hand out to my students that I wrote in Microsoft Word years ago. Luckily, I can easily convert this over to Moodle. What's great about converting a glossary over to Moodle is that:

◆ A glossary entry can be much more than just text: you can use the skills and experience you have learned as you have worked through this book to include graphics and embed multimedia.

◆ Students can add entries to the glossary. By converting to Moodle, I can make creating and enhancing my glossary a class activity. Moodle further supports this by allowing me to grade glossary entries.

◆ Moodle can be configured so that wherever a word or phrase appears on my course that is included in the glossary, then that text is highlighted, I can click on it, and the glossary entry is displayed. It's called glossary auto-linking, and we'll be looking at setting this up later in this section.

◆ Glossaries can be imported and exported, meaning they are easy to share and develop with colleagues.

A glossary doesn't have to be just a dictionary of course-related technical terms. Here are some examples of good Moodle glossary use:

◆ Language dictionaries. For example, use auto-linking to highlight words and phrases in English and populate a glossary with the Spanish translations. The glossary entry could include an embedded audio file of the word translated, perhaps then followed by a sentence containing the word in context.

◆ Glossary of favorite websites. Another alternative to the uploaded Word document or the wiki is a glossary of web links.

◆ Quiz questions. Have your students add glossary entries containing quiz questions they have written. Here's the clever part: you can export the glossary and then, with a little adjustment to the exported file, import the questions back into your quiz question bank.

◆ Glossary explaining the meaning of terms students need to understand when they are writing assignments—for example, the meaning of "interpret" or "demonstrate your understanding" in the context of writing up their reports.

Let's start converting my glossary to Moodle right now.

Adding a glossary

Adding a glossary is easy. Configuration is a little more subtle, but I'll explain things as we are going along. I'll start by mentioning that there are two types of glossary that you can include in a course:

◆ **Main glossary**: You are only allowed one per course and students aren't allowed to edit it, only teachers.

◆ **Secondary glossary**: You can have as many as you like and anyone can edit them.

Why have Secondary and Main glossaries? That's so that students can add to Secondary glossaries and then teachers can take the best entries from them and include those entries in the Main glossary. You don't have to use glossaries in this fashion: if you just want a basic glossary then stick to Secondary glossaries.

With that explained, let's now get on and add a Secondary glossary into our course—a glossary that anyone can edit.

Time for action – including a glossary

1. Ensuring that editing is turned on, choose the topic you want to add your glossary to, click on **Add an activity...** and select **Glossary** from the list.

2. You need to give your glossary a name and describe its purpose. Mine is a glossary of ballistics-related terms to help you as you work through the course. In the description, I'm also going to mention that anyone can add to this glossary.

3. We can leave the rest of the glossary configuration settings set to the default, but if you want to experiment with them, remember that you won't break anything. When you are happy with the settings, press the **Save and display** button. Your new glossary is now ready to have entries added to it:

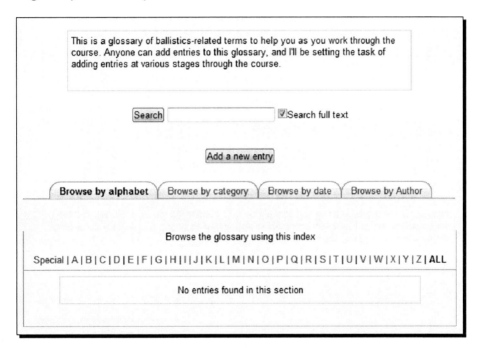

What just happened?

We've just completed adding a glossary to our course—a Secondary glossary that everyone can add entries too, and I've also configured it so that entries can be rated by everyone.

How do you add entries into the glossary?

Time for action – adding a glossary entry

1. Press the **Add a new entry** button.

2. The concept is the word or phrase that you want to explain.

3. Use the **Definition box** to give your explanation. Remember that you can use the skills you have learned so far to make a simple glossary entry a truly multimedia experience.

4. Do you want this particular glossary entry auto-linked, so that wherever it appears in your course a student can click on it to display your explanation? If so, then make sure **This entry should be automatically linked** is ticked.

5. When you are ready, scroll down to the bottom of the page and press the **Save changes** button. You now have a new entry added to your glossary:

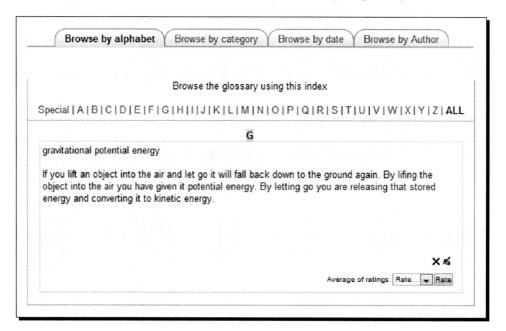

What just happened?

We've just seen how easy it is to add an entry to the glossary. Try to keep glossary entries concise. If your glossary entries start to become more complex than just a few sentences, an image or two, and perhaps a little embedded multimedia, then think about using a wiki instead.

Glossary auto-linking

When you added your first glossary entry, did you enable auto-linking for that entry? If everything worked as it should then whenever the concept (the word or phrase that represents your glossary entry) appears in your course, then it is highlighted (by default) with a subtle gray background:

> As the ball flies up into the air kinetic energy (KE) is tranferred into gravitational potential energy (GPE). When all of the KE is converted to GPE the ball stops momentarily in mid-air.

Click on the highlighted text and the glossary entry will be displayed in a pop-up window.

But there are situations when auto-linking doesn't work:

♦ When the administrator hasn't yet enabled glossary auto-linking for your site. Check out the *Ask the admin* section at the end of this chapter if this is happening to you.

♦ Auto-linking doesn't work on texts on external websites and on texts in uploaded documents. Moodle doesn't know what is actually inside those documents so it can't link your glossary to them.

Glossary block

If you return to your course front page and, with editing turned on, you can add a new **Random glossary entry block** to the course front page. This block does as its name suggests and chooses an entry from the glossary you specify at random and displays it. If your glossary contains inspirational quotes, the biographies of characters from a book your class is studying, or an illustrated vocabulary, then the random glossary entry block is an engaging and entertaining tool.

Have a go hero – allowing students to rate entries

Because students are adding entries to this glossary, I'm going to allow all entries to be rated by them (I need to be vigilant and ensure that there is no favoritism or special deals going on), with a maximum "grade" being a mark out of 5.

Click on **Edit settings**, under **Glossary administration** in the **Settings** block. In the **Ratings** box, select an aggregate type and then ensure the **Scale** is out of 5.

To allow students to rate entries, click on **Permissions** in the **Settings** block, scroll down to the **Rate entries** capability (listed under "Activities: Glossary") and press the Allow icon:

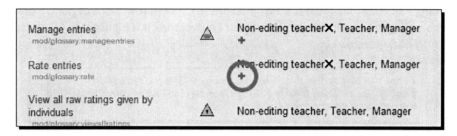

On the next page, ensure **Student** is selected in the **Select role** drop-down menu and press the **Allow** button.

Choice

A simple, powerful, but often overlooked activity: the choice activity.

I often use straw polls in my class to stimulate thinking. For example: If I light a candle in space what shape will the flame take? It then display a list of choices on the interactive white board. Take a vote on each choice, and spend time discussing each answer.

What are the benefits of converting such a simple activity over to Moodle? Here are just a few:

- It makes it easier to record which student makes which choice: voting in straw polls can be either anonymous or named
- Choices can be updated, allowing students to change their mind if they are given a little time to think about their answer
- It is easy to see which students didn't answer the question at all

So how do I go about converting my candle question over to Moodle?

Time for action – adding a choice activity

1. With editing turned on, choose a topic, then click on **Add an activity...** and select **Choice** from the list.

2. Give the new activity a name.

3. Type a question into the **Choice** text box.

4. Use the **Choice** boxes to specify the possible answers you want your students to choose from.

5. In the **Miscellaneous Settings** box, you can configure how results are displayed, if results are to be displayed to students, and—if they are given to students—you can specify whether the results are to be anonymous:

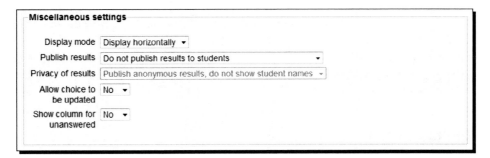

6. When you are finished, press the **Save changes** button at the bottom of the page.

What just happened?

We've just added a poll to our course using a choice activity. I use straw polls to stimulate thinking in a class—they are the ideal tool to engender discussion and debate.

You can restrict when a choice activity is available, or you can simply hide the activity on the course front page (remember: click on the hide icon—usually an eyeball—to hide an activity).

To view the results of a poll, simply click on the activity in the course front page, then click on the **View responses** link in the top right-hand corner of the page:

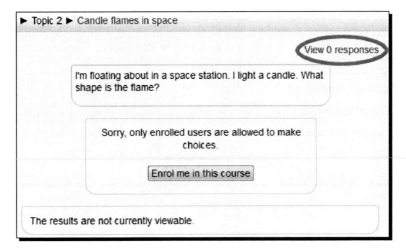

A learning journey

There is nothing at all wrong with a Moodle course starting as a list of links to other resources, for example resources uploaded to Moodle or those that exist already somewhere on the Internet—indeed, that's how we began this book. As we want to include a quiz, or a forum, or a peer review workshop, then it becomes more critical that, rather than our students dipping in to a basin of knowledge and spooning out what they fancy, we would want to be careful that they make more of a formal "learning journey". How do we know that students have viewed a resource or attempted a particular activity? That's the purpose of the completion tracking feature. How do we guide our learners on their learning journey? That's the purpose of conditional activities. Completion tracking and conditional activities are described in the next two sections.

Completion tracking

There are two parts to completion tracking:

1. Completing a resource or activity
2. Completing the course

Let's configure our Moodle course so that when students themselves consider that they are ready to move on from a resource or activity, they can mark it as "completed".

 At the time of writing, the completion tracking feature is disabled by default. You'll need to ask your Moodle administrator to enable this functionality for you. See the *Ask the admin* section at the end of this chapter.

Return to your Moodle course main page and in the **Settings** block, under **Course administration**, click on **Edit settings**. Scroll down to the Student progress section. Click on the **Completion tracking** drop-down menu and select **Enabled, control via completion and activity settings** from the list:

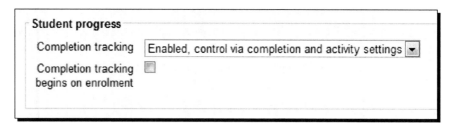

I'm not going to enforce course (rather than activity—we'll come on to that shortly) completion tracking on my course, put simply; mine isn't that kind of course. There are, however, good examples of where you would want course completion tracking enabled by default: one is any Moodle course in work-based learning (rather than in a school). Imagine my course was on manual handling—a mandatory course that all new employees had to sit through... and pass. That our students had completed every activity and had indicated that they had read and digested every static resource (through the completion tracking feature) then becomes an important part of their employee record.

Scroll down to the bottom of the **Edit course settings** page and press the **Save changes** button.

In the **Settings** block, under **Course administration** a new link has been added: Completion tracking. Click on that now to display the **Edit course completion** settings page.

Because I'm not going to force the completion tracking feature on my students from the moment they enroll, I'm going to enable the **Manual self completion** feature:

and that's it for this screen. For more information on the many other settings on this page, remember to check out the Moodle docs at `http://docs.moodle.org/20/en/ course/completion`. I'm going to scroll down to the bottom of the page and press the **Save changes** button.

The final step is to add the Self completion block onto the course page, because without it course completion tracking isn't fully enabled the way I want it. Ensure you have editing turned on and from the **Add a block** select **Self completion** from the drop-down list:

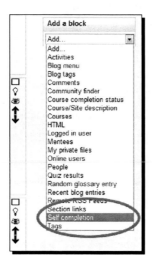

Once added, I'm going to move the Completion tracking block to the left of the page, just under the Navigation block:

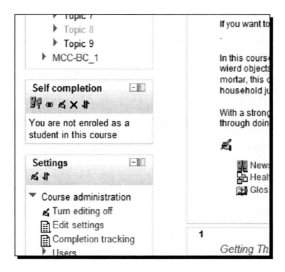

That now allows students to state (in Moodle) when they consider that they have finished the course. We'll come back to this block later in this chapter. But what about individual activities? That needs to be configured on a per activity basis. For example, how do I allow students to mark that they have read the Sources of Energy handout?

Time for action – enabling completion tracking on an activity

1. With editing turned on, click on the Update icon next to the Sources of Energy link.

2. Now that we have completion tracking enabled on our course, we can now scroll down to the **Activity completion** section:

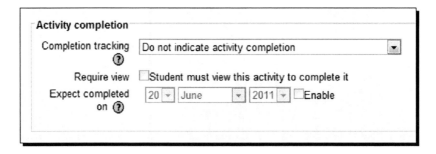

3. From the **Completion tracking** drop-down menu, I'm going to select **Students can manually mark the activity as completed**:

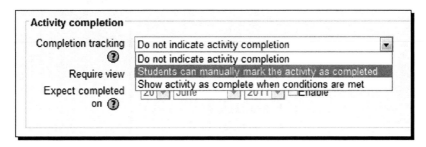

4. Scroll down to the bottom of the page and press the **Save and return to course** button.

5. That's it! We're done.

What just happened?

Now we've returned to the course page, track across to the right of the Sources of Energy resource and you'll see a little gray check mark:

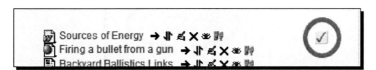

This is what completion tracking looks like from a student's point of view. For example, once he considers it read, John Smith can click on the checkbox:

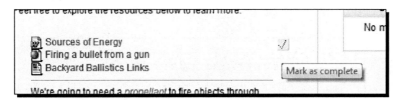

And I can track which students have indicated they have read the Sources of Energy handout through course reports. In the **Navigation** block, under **My courses**, click on the short name for your course and select **Reports**. Then, click on **Activity completion**:

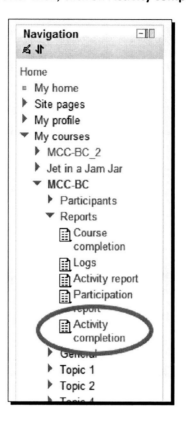

You'll see a list of your enrolled students and an indication of who has completed which activity:

Check out the activity completion report download options (see previous screenshot). These are really useful if you need to analyse activity completion data in more detail, for example in Excel.

Automatic activity completion

In my course, I'm happy for my students to indicate that they have completed an activity. The dynamic in my group of students is such that it quickly becomes obvious when someone hasn't done their homework (mainly due to the fact that it's a small group). What about having Moodle mark an activity as complete? Moodle can automatically mark an activity as complete but, obviously, what you define as "complete" depends on the activity. For example, for my Sources of Energy handout, Moodle can record the activity as complete when a student has viewed the handout:

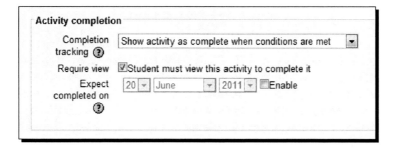

However, for a forum activity we can specify the number of posts a student must make in order to "complete" the task. We can also distinguish between starting new discussions and replying to other posts:

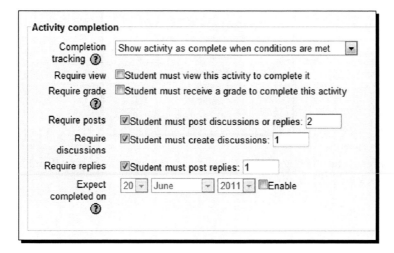

Note that we can also specify a completion deadline to really keep our students on their toes.

Rather than attempting to describe the raft of different completion options for all of the resources and activities available in Moodle, I'm going to direct you to the Moodle docs at `http://docs.moodle.org/20/en/Teacher_documentation`.

More on course completion

I have my course configured so that students can indicate when they think they have completed it—by clicking on **Complete course** in the **Self completion** block:

Clicking on the link allows the student to specify whether they have completed the course (two buttons are displayed, "**Yes**" and "**No**"). But now that I have started to configure activity completion on individual tasks in my course (for example, reading the Sources of Energy handout and posting to a forum), now I can, if I wish, configure automatic course completion. In the **Settings** block, under **Course administration**, click on **Completion tracking**. Scroll down to the **Activities completed** and you will see listed those tasks that have activity completion enabled:

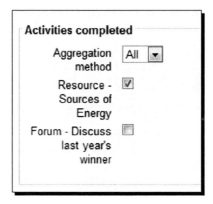

Note that students can still record that they have completed the course if you leave the Self completion block on your course page.

Conditional activities

Of course, guided learning isn't just about us insisting that our learners have to understand one concept before being allowed to attempt an activity (for example, there's no point trying to learn about calculus if you don't understand rates of change). In much the same way that in the classroom we guide our students to other activities they might find interesting—or will enrich their current understanding—we can do the same in Moodle. Also, don't necessarily think of conditional activities as being a replacement for the lesson activity. Lessons are primary for exploring scenarios. Conditional activities are for learning journeys.

So, how do we configure access to one activity being conditional on completing another? Firstly, you have to ensure that conditional activities is enabled on your Moodle. Check out the *Ask the admin* section at the end of this chapter. Let's assume I want to ensure students have read the Sources of Energy handout before they get access to the **Firing a bullet from a gun** link:

> - by making things lighter than air
> - by converting stored *energy*
>
> Feel free to explore the resources below to learn more.
>
> 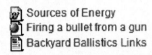 Sources of Energy
> Firing a bullet from a gun
> Backyard Ballistics Links
>
> We're going to need a *propellant* to fire objects through the air. Test your knowledge of fuels - and all things explosive - by trying the quick-fire quiz below...

We can control access to tasks based on grade, date, or completion. I want to ensure that the Sources on Energy handout has (at the very least) been clicked on to view so I'm going to configure access to Firing a bullet from a gun based on the student having viewed Sources of Energy. Note that I'll need **Activity completion** enabled on the Sources of Energy handout to be able to follow the steps outlined in the next Time for action.

Time for action – configuring conditional activities

1. With editing turned on, click on the Update icon next to the Firing a bullet from a gun resource.

2. Scroll down to the **Restrict access** section (note that this section is only available if the conditional activities feature is switched on in your Moodle):

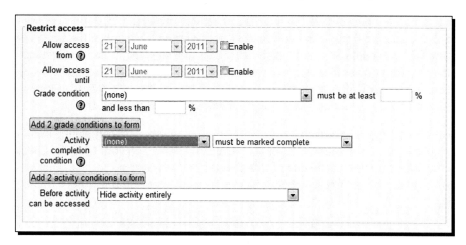

3. From the **Activity completion condition** drop-down menu, I'm going to choose **Sources of Energy**, which "must be marked complete":

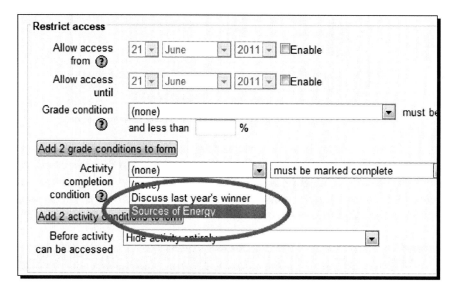

4. Scroll down to the bottom of the page and press the **Save and return to course** button.

5. We can see that access to the Firing a bullet from a gun resource is now restricted:

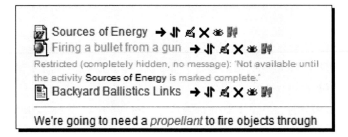

What just happened?

I've just configured access to a resource to be conditional on having viewed another resource. As you can imagine, there are a myriad of ways of configuring conditional activities so I thought it best to show you the simplest kind of controlling access—meaning you can't do A without attempting B.

Notice that you can configure more than one condition – meaning you can't access A without having attempted X, Y, and Z. Or the grade condition of A must be above a certain level and you have attempted to access B.

Like all journeys, the recommendation is that you plan your student's learning journey before you begin configuring it in Moodle.

Have a go hero – only allowing access to resources and activities when learners have agreed with the rules

It makes sense to prevent your learners from accessing resources and activities until they've agreed to the class rules. Have a go at configuring your course to implement this restriction.

Ask the admin

In this section, you'll find guidance on what to ask your administrator if you need to allow teachers to access questions in question banks outside of their Moodle course, turn on support for glossary auto-linking, and have completion tracking and/or conditional activities enabled in order to present your Moodle course.

Allowing teachers access to questions outside of their courses

Your admin needs to give you the role of teacher at the course category level. Your admin will need to:

1. Return to the Settings block and under **Site administration** click on **Users | Permissions | Define roles**.

2. Press the **Add a new role** button.

3. Create a new role called **Shared question user**, which can be assigned at the Category context:

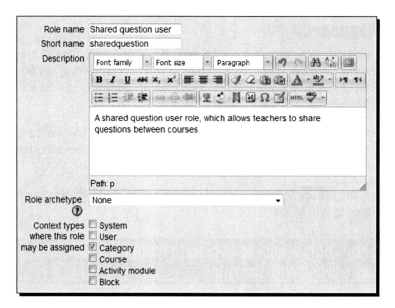

4. Scroll down the list of capabilities and Allow:

    ❑ moodle/question:add

    ❑ moodle/question:useall

    ❑ moodle/question:usemine

    ❑ moodle/question:editall

    ❑ moodle/question:editmine

    ❑ moodle/question:viewall

    ❑ moodle/question:viewmine

    ❑ moodle/question:moveall

    ❑ moodle/question:movemine

    ❑ moodle/question:managecategory

5. Scroll down to the bottom of the page and press the **Create this role** button.

6. Again under Site administration, select **Courses | Add/edit courses**, then click on the parent category for your course—in my case Faculty of Science.

7. In the Settings block, under the name of your category (not under Site administration) click on **Assign Roles**.

8. Assign your username to the Shared question user role.

Once your admin has done this for you, go back to your course question bank, click on **Categories** and check to see whether you can view question bank categories outside of your own course.

Configuring glossary auto-linking

Tell your admin that to enable the glossary auto-linking feature they need to:

1. Go to the **Site administration** menu in the Settings block, click on **Plugins**, then **Filters**, and finally select **Manage filters**.

2. In the **Active?** column, make sure glossary auto-linking is set to **On** (they'll know what you mean when they're on that page).

With that done, you should now be able to go back to your course to check that auto-linking is working.

Configuring completion tracking

Enabling the completion tracking feature is easy. Under the **Site administration** menu in the Settings block, click on **Advanced features**. Scroll down to the **Enable completion tracking** option and ensure that it's checked. Scroll down to the bottom of the page and press the **Save changes** button.

It's also worth thinking about the default settings for new courses. Under **Site administration**, click on **Courses**, then **Course default settings**. Towards the bottom of the page, under the section Student progress, are the default settings for any new course. For example, if tracking their completion is an activity that you wish all your students to engage in, then the **Completion tracking begins on enrollment** setting can be ticked. Note that these are the default settings so a teacher can alter them as they require on their Moodle course.

Configuring conditional activities

Open out the **Site administration** menu in the **Settings** block and click on **Advanced features**. Scroll down towards the bottom of the page and ensure the **Enable conditional access** option is checked. Scroll down to the bottom of the page and press the **Save changes** button. That's it! Conditional activities is now enabled.

Summary

We learned a lot in this chapter about enhancing our teaching using some of the more advanced Moodle modules.

Specifically, we covered:

- How to convert a test to a Moodle quiz using the quiz activity. We learned how each course has its own question bank, and that including a quiz on our course involves adding questions to the question bank and then adding questions from the question bank into our quiz. That way we can reuse questions easily—and easily share questions with our colleagues.

- How to convert role-playing games, quandaries, and scenarios over to Moodle using the lesson activity. Lessons can take some time to set up, so it is often best to use them to support classroom-based teaching.

- Allowing students to collaborate online with project work using the wiki activity. We saw how the wiki system makes creating new pages fast and easy. We also learned that you can specify a template: useful if there are forms for students to fill in and you want to provide a guide.

- Setting up an online multimedia dictionary using the glossary activity. We saw that not only could I convert my handout of ballistics-related terms to something a little more engaging, but students can also work together on a Moodle glossary, allowing me to turn this into a teaching activity.

- How straw polls can be converted to Moodle using the choice activity. By converting to Moodle I can better monitor which students are actively getting involved in the class and which students might need a little more encouragement.

Along the way, we discussed how to use our newly honed skills in making online content engaging and entertaining—especially when it came to configuring the activities we have been learning about in this chapter.

Now that we've learned about Moodle's more advanced activities, we're ready to start putting it all together—which is the topic of the next chapter.

9
Putting it All Together

Just think about all that we've covered together in previous chapters.

We started, in Chapter 2, Setting up your Courses by learning how to configure a Moodle course and how to make it ready for our teaching materials.

In Chapter 3, Adding Documents and Handouts we began the process of converting our teaching materials over to Moodle, and learned how, by doing so we could not only store and manage those materials more easily, but we also saw how easy it was to hand out resources to students from the course front page.

After learning how to hand out work in Moodle we looked, in the bonus chapter, Handing in Work through Moodle at how easily we can have our students hand in their work via Moodle, a topic we returned to in detail in Chapter 6, Managing Student Work.

In Chapter 4, Sound and Vision—Including Multimedia Content and Chapter 5, Moodle Makeover we saw how we could use graphics, video, and audio to make our Moodle courses much more engaging and entertaining.

Not only can we convert our resources to Moodle, we learned in Chapter 6, Managing Student Work that we can manage student work online, too.

We can also convert classroom discussions over to Moodle using forums and chats, and we explored just a few of the benefits of doing so in Chapter 7, Communicating Online.

In the previous chapter we looked at just five of the many Activity modules Moodle provides. We looked on these as a great ways of enhancing your online teaching:

◆ Quizzes

◆ Moodle lessons for exploring scenarios

◆ Workshops for peer review

◆ Wikis for collaborative working

◆ Glossaries

◆ Choices

In this chapter we are going to bring all of this together and look at possible ways of structuring a course that has been converted to Moodle.

In this chapter we shall be answering the vital question: where do I go from here? We will look at:

◆ Structuring an online course to support face-to-face teaching (so-called "blended learning")

◆ Converting group working to Moodle, how to manage groups online

◆ How to check student progress

◆ To make sure we don't lose all of our hard work

◆ How to back up and restore courses.

There's a lot to cover, so let's make a start by looking at how you can use Moodle to support face-to-face learning.

Blended learning with Moodle

Blended learning is when you support your face-to-face teaching with online resources and activities. In this section we will learn how we can achieve this using the skills and techniques we have learned so far.

Why blended learning

In this book we've been working together as I've been converting my Backyard Ballistics course over to Moodle. Yet another course I run with my students is a two-week project on jet engines, culminating with us building working pulse jets and maintaining/developing a bench-size turbo jet engine.

How might I want to support that project with Moodle? Well, by converting to Moodle I can:

- Manage all of my teaching resources in one place and have full control over how they are presented to students (*Chapter 3, Adding Documents and Handouts*, *Chapter 4, Sound and Vision—Including Multimedia Content* , and *Chapter 5, Moodle Makeover*)
- Encourage discussion and debate using the online communication skills we experienced in *Chapter 7, Communicating Online*

The students on my Jet Engine course don't know each other before the course starts. Moodle provides the ideal way to make introductions (I can register them on Moodle when they sign up for the course), and a great way for them to communicate after the face-to-face sessions have ended.

Because our time together is so short, they can get guidance and support with the project work they have to carry out to gain their final certificate using both *Chapter 7, Communicating Online* (forums and chats) and in the bonus chapter, *Handing in Work through Moodle* and *Chapter 6, Managing Student Work* (where we learned how to manage student work).

I've spoken to my Moodle administrator about creating a new course for me; she's done this and now I'm ready to start converting.

Structuring your course – Modifying the course settings

The first task is to alter the course settings to fit the course we are about to give. My admin has basically just added the new course to the **Faculty of Science** category and made me a teacher. This means I've got a little bit of setting up to do before I start uploading my resources.

Time for action – new course quick configuration

1. Go to your course front page. In the course **Settings** block, under **Administration** block click on **Edit settings**.

2. Give your new course a name and a short name. Remember that the short name must be unique.

> Have you discussed with your colleges a naming convention for course short names? If you haven't then this might be a good idea. Having a convention will make it easier for students to navigate around your Moodle site. It will also make it easier if your admin ever wants to have students enrolled on courses automatically.

3. Think of a description for your new course. Try to make it inviting, it's the first thing students will see before they are actually enrolled on your course. Try not to make it too elaborate, you know how to use the Moodle Editor and you know how to include graphics, audio, and video in your course summary if you wanted to. Try to resist going overboard using these techniques in the course summary, it will put students off when they are trying to look through the list of courses in our course category. I've included an animated GIF, but I've arranged the layout so that it is over on the right-hand side of the summary:

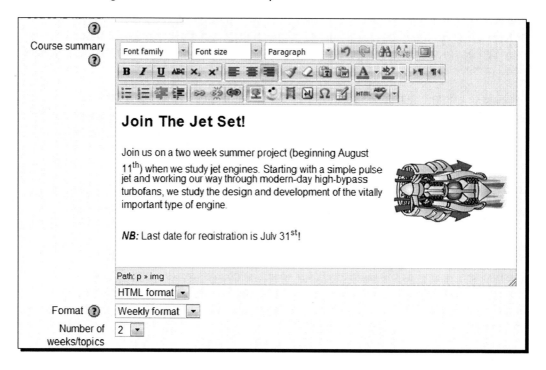

When my course appears in the list of courses in this category, having the image over on the right-hand side makes the list of courses easier to read through.

4. Set the course format. Mine's a two-week course starting in August. I'm going to set the configuration accordingly:

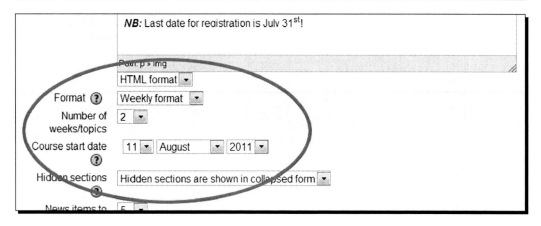

5. Scroll down to the bottom of the page and press the **Save changes** button. That's the course set up as I need it and here's how my new course is listed, along with other courses, on the site's front page:

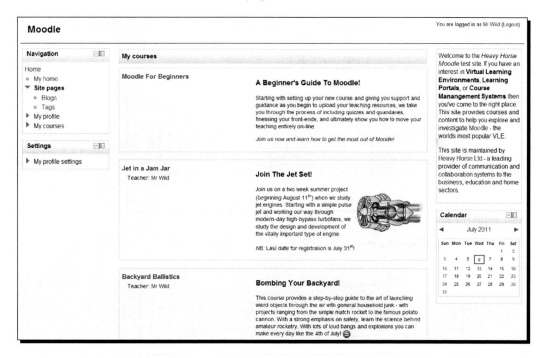

6. Next, I need to specify an enrollment key. Return to the course and in the **Settings** block under **Course administration**, click on **Users** then **Enrolment methods**:

7. Ensure **Self enrolment (Student)** is enabled (poke it in the eye) and click on the edit icon:

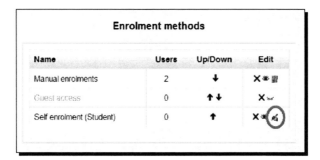

8. Specify an **Enrolment key**:

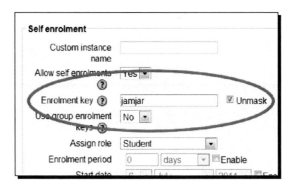

9. Scroll down to the bottom of the page and press the **Save changes** button.

10. That's it. we're done!

What just happened?

I've just set up my new course ready for me to start uploading resources. I've given my course a brief summary, kept it as a weekly format but cut it down to two weeks. I've also specified an enrollment key so that new students can't get in. I haven't hidden this course from my students: I could have done, but I wanted to let students know it's there (what's stopping them from getting in is their not knowing the enrollment key). I want to get my students interested in this course.

Introducing your course

We saw in *Chapter 2, Setting up your Courses* that it is a good idea to make "**Summary of General**" (which is how Moodle refers to the section at the very top of the course page) a place where students can find out about the course and also find out about each other.

Check out *Chapter 4, Sound and Vision—Including Multimedia Content* where we created a photo montage using Slide.com (see Picture Shows Using Slide.com). I've got lots of photographs from when I've run this project in previous years. I've uploaded these to Slide.com and I'm going to include a Slide.com slide show in Summary of General, so my new students can know what they are letting themselves in for:

I'm also going to include an Introductions forum (see *Chapter 7, Communicating Online*), so that before they meet for the first time all the members of the group have a chance to get to know one another (and me). After only thirty minutes (I know because I timed it), using all the techniques we have learned in this book to create my Summary of General, here's how my course now looks (to a student):

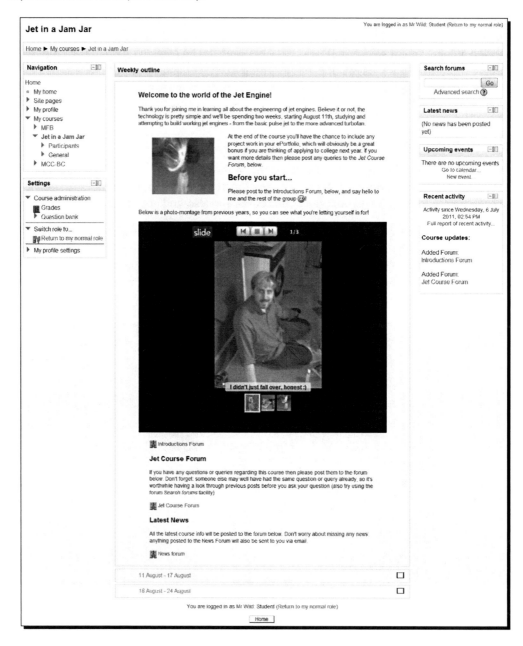

Pop quiz – using labels

Remember how we discussed using labels in *Chapter 5*, *Moodle Makeover*? We saw that labels are the glue that hold courses together. Can you tell where I've used labels in my Summary of General?

Using multimedia sharing services

I used `Slide.com` in the previous example but there are, of course, many other online sharing sites for sharing all manner and types of multimedia content. Think about the possibilities of using Google Picasa, Flickr, and YouTube, for instance. Remember to ensure that the service you choose is actually available to your students. For instance, students are often blocked from accessing YouTube, even if members of staff are allowed access. Check out *Chapter 4*, *Sound and Vision—Including Multimedia Content* for more advice on including multimedia in your courses.

Arranging activities

Let's look at how I'm going to arrange Week 1 (I'm going to arrange Week 2 in much the same way). Let's start the online activities by asking the students a simple question to test their understanding, let's give them a choice. We saw how to include and configure a choice activity in *Chapter 8*, *Enhancing Your Teaching*. My question is: "Does a liquid have to be highly flammable to be explosive?". Here is the choice activity I've created:

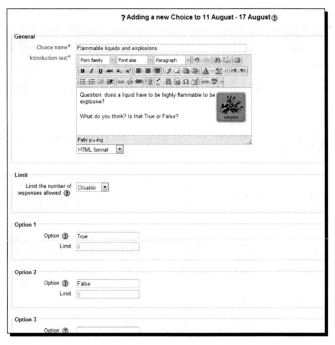

And I've configured this choice so that it is only open on the very first day of the course with the results being automatically published when the polling has closed:

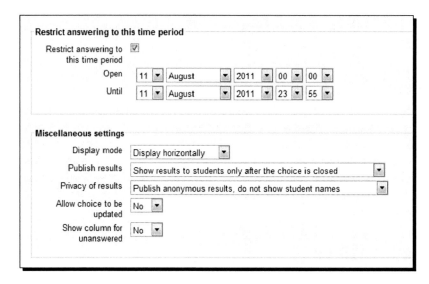

I'm going to add a forum next, so that we can discuss the results. The trick is that I'm going to hide this new forum until the results are in.

Then I'm going to upload my instructions for making a Jam Jar Jet. I made this handout a couple of years ago using Microsoft Word. For now I'm simply going to upload this file as it is.

I've also got another handout, a crossword that I created using Hot Potatoes. That suite of programs contains a crossword generator, so using Hot Potatoes I'm going to convert a crossword to Moodle (for more information on Hot Potatoes visit `http://hotpot.uvic.ca/`).

 If you want to import Hot Potatoes' activities so that they are graded by Moodle then we need to export it as a SCORM 1.2 activity.

Time for action – converting a crossword to Moodle

1. First, create your crossword with JCross:

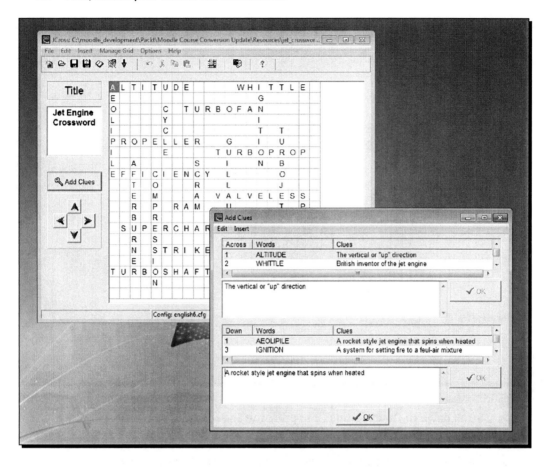

2. We next need to export the crossword as a SCORM activity. From the JCross main menu select **File** then slide down to **Create Scorm 1.2 Package**.

3. Back in your Moodle course, in the correct week I need to click on the **Add an activity...** drop-down and select **SCORM package**.

4. In the **General** box, give the activity a name and description, then choose the SCORM package file we just created:

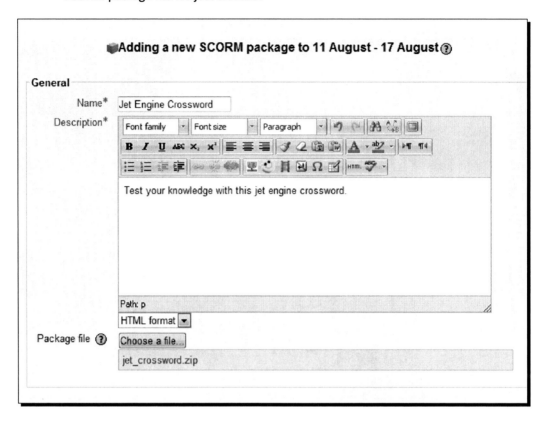

5. Scroll down to **Other settings** and press the **Show advanced** button. I'm going to display the crossword in a new window and allow that window to be resized.

6. Scroll down to the bottom of the page and press the **Save and display** button.

7. Here's how my crossword looks now that it has been converted to Moodle:

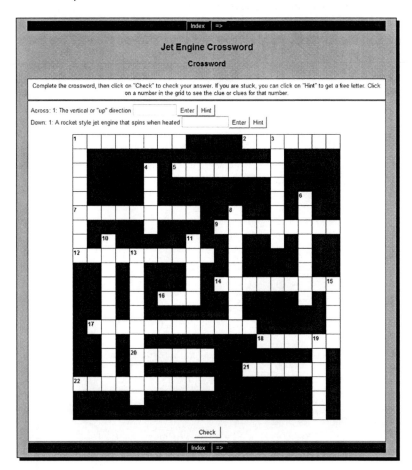

What just happened?

We've just followed the process of me converting my Jet Engine Crossword to Moodle. Here are the advantages of me doing so:

♦ I don't have to worry about collecting pieces of paper, looking after them, marking them, and handing them back again

♦ The crossword is marked automatically

♦ By clicking on **Grades** from the course Administration block I can see at a glance who has attempted the crossword and how well they did (there's more on the course Gradebook in the second half of this chapter)

Now I've got my students thinking about the technical terms associated with jet engines (and a lot of the terms are quite complicated if you haven't come across them before), they can work on creating an online glossary together. Let's add in a secondary glossary, and I'm going to allow comments on glossary entries and allow students to rate the entries (a mark out of 5):

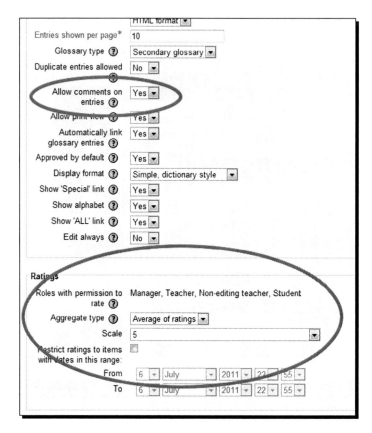

Note that I've allowed students to rate entries in this glossary through the Permissions screen (via the **Settings** block under **Glossary administration**).

We'll start with the glossary empty so that we can fill this out as we are working through Week 1 together.

I also want us all to work together on a pulse jet Wiki, which can then form a part of the student's e-Portfolios. I've already got a document structure that they can follow, so I'm going to follow the instructions in *Chapter 8, Enhancing Your Teaching*, to this time create a Group wiki, but also specify a start page so the students have a structure to follow (important for their ePortfolio).

Finally, and because this is a fairly practical course that I'm supporting with Moodle, I want to give the students an opportunity to upload their photographs. At the moment they hand me USB memory sticks, the memory cards from digital cameras or, if we are feeling particularly adventurous, they attempt to bluetooth the image files to me. Let's convert this to Moodle using an assignment. In fact, let's use the Advanced uploading of files assignment we first encountered in *Chapter 6, Managing Student Work*. The advantages are:

- If the students have got any photographs they want to give me they can upload them straight to Moodle themselves
- I can manage how many photographs come from each student, and easily check to see who hasn't managed to upload any

But, most importantly:

- I don't have to try and work out how to use their mobile phones

At the moment those are the only aspects of my Jet Engine course that I want to convert to Moodle, so let's stop there and take a look at my Week 1 so far:

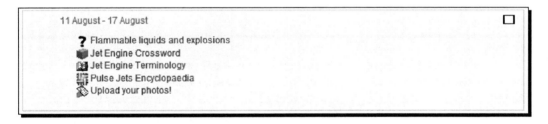

What are lacking here are a summary and some kind of indication to the students of how these activities fit together. Let's use some labels and a few of the tips and tricks from *Chapter 5, Moodle Makeover* to finesse our HTML:

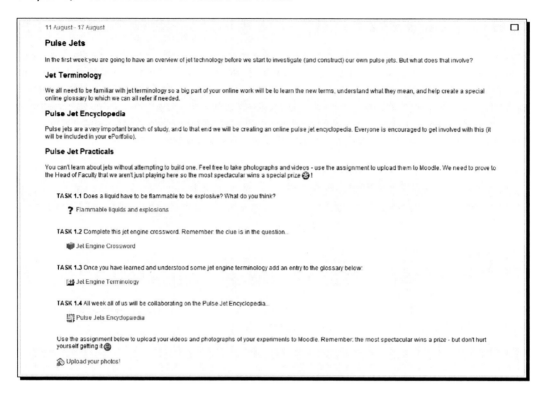

The Moodle philosophy suggests that learners can meander (or "moodle") their way through the resources and activities any way they choose. However, I want to manage how my students work their way through the first week of my course. The easiest way to do that is to hide everything and then show things as I want my students to do them. But remember, that in Moodle I can make access to activities conditional on other activities having been completed, although that may be an overcomplication. This approach may also contradict the basic Moodle pedagogy, but there are three important reasons I have come across to explain why you would want to control access to work:

- to prevent your students from getting worried about what they see as difficult work coming up in the future

- to avoid being asked questions on topics that you haven't covered yet

- to avoid being asked questions by parents who are checking to see what their children will be doing when they take the course (sounds bizarre, but I've come across this problem many times)

You can see from the previous screenshot that in fact I'm not doing that. I'm giving all of the tasks in my Moodle course a number (1.1, 1.2, and so on), which I can then refer to as I'm working with the students.

All of the work you can see in this section of this chapter took just over an hour. It really doesn't take long to start to convert to Moodle. I needn't have used Moodle for any of this work (I didn't up until now). But, hopefully you can see that by converting just a few aspects of my course to Moodle, how I can both make my life easier and the student's experience more entertaining. There's more advice on converting to Moodle at the end of this chapter.

Converting to fully online courses

Up to now we have been discussing converting to Moodle but we have always assumed that there will be at least some face-to-face elements to your teaching. However, at this stage there is really nothing stopping us from thinking about moving our courses entirely online. There are two further issues we need to address before we are completely electric:

♦ How to group students and manage them online
♦ How to manage and organize grades

Let's look at the first of these issues in the next section.

Managing groups of students

If I've got a group of students (especially if they are of mixed ability) then I like to split them into groups. Not only does this make them easier to manage from my point of view, but I also put students into groups if they don't know each other that well (a way of getting them to mix socially). Whether or not you are moving fully online, being able to group students, and then to hand out work depending on what group they are in, is something that you will very likely want to do; in this section we learn how.

Creating Groups

I'm going to divide the students on my Jet Engine course into two groups, the Turbo group and the Pulse Group:

Time for action – creating student groups

1. Return to the course front page. Click on the **Groups** link in the **Settings** block under **Course administration**, then **Users**:

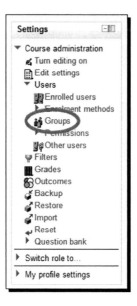

2. Press the **Create group** button:

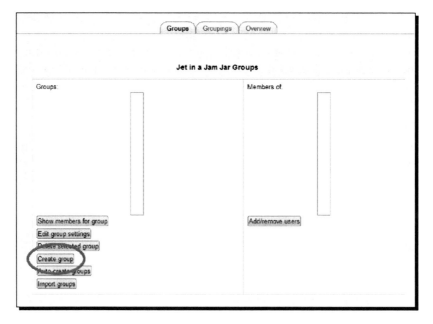

3. Give your group a name and, optionally a description (more on this shortly).

4. You can optionally specify a picture to represent the group (again, more on this in a moment).

5. When you are done press the **Save changes** button. Your new group is now added to the list of available groups (the number in brackets after the group name indicates how many users are in it):

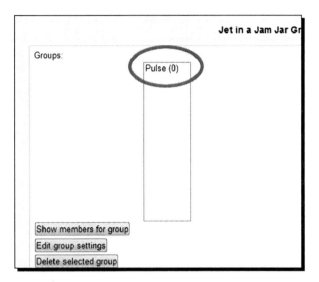

What just happened?

We've just created a new group, albeit so far with no one in it. As with most things in Moodle you aren't committing yourself when you specify configuration settings. When configuring groups there are usually two settings that I return to once the group has some members:

- I start leaving the group description blank and then ask the group, when they first get together, how they would like to describe themselves. If the course is converted to be entirely online then we'll either have a chat or (more usually) I'll start a forum discussion.

- Likewise with the group picture, either I will take a group picture, or the group can choose a mascot for themselves, which I can then specify with the **New picture** setting.

I'm going to repeat the previous process to create the Turbo group, and then I'm going to start adding students into my groups (the topic of the next section).

Adding students to groups

This can be achieved in two ways:

- ◆ I manually add students to the group
- ◆ The students enroll on the course and automatically join their group

Let's look at the first of these now.

Time for action – manually adding students to a group

1. Return to the course front page and select **Groups** from the **Administration** block.

2. Click on the name of the group you want to add members to and press the **Show members for group** button.

3. Press the **Add/remove users** button.

4. Select the users you want to add into the group (you can select more than one at a time) and press the **Add** button:

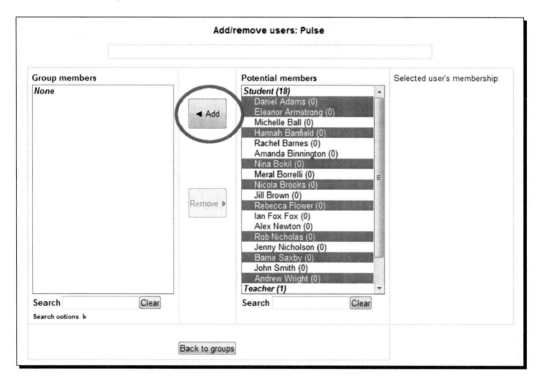

5. Note that the users are immediately added to the group. If you then press the **Back to groups** button you will see the brackets after the group name now tells you how many users are in the group. If I click on the name then the members are listed in the Members of list:

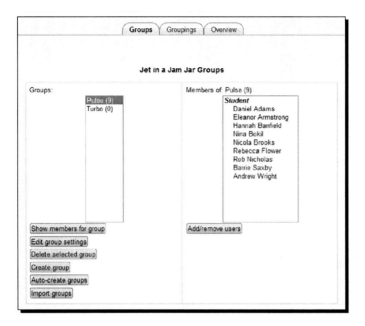

6. That's it. We're done!

What just happened?

We've just seen how easy it is to manually add a student to a group and removing a student from a group is as easy (did you spot the **Remove** button as you were adding users?).

If you've a lot of students then that method can become cumbersome. The more typical way of grouping students is via the group enrollment key. Let's see how to make that work now.

Time for action – specifying a group enrollment key

1. Return to your course front page and click on **Groups**, under **Course Administration** then **Users** in the **Settings** block.

2. Select the group you want to edit and press the **Edit group settings** button.

3. Specify a group enrollment key. This can be anything you like. To reveal the key you have just typed (so you can read it) ensure the **Unmask** setting is ticked. It's useful in a school situation to have this as the name of the class for any course, for example, 9A, 9B, and so on.

4. Press the **Save changes** button and you're done.

What just happened?

We've just specified an enrollment key for the group. This means that I can give a student the group enrollment key and when they come to enroll they use the group key (rather than the course key) to get on the course. This not only registers them on the course but also automatically adds them to the right group.

Different groups can have different keys, and if I don't want particular students added to any group at all then I just give them the course enrollment key.

But once students are grouped, how do I manage their work? Let's look at how you would make an activity a group activity.

Collaborating in groups

To show how we can manage group work in Moodle we need to look at a collaborative activity. The process we're about to run through applies to any collaborative activity, but let's take a forum as an example:

Time for action – group work in a forum

1. Choose a topic or week in your course, and with editing turned on click on **Add an activity...** and select **Forum** from the list.

2. Give the forum a name and an introduction.

3. Scroll down to the bottom of the page to the **Common module settings** box. The **Group mode** settings gives you three options:

   ❑ **No groups**: This is the default. Student's can see everyone's work, regardless of which group they are in.

   ❑ **Separate groups**: Students can only see the work of students in their group. As far as they are concerned they have their own forum.

   ❑ **Visible groups**: Students can see the work of students in the other groups but they can only interact with students in their own group. It's rather like splitting a class in two where both groups can see what the other is doing but they can't interfere with their work.

4. When you have made your choice press the **Save and display** button.

5. If you have specified one of the two group modes then you can choose which group you want to work with using the drop-down list at the top left-hand corner of the forum page:

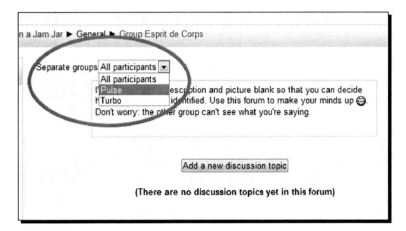

What just happened?

We've just seen how easy it is to manage group work in Moodle, using a forum as an example (but the principle is the same for all collaborative activities).

Once we've got our students working in groups then it's natural at some stage to want to hand out different work to different groups. Let's spend the next section looking at this task.

Handing out group-specific work

"Groupings" is Moodle's way of allowing you to dish out different work to different groups. Let's work through the process of creating groupings now:

Time for action – create groupings

1. Return to the course front page and click on **Groups** under **Course administration**, then **Users** in the **Settings** block.

2. Do you see a **Groupings** tab at the top of the **Groups** page?

3. If not then you need to speak to your Moodle administrator (refer to the *Ask the admin* section following on from this one). If you do then click on it.

4. Press the **Create grouping** button.

5. Give the grouping a name and, optionally, a description.

6. Press the **Save changes** button.

7. We have now created a grouping, but there aren't yet any groups in it:

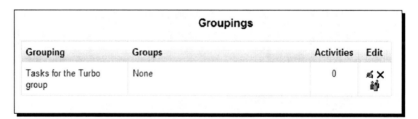

8. Click on the show groups in grouping icon:

9. Select the group you want to add into the grouping from the Potential members list. Then press the **Add** button:

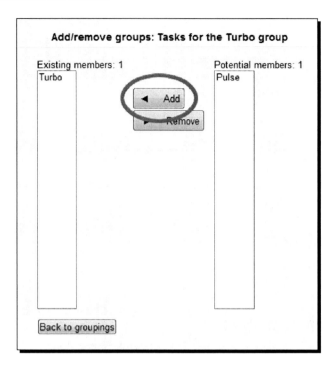

10. When you are done press the **Back to groupings** button.

Now I'm going to return to the forum I just created and press the **Update this forum** button to go back to the **Editing forum** page.

11. Once you are back to the **Editing forum** page, scroll down the page to the **Common module settings** box. Click on the **Show Advanced** button in the top-right corner of the box:

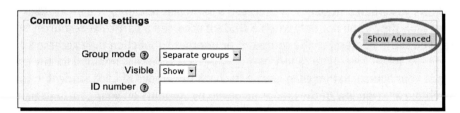

12. The **Grouping** settings will now be revealed. To ensure that my forum is only available to students in a particular grouping then select the grouping from the drop-down list and ensure the **Available for group members only** setting is ticked:

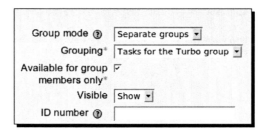

13. That's it! This forum is now only available to students in the groups that are contained in the Tasks for the Turbo group grouping.

What just happened?

We've just converted a vital part of face-to-face group teaching, handing out different work to different groups, to Moodle.

Checking student progress

Even if you aren't converting courses to be run completely online there may still be instances when you want to monitor student activity. For example, if you are keen to develop your course as students are using it you may want to monitor how many students are accessing a particular resource. So how do you tell where students have been and how long they spent there?

Monitoring student participation

Return to your course front page and look for the **People** block (it's usually at the top-left corner of the course front page). Click on the **Participants** link in the **People** block. Select a name from the list of participants and then click on the **Activity reports** tab. The **Outline** report shows you when a student last accessed a particular resource or activity. Clicking on the **All logs** tab shows you not only when a student accessed a particular resource, but also the ID (called the IP address) of the computer or Internet connection they accessed it from. The **Grade** tab shows an outline report of the grades a student has attained for the gradable activities in your course. Rather than having to check the grades of each student in turn, you can obtain an overview of the grades achieved by students on your course using the Moodle gradebook.

Using the Moodle gradebook

Let's take another visit to the gradebook we first encountered in *Chapter 6, Managing Student Work*. The gradebook is a very powerful feature of Moodle, and if you are going to be converting your course to be fully online then you will want to know how to use it well. That said, most of the gradebook is self-explanatory. As you add activities to your course you will see them added to the grader report and see student results displayed there.

Most educators are more than happy to use the gradebook as it is. However, you can insert custom grade items into your gradebook (you aren't just limited to activities you've added into your course), you can change the way grades are calculated, and you can categorize grades (grouping grades and even calculating an overall grade for that category).

To access the gradebook for your course you will need to return to the course front page and select **Grades** from the **Settings** block, under **Course administration**.

Once on the **Grader report** page, click on the **Grader report...** drop-down menu to see the kind of options that are available to you:

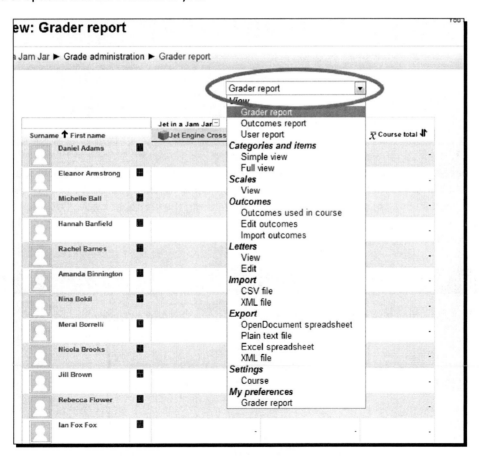

Clearly you can:

- import grades
- export grades
- specify grade letters (grades are by default numeric but you can easily convert an overall course grade to a letter if you wish)
- edit categories and items

Let's briefly take up the last item in the list: editing categories and items. Under **Categories and items** from the drop-down menu select **Full view**. You are presented with the **Full view** page, but this now lets us edit the categories and items contained in the gradebook:

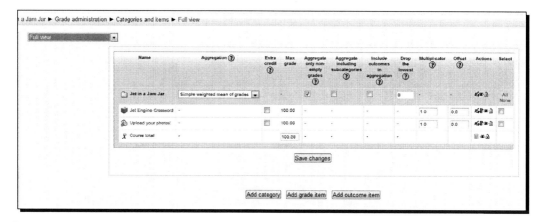

This page displays the structure of the grader report in tree form, although that fact may not be that clear at the moment. I give grades to my students for their practical work (for safety, design, and so on). Let's have a quick go at reconfiguring the gradebook now. I'm going to add two categories; one to contain marks for practical work and one that contains marks for the Moodle course activities.

Time for action – configuring the gradebook

1. Assuming you are still on the same page, press the **Add category** button:

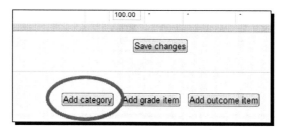

2. Give your category a name. I'm going to call mine "Marks for practical".

3. Press the **Show Advanced** button. You will see a few extra settings appear. I'm not going to worry about them now, but feel free to investigate. Remember: you won't break anything and you can always refer to Moodle Docs for guidance.

4. When you are done press the **Save changes** button.

5. I'm now going to repeat the process and create a category called "Marks for Moodle activities". My tree of categories and items now looks like this:

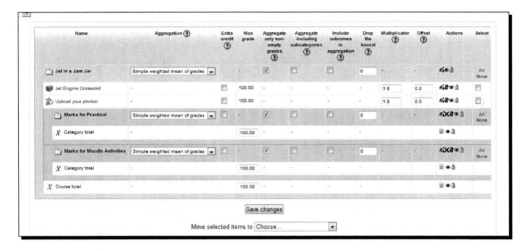

6. Using the move icon (or by clicking and dragging, depending on how your site is set up) I can then move the Moodle activities under the "Marks for Moodle activities" category in just the same way as we can shuffle activities and resources about in a Moodle course. Here's how my tree looks now:

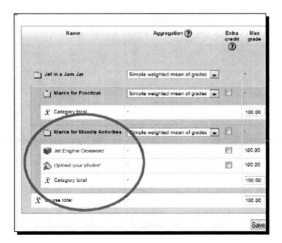

Now I can start adding grade items for the practical work the students are going to undertake.

7. Press the **Add grade item** button.

8. Give the grade item a name, for example "Planning and design".

9. Specify the grade type. You can use a custom scale if you want to (see *Chapter 6, Managing Student Work*).

10. Use the Parent category drop-down list to specify the category you want your grade item to be included in.

11. Press the **Save changes** button. My new grade item is now added to the tree:

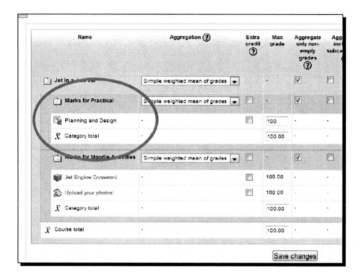

12. If I then click on the **Choose an action...** drop-down in the top left-hand corner and select **Grader report** (under the View heading) then you will see how we have restructured the gradebook:

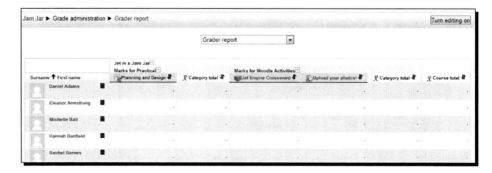

What just happened?

I've just restructured my course gradebook to include two categories, "Marks for practical" and "Marks for Moodle Activities". You've also seen how I can add in my own custom grades, which means my gradebook doesn't just have to contain the grades for Moodle activities. You can add in your own grades if you want to.

Have a go hero – including custom outcomes

Not only can you add in custom grades but you can also include custom outcomes; vital if you are converting a course that judges student achievement using attainment targets or learning descriptors.

> **Hint on including custom outcomes**
>
> Before you start specifying attainment targets in your gradebook you will need to create custom scales. Check out *Chapter 6, Managing Student Work* for details.

Return to the **Edit categories and items** page. Press the **Add outcome item** button. See if you can add a custom outcome to your gradebook. Remember that you will need to create and configure a custom outcome before you start.

Backup and Restore

We are nearly at the end of our journey together and the very last thing I want to happen now is that you lose all of your work (and mine!). Return to your course front page and look down the options in the **Settings** block under **Course administration**. Two options listed are **Backup** and **Restore**. Choose **Backup** (we'll look at restoring shortly) and let's get all the hard work we've done so far backed up; it's better to be safe than sorry.

Backing up your course

You'll find many, many options you can choose as we run through the backup procedure. At this stage it's best just to stick with the defaults and back up everything. Let's run through the process now:

Time for action – back up your course

1. Once you've selected **Backup** from the **Settings** block you are taken to the first page of the **Backup wizard** ("**Initial settings**"). Simply leave the defaults as they are, scroll down to the bottom of the page and press **Next**.

2. The next page ("**Schema settings**") allows you to choose what you want to back up. Again, scroll down to the bottom of the page and click **Next**.

3. The "**Confirmation and review**" page allows you to check your choices and also to change the name of the backup file Moodle is about to create. If all is well, press the **Perform backup** button at the bottom of the page. Once the backup has been performed, press the **Continue** button and Moodle now displays your backup files. You can see that I have backed up both my Backyard Ballistics and my Jet in a Jam Jar courses:

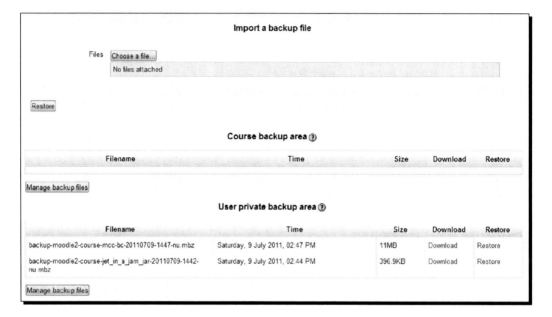

4. You can see that Moodle has backed up your entire course into a single file and put it in your User private backup area. That's fine, but if something goes wrong with the computer Moodle is running on that isn't much help. Click on the **Download** link along from the name of the file. You are given the option to either open it or save it. Choose **Save** and save the file to your computer, USB memory stick, or portable hard drive. Keep it safe:

What just happened?

I think I would probably burst into tears if I'd have lost all of the work that I've done so far. Thank goodness that backing up my course is easy. I simply select **Backup** from the course from page (via the **Settings** block) and follow the instructions. There are lots of settings allowing me to choose what I actually back up, but at the moment I'm just wanting to back up everything; there really isn't any harm in doing that.

Do you want to give your course to a colleague? The best way to do that is to back it up, following the previous procedure, and give them the backup .MBZ file. And how do they restore this file? That's the topic of the next section.

Restoring a course

What about when the worst happens and I need to restore my course? That's straightforward too. Let's imagine the nightmare scenario that your course, for whatever reason, has gone completely. Before you restore your course you will need to ask your admin to create an empty course for you, unless you are a course creator, because then you can create your own. Open up your new course, find the course **Administration** block and click **Restore**.

Time for action – restore a course

1. Clicking on **Restore** under **Course administration** in the **Settings** block takes you to the **Import a backup file** page.

2. Import your backup file if you need to. The procedure for uploading this file is exactly the same as uploading a resource:

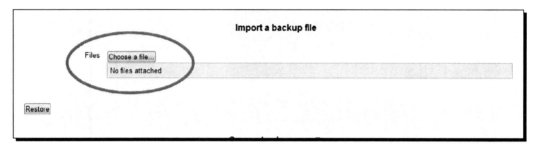

3. Once your file is uploaded press the **Restore** button.

4. You are taken to the first page of the Restore wizard ("**Confirm**"). The contents of the backup file are displayed. If you are happy then scroll down to the bottom of the page and press the **Continue** button.

5. The next page allows you to specify the destination. Importantly, you are also asked if you want to:

   ❑ Merge the contents of the backup into the course

   ❑ Delete the contents of a course and replace it with the contents of the backup

   and, if you have course creator privileges:

   ❑ Create a brand new course

   You will need to make sure the correct option is chosen. Then scroll down to the bottom of the page and press the appropriate **Continue** button:

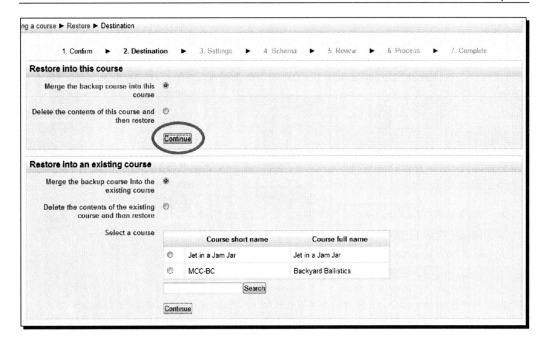

6. Confirm the settings and press the **Next** button.

7. The "**Schema**" page allows you to confirm (or alter) the course name and short name (remember short names must be unique), and also allows you to choose what resources and activities will be restored out of the backup file. Scroll down to the bottom of the page and press the **Next** button.

8. Review your choices before pressing the **Perform restore** button at the bottom of the page.

9. When the restore is complete press the **Continue** button. You are now returned to the course front page. And that's it, you're done!

What just happened?

If the worst happens and I need to restore my course then luckily the process is easy. Simply click on **Restore** under **Course administration** in the **Settings** block, upload the backup file, click on **Restore**, follow the instruction and Moodle does the rest.

The great thing about Backup and Restore is that it can be used to share Moodle courses. If ever you are given a Moodle course by a colleague and you are wondering how to get that course on to your Moodle then it's highly likely that what your colleague has given you is a course backup.

Copying activities from one course to another

To quickly copy activities from one course to another it is better to use **Import**, also available under **Course administration** from the **Settings** block.

Summary

We learned a lot in this chapter about how converting to Moodle can help support face-to-face learning. Specifically, we covered:

- How quickly a new course can be configured so that it is ready for content
- How to structure a course, including specifically how to structure an introduction and how to arrange activities
- How quickly courses can start to take shape

We also saw how we could convert to fully online courses, with particular emphasis on learning about how we can convert group, or team working over to Moodle, specifically:

- How to manage groups of students online
- How to create groups and how to add students to them
- How to hand out group specific work (using Groupings)

We saw how we can monitor student progress, and how we can see where students have been on our course (and even from which computer). That led us on to a discussion about the Moodle gradebook. We barely scratched the surface of this tool, but we did see how you can categorize grades and even add in your own grading items (so that you are not limited to only grades from course activities).

Finally, we learned how to back up and restore courses, meaning we can preserve all of the hard work you have done so far!

Pop Quiz Answers

Chapter 1, Going Electric

- Moodle is an acronym but what does it stand for? When thinking about your Moodle doing what you need it to do to support your teaching, why is the 'M' in Moodle so important?

    - **Answer**: Modular Object Oriented Dynamic Learning Environment. That Moodle is 'M'odular means if Moodle doesn't do something you need it to then, chances are, there is a module available that will let you do it.

- I've just clicked on a category to view the courses in it. I see that there is a button marked **Add a new course**. What's my role in this context?

    - **Answer**: Course creator

Chapter 2, Setting up your Courses

- What is the difference between a course creator and a manager?

    - **Answer**: A course creator has fewer permissions than a manager. For example, a course creator can create new courses but a manager can delete them, too!

- How do you change the format of your course from topics to weekly?

    - **Answer**: By going to your **Course settings** page (via the **Settings** block by clicking on **Edit settings**) and selecting the desired type from the **Format** drop-down list.

Chapter 3, Adding Documents and Handouts

◆ Do your students have direct access to your Private files area? How do you provide a link to a file in your Private files area?

❏ **Answer**: Students do not have access to your Private files area. Select the file you wish to hand out using the file picker.

◆ The size of PowerPoint files can be greatly reduced by cropping and compressing any images contained in the presentation. Can you remember the steps to compress images?

❏ **Answer**: Look back through this chapter to check your knowledge.

◆ If you've just cut and pasted text from a Word document then there's a special button in the HTML editor that is worthwhile pressing before you go any further. What's the name of that button?

❏ **Answer**: You can use the **Cleanup messy code** button.

Index

Thank you for buying
Moodle 2.0 Course Conversion Beginner's Guide

About Packt Publishing

Packt, pronounced 'packed', published its first book "*Mastering phpMyAdmin for Effective MySQL Management*" in April 2004 and subsequently continued to specialize in publishing highly focused books on specific technologies and solutions.

Our books and publications share the experiences of your fellow IT professionals in adapting and customizing today's systems, applications, and frameworks. Our solution based books give you the knowledge and power to customize the software and technologies you're using to get the job done. Packt books are more specific and less general than the IT books you have seen in the past. Our unique business model allows us to bring you more focused information, giving you more of what you need to know, and less of what you don't.

Packt is a modern, yet unique publishing company, which focuses on producing quality, cutting-edge books for communities of developers, administrators, and newbies alike. For more information, please visit our website: www.packtpub.com.

About Packt Open Source

In 2010, Packt launched two new brands, Packt Open Source and Packt Enterprise, in order to continue its focus on specialization. This book is part of the Packt Open Source brand, home to books published on software built around Open Source licences, and offering information to anybody from advanced developers to budding web designers. The Open Source brand also runs Packt's Open Source Royalty Scheme, by which Packt gives a royalty to each Open Source project about whose software a book is sold.

Writing for Packt

We welcome all inquiries from people who are interested in authoring. Book proposals should be sent to author@packtpub.com. If your book idea is still at an early stage and you would like to discuss it first before writing a formal book proposal, contact us; one of our commissioning editors will get in touch with you.

We're not just looking for published authors; if you have strong technical skills but no writing experience, our experienced editors can help you develop a writing career, or simply get some additional reward for your expertise.

Science Teaching with Moodle 2.0

ISBN: 978-1-84951-148-3   Paperback: 296 pages

Create interactive lessons and activities in Moodle to enhance your students' understanding and enjoyment of science

1. Follow a sample course to see how lessons, groups, and forums are created

2. Make your student's homework more exciting by enabling them to watch videos, participate in group discussions, and complete quizzes from home

3. Simplify the teaching of difficult scientific notation using animations

4. Monitor your students' progress using Gradebook

Moodle 2.0 for Business Beginner's Guide

ISBN: 978-1-84951-420-0   Paperback: 324 pages

Implement Moodle in your business to streamline your interview, training, and internal communication processes

1. The first book that shows how to use Moodle in a corporate environment

2. Practical examples allow you to set up Moodle in your business with ease

3. Well-known companies that have implemented Moodle for staff training share their experiences in the form of case studies

4. Use Moodle for recruitment, training, group activities, and much more

Please check **www.PacktPub.com** for information on our titles

Moodle JavaScript Cookbook

ISBN: 978-1-84951-190-2   Paperback: 180 pages

Over 50 recipes for making your Moodle system more dynamic and responsive with JavaScript

1. Learn why, where, and how to add to add JavaScript to your Moodle site

2. Get the most out of Moodle's built-in extra—the Yahoo! User Interface Library (YUI)

3. Explore a wide range of modern interactive features, from AJAX to Animation

4. Integrate external libraries like jQuery framework with Moodle

Moodle 2 Administration

ISBN: 978-1-84951-604-4   Paperback: 427 pages

An administrator's guide to configuring, securing, customizing, and extending Moodle

1. A complete guide for planning, installing, optimizing, customizing, and configuring Moodle

2. Learn how to network and extend Moodle for your needs and integrate with other systems

3. A complete reference of all Moodle system settings

Please check **www.PacktPub.com** for information on our titles

Lightning Source UK Ltd.
Milton Keynes UK
UKOW010726070112

184881UK00001B/6/P